LEVEL ZERO HEROES

LEVEL ZERO HEROES

The Story of U.S. Marine Special Operations
in Bala Murghab, Afghanistan

MICHAEL GOLEMBESKY
AND JOHN R. BRUNING

 ST. MARTIN'S GRIFFIN NEW YORK

LEVEL ZERO HEROES. Copyright © 2014 by Michael Golembesky and John R. Bruning. Fore-word copyright © 2014 by Fred Galvin. All rights reserved. Printed in the United States of America. For information, address St. Martin's Press, 175 Fifth Avenue, New York, N.Y. 10010.

Map and Level Zero Heroes logo © copyright 2014 by Level Zero Heroes LLC.

www.stmartins.com

The Library of Congress has cataloged the hardcover edition as follows:

Golembesky, Michael.
    Level zero heroes : the story of U.S. Marine Special Operations in Bala Murghab, Afghanistan / Michael Golembesky with John R. Bruning. — First edition.
        p. cm.
    Includes bibliographical references.
    ISBN 978-1-250-03040-5 (hardcover)
    ISBN 978-1-250-03041-2 (e-book)
    1. Golembesky, Michael.   2. Afghan War, 2001—Personal narratives, American.
3. Afghan War, 2001—Campaigns—Afghanistan—Badghis.   4. United States. Marine Special Operations Command. Marine Special Operations Team 8222—Biography.
5. United States Marine Corps—Non-commissioned officers—Biography.   6. Close air support—History—21st century.   7. Taliban.   8. Murgab River Region (Afghanistan and Turkmenistan)—History, Military.   9. Badghis (Afghanistan)—History, Military.
I. Bruning, John R.   II. Title.   III. Title: Story of U.S. Marine Special Operations in Bala Murghab, Afghanistan.
    DS371.413.G68 2014
    958.104'745—dc23   2014016597

ISBN 978-1-250-07029-6 (trade paperback)

St. Martin's Griffin books may be purchased for educational, business, or promotional use. For information on bulk purchases, please contact the Macmillan Corporate and Premium Sales Department at 1-800-221-7945, extension 5442, or write to specialmarkets@macmillan.com.

First St. Martin's Griffin Edition: September 2015

10 9 8 7 6 5 4 3 2 1

To the men of Marine Special Operations Team 8222

and everyone who lived, fought, and died

in the Bala Murghab River Valley.

★ ★ ★

Always Faithful, Always Forward

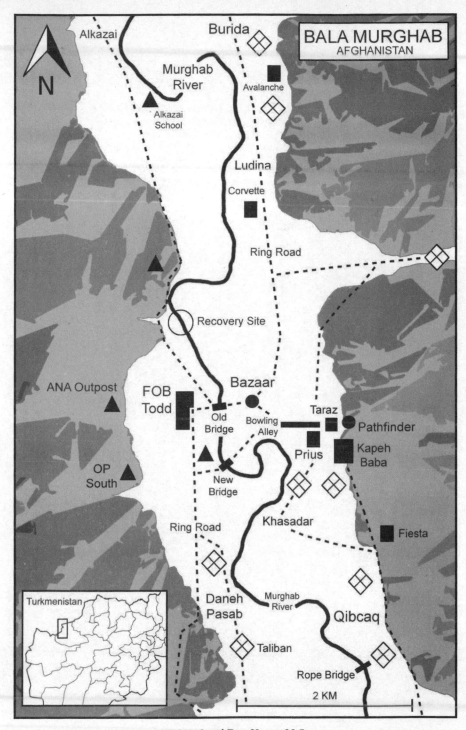

BALA MURGHAB
AFGHANISTAN

Alkazai
Burida
Murghab River
Avalanche
Alkazai School
Ludina
Corvette
Ring Road
Recovery Site
ANA Outpost
FOB Todd
Bazaar
Old Bridge
Bowling Alley
Taraz
Pathfinder
Prius
Kapeh Baba
OP South
New Bridge
Khasadar
Fiesta
Ring Road
Daneh Pasab
Murghab River
Qibcaq
Turkmenistan
Taliban
Rope Bridge
2 KM

© 2014 Level Zero Heroes LLC

★ Contents ★

The art of war is simple enough. Find out where your enemy is. Get at him as soon as you can. Strike him as hard as you can, and keep moving on.

—Ulysses S. Grant

★ AUTHOR'S NOTE ★

Before we left Afghanistan, I promised the men of my Marine Special Operations Team that if we lived through this experience I would find a way to share our story with the American people. I promised I wouldn't sugarcoat it, or turn it into a feel-good story like some of that sexy high-speed recruiting shit that Hollywood is known to produce. I wanted to tell the truth, even if the truth was something hard to swallow. The story of our team is a chronicle of a small group of extraordinary men thrown into a hopeless situation and asked to go win a war.

The men of MSOT 8222, call sign Dagger 22, represent the very best of what the Marine Corps brings to the Special Operations community. As the newest component of SOCOM, activated on February 24, 2006, Marine Corps Special Operations Command (MARSOC) hit the ground running with endless deployment cycles in support of operations in Afghanistan.

The Marines and sailors who make up these small and elite teams are asked to do nothing less than to be pioneers who will write a new chapter in Marine Corps history. The black granite blocks that sit in front of the MARSOC HQ building at Stone Bay, North Carolina, already bear the names of twenty-nine operators who have willingly given their lives performing the job that they loved, for the people they loved, and for a nation that will always be in their debt. Sadly, there is still plenty of blank space for more names to be added.

The story of Bala Murghab Valley is the story of the Afghan War in microcosm. Our struggle to liberate the valley from Taliban control reflects the challenges and trials of every unit throughout the country. Our chunk of Afghanistan happened to be an area once thought secure, and so little attention was paid to it. We arrived to discover the truth that the Bala Murghab Valley had never been secure. Instead, accommodations were made between the International Security Assistance Force (ISAF) and the enemy to live and let live. Our arrival, along with the U.S. Army's 82nd Airborne Division, changed all that.

It was my greatest privilege to have served alongside these men in some of the most hostile real estate in Afghanistan. We discovered a hidden hornet's nest of Taliban fighters operating freely and without retribution. There would be no accommodating them this time. What followed was six months of firefights, night raids, and offensives. We dropped more bombs in BMG than the Army, Marines, and Air Force did during the largest battle of the Iraq War, Second Fallujah (fact).

When our days in battle came to an end, the members of Dagger 22 were recognized as the highest-decorated Marine Special Operations Team to date with eight Purple Hearts, one Silver Star, and thirteen Medals for Valor awarded to the twenty-three-man team.

To protect the identities of the people in this story, only first names have been used, with the exception of those who are deceased. Those who fell—well, I want everyone who reads this book to know their names.

As for the individuals whose actions earned our contempt, I have changed their names fully for their sake. This book was not an opportunity to take cheap shots or to point out someone else's shortfalls. God knows I have my share of those. That is something those individuals will have to live with and played absolutely no part in the truthful and accurate telling of this incredible story. But the truth is the truth, and the destructive actions of some played a significant role in what Dagger 22 experienced. To delete them from the story would be offering a sanitized version of our history, and that would diminish the accomplishments of those who withstood the fires of battle with stout and noble hearts.

This book has no political agenda on failed foreign policies or the handling of the war. I would not disrespect the men in this story by associating them with any idealism or position on these topics. I wrote the story as it happened. You be the judge of what's right and wrong. That said, we were hampered constantly by the rules with which our nation's leaders have decided to fight the war in Afghanistan. Politics and the strategy that has emerged from that quagmire have cost us lives. I will not dishonor their memories by sugarcoating that reality.

War is easy. You either choose to fight or you choose not to. Afghanistan has no winners and losers, just those who survive and those who die. The Afghans, more than anyone else, know this truth, as it has been the fundamental current within their culture for centuries.

When we left the valley, we had learned it, too. We went in eager for victory. We chose to fight, we won our battles. In the end, none of it seemed to matter. None of it, except the most important thing: We did our damn best to bring everyone home.

To the team members of Dagger 22, this book is for you.

—Ski

★ FOREWORD ★

By Maj. Fred Galvin, USMC (Ret.)
Former Marine Special Operations Company F commander

Level Zero Heroes describes the shared sacrifices of Marine Special Operations Team 8222 as they lived, trained, and fought together in preparation for and during their combat operations in Bala Murghab, Afghanistan. If readers can see beyond the criticism of modified grooming standards and unapologetic combat vocabulary, the greater issues of Marines succeeding in combat become clear.

Prior to September 11, 2001, Marine Corps Force Reconnaissance Teams were not officially authorized to control aviation ordnance without having a qualified Forward Air Controller, which at the time were hard to come by. While serving as Reconnaissance Instructor and Joint Terminal Attack Controller in 2001 at the Weapons and Tactics Instructors course in Arizona, a former commanding officer of mine, Colonel Jeffrey Powers, visited our squadron to coordinate our course curriculums. He was a no-nonsense combat-experienced warrior who had served several tours in Marine Reconnaissance units. We both agreed that small teams with the ability to control precision munitions were vital to success in combat. But the fact was that enlisted Marines still were not legally authorized to control aviation ordnance.

As the Director of Training, Expeditionary Warfare Training Group Pacific, where aviation officers are trained to become ground controllers, Powers was on a new mission to have enlisted Marines qualified to control firepower and shape future fights. Shortly after returning to his schoolhouse, the first enlisted reconnaissance Marine officially attended the course and became a qualified air controller. Powers's forward thinking led directly to the increase in survivability for reconnaissance and Special Operations teams throughout the following thirteen years of combat.

Powers had opened the door; enlisted Marines were now able to become qualified to control aviation ordnance. This forever changed the landscape of precision air strikes.

Staff Sergeant Golembesky's qualifications and execution of combat controls in Afghanistan during 2009–10 portray the evolution and strategic advantage of enlisted Marines in this once officer-dominated role.

Level Zero Heroes also describes the evolution of MARSOC teams' incorporation of all-source intelligence fusion and integration with joint service Special Operations Forces and conventional forces in their pursuit of America's enemies.

MSOT 8222's battlefield account places the reader in the team, experiencing how they lived and fought. MSOT 8222 experienced combat proactively, not waiting to be engaged by the enemy on their terms.

The Marines, corpsmen, and officer of MSOT 8222 demonstrated courage under fire, swift decision making, brilliant coordination abilities with adjacent ground units and aviation assets, as well as an indomitable fighting spirit, which shattered the local Taliban forces during their tour in Bala Murghab, thus bringing hope to a hopeless situation.

For seven months the MARSOC warriors aggressively synchronized their intelligence, offensive tactics, and aviation firepower with the local units they supported and sought out the enemy.

This unvarnished account openly depicts the dark valleys of our war in Afghanistan through a battlefield description of NATO forces conceding and colluding with the Taliban.

Golembesky also recalls the friction of their fights and the frustration of how restrictive rules of engagement (ROE) and concepts of "battlefield restraint" hamstrung our warfighters' ability to win battles.

Level Zero Heroes illustrates how the failed counterinsurgency concept of "killing our enemies through kindness," while briefed exceptionally well to the U.S. and international press, in its battlefield application led to hesitation, which cost countless Coalition lives. Golembesky explains how our patriots were continuously placed under the zero-mistakes microscope and second-guessed on their battlefield decisions, culminating in prolonged official investigations. This self-induced restraint has empowered and emboldened our enemies. America is still allowing for the accountability of strategy failures at the command level to go unanswered.

Golembesky integrates his unique skill as a qualified air controller to connect his team with the aviation arsenal that was often the only option to overcoming a well-trained and violent enemy. He clearly communicates how highly advanced and deliberate our enemy has become in their battles with Coalition forces. The book provides firsthand experiences of the Taliban's cunning tactics of controlling shadow governments in villages, as well as exploiting leaders on both sides.

Golembesky intimately describes overcoming his personal fears and mastering the controlling of aviation firepower so that he would never fail the men he fought beside. His meticulous preparation for combat using the entire fixed-wing attack arsenal, coupled with the lethality of his team's tactics when engaging the enemy, only confirmed MSOT 8222's commitment to defeating the Taliban in their area.

The Taliban mastered the use of natural and urban terrain, fighting with improvised explosive devices and indirectly through the intimidation and assassination of Afghan civilians, including the families of Afghan National Army soldiers. This is all in an effort to defeat the development of the Afghans' internal defense capability, which has become our exit strategy to the war.

Level Zero Heroes' account of American Special Operators, who sacrificed the stability of their personal lives and families through demanding pre-deployment training and dangerous combat deployments, also includes vivid descriptions of the intimate bonds created during tumultuous and uncertain circumstances. It provides seldom disclosed personal accounts of their understanding of the brutal enemy they faced.

MSOT 8222 continuously demonstrated steadfast professionalism during numerous enemy engagements. Their problem-solving abilities were able to keep them focused on defeating an enemy that is often invisible— hiding—fighting from within the Afghan population.

Level Zero Heroes' honest portrayal of personal and collective mistakes shows how these warfighters faced the music and turned a deficiency into strength. This only highlights the honor and openness of these warriors, who never allowed anything to prevent them from winning the day.

Golembesky's unapologetic description of the "ground truth" in Afghanistan is refreshing and many times disturbing. He sheds light on the reckless abuse of authority in a hazardous environment where rank rules and often goes unquestioned, and chillingly describes how a commander compromised his commitment to his men and allowed an all too often focus on politics to needlessly risk the lives of Coalition forces in the valley.

The multiple accounts of assertive tactical ingenuity among key members of the team, such as Licon's critical skill at defeating explosive devices; Mark's striving to be the deadliest precision rifle on the battlefield; and King's unrelenting work ethic in pursuing accurate intelligence aspects to target the enemy reveal the Marine Corps' still-alive gung ho Raider spirit.

Work together.

The Raider concept is based upon a Chinese rebel tactic for how small separate forces are capable of defeating a larger force through working harmoniously together as one force aimed toward a united objective.

This is evident through MARSOC's training, which instills a commitment to progress each day in all areas. We see evidence of this training in an assaulter's actions during a gun battle of immediately transitioning from one weapon system to the next to achieve the most effective firepower against the enemy.

The tactics and techniques used by MSOT 8222 are not developed through simplified shortcuts and easy reference handbooks. It is not about being high-speed or having the coolest gear. It's about the raw lessons of combat that have been learned by the men that have come before. It's about having heart.

Effective combat capabilities are developed through realistic and challenging training that requires the most dedicated professionals to commit everything in order to be worthy of a position on a team.

This book offers a candid and direct description of tactical MARSOC leaders who displayed calmness during near catastrophic conditions, sound decision making, and clear and confident commands during gun battles: leadership traits that are evident throughout MSOT 8222's firefights.

Level Zero Heroes accurately portrays the impact that combat has across various levels within a team. Golembesky openly describes the disabling effect that combat stress has on team members during sustained combat operations. The experiences of our warriors create long-lasting and often negative changes to both individuals and families. American Veterans of Foreign Wars over the past century, especially the Vietnam

Veterans, have greatly advanced Americans' patriotism and honorable treatment of our nation's combat veterans.

The story of MSOT 8222 reinforces this patriotic spirit and connects readers with our warriors' humanness, described through Golembesky's sensitive accounts of striving to prevent the needless loss of American and Afghan lives, as well as through his enthusiasm to return to his family and a simpler life.

The indescribable sacrifices of MARSOC units in Afghanistan and across the globe have significantly increased our nation's security. These sacrifices are remembered in the shared sufferings of our patriots who have voluntarily laid down their lives simply because the American people asked them to. *Level Zero Heroes* brilliantly illustrates the depth of friendships developed through the team overcoming challenging circumstances, the sharing of personal confidences, and fighting a ruthless and determined enemy.

This is the story of America's trench-line fighters. As a nation, we could not be prouder of these warriors, and it is an honor to call them our own.

★ PROLOGUE ★

Dust churning in our wake, we rolled along a rutted dirt road that wound through countryside that could have passed for the set of *Dust Up*. A flat, empty wasteland greeted our eyes to the north and south. Wadis and arroyos furrowed the landscape. Here and there, a few hardy plants and trees tried valiantly to make a go of it. Brown grass grew in tufts and waved in the gentle breeze. Behind us, snowcapped mountains rose out of this postapocalyptic nothingness to provide a dramatic backdrop.

Our drivers were going flat out as our gunners rode high in their turrets. We'd been equipped with light armored trucks called Ground Mobility Vehicles (GMV)—basically souped-up Humvees with pickup-truck-style beds behind the cabs. They were designed exclusively for Special Operations units, and they bristled with weaponry. The turrets sported .50 caliber machine guns or 40mm grenade launchers, while the guys in back manned a pair of 7.62mm machine guns. Humvees had a third of our firepower.

The dirt road dumped us onto a black strip of asphalt that cut east–west through the desert. We swung left and blasted down the hardball, speedometers touching sixty-five. I rode in the back bed of our GMV, watching our little convoy of gun trucks and enjoying the wind on my sunburned face. It'd been a long day in full battle gear, and I was sweaty, rank, and dust-covered. Hours of wearing my helmet had left the back of my neck sore, as was my ass from sitting on the hard bench in the back of this truck. A few spent shell casings rattled around at our boots. We'd have to clean the brass out later.

The diesels roared. The sun dropped lower on the horizon, growing redder and more defined as sunset approached. We passed a reservoir haloed by green trees and grass, and it reminded me of an oasis in a Foreign Legion movie.

Another twenty minutes, and the desert gave way to irrigated farmland sustained by the reservoir. Orderly and well tended, the farms fanned out for miles on either side of the highway, a few homes interspersed among the fields.

A small town came into view up ahead, shimmering in the heat radiating off the asphalt. Some old buildings and a gas station—that was about it. Our lead truck pulled into the station and stopped at the pump island as the rest of us lined up to take a turn as well. After all the driving we'd done that day, all four of our GMVs needed to be topped off.

A few locals were busy gassing up their sedans and pickup trucks. When we dismounted from our armored vehicles, they snatched uneasy glances at us; others gaped in surprise. I doubted any of them had seen a Marine Special Operations Team blow into their little town before like this. When I climbed out of the back of our GMV to stretch my legs, the .45 caliber MEU(SOC) pistol I wore attracted some looks. Or maybe it was the body armor.

Pat, one of our Recon operators, slipped out of his turret, face covered in camouflage paint. I'd only been with the team a short time, and I barely knew its members but already Pat stood out. Energetic and passionate about all things military, he had been among the first to welcome me aboard. He was also the only one of us to put on cami paint. He wore it all the time, through every mission. When we hit the casinos in Reno after training missions, he'd show up with the stuff still in the creases behind his ears and along his hairline, even after showering.

"Let's go get some food," he said as he walked past me.

I followed him and the others into the gas station's minimart, where a thirtysomething woman at the cash register greeted us with wide eyes. She was a stocky woman with bad teeth and a nametag on her shirt.

Tough life out here on the edge of nowhere. Probably makes less than eight bucks an hour.

That was me once, toiling away in a meaningless job, saving every dime I had to get out of the dead-end shithole existence I lived in back in Levittown, Pennsylvania. I achieved escape velocity and never looked back. I wondered about her. Was she saving, or simply surviving?

I nodded to her as we streamed past on our way to the beer cooler.
"Coffee's free for you boys," she said to us.

We thanked her, and a couple of us peeled off and went for the pots
brewing on a side counter. The rest of us grabbed boxes of Budweiser, Coors
Light, and Miller and stacked them next to her register. A few more of the
guys grabbed a bunch of Ball Park Franks and buns. Soon, we had a pile of
dogs, buns, beer, and condiments heaped in front of the cashier. She began
ringing it up as the rest of us grabbed some coffee.

We stood in line and waited as the cashier totaled out our munchies.

"Hey Ski, can I ask you something," Pat said.

"Sure."

I'd seen him looking at the tattoo on my arm earlier, so I was expecting some sort of remark. It always got remarks. He nodded down at it and
said, "What's that shit on your arm say?"

"Kill Whitey. In Hindi"

He blinked. "Dude, that's fucked up."

It actually says "Peace" in Hindi, but I wasn't about to tell a bunch of
Special Ops Recon guys I'd just met something like that. I was already
the black sheep of this bunch, I didn't need to make it worse.

The cashier gave us our total, and Pat paid up. She handed him the receipt, which he stuck absently in his pocket. That little scrap of paper later
came back to haunt us, but we didn't know it then.

Moments later, twenty Marines in full combat kit burst out of the local
Kwik-E-Mart toting boxes of beer and sacks of grub. We threw them aboard
the GMVs and mounted up. Traffic in this little burg on the outskirts of
Fallon, Nevada, was light that day, but cars stopped to let us have the right
of way as we pulled out onto the main highway. After all, who wouldn't
break for armored gun trucks? Well, besides Iraqi drivers and guys em-
placing IEDs (improvised explosive devices).

Gas, food, booze; we were all set. We put the sunset to our six and
double-backed toward the wasteland of Dixie Valley. We hadn't gone far
when Pat ducked down in his turret, then reappeared with a Budweiser in
hand. He cracked it open and took a long pull.

*Do the open container laws extend to machine gun turrets on armored
vehicles?*

We had been training in Nevada now for several weeks as part of our

pre-deployment workup for Afghanistan. Our Marine Special Operations Company (MSOC) was next in line to deploy to that country. The
teams had been formed only a few years before, and now we were in the
full-up rotation of deployments to Afghanistan like the rest of the SOCOM
(Special Operations Command) elements.

To stand up MARSOC, the Corps culled the ranks of the Force Recon
battalions, which up to that time had been the elite of the Marine infantry (MOS 0321). I was one of the only non-Recon guy on the team, which
made me instantly suspect to the others. That was okay. I'd been an outsider all my life; nothing new here.

We reached the dirt road just as it grew dark. Headlights on, we
bounced and shuddered into Dixie Valley as naval jet fighters streaked
overhead. The valley was part of the vast naval airbase at Fallon, and the
aviators used it for simulated bombing runs and low-altitude combat ma-
neuvers. We'd been out at the ranges all day, shooting up targets as we
practiced firing from our moving GMVs.

When we'd planned our operations in Dixie Valley, we'd discovered a
couple of derelict buildings large enough to be seen on our satellite maps.
Seemed like a good place for some team bonding. We decided to spend
the night there.

We found the site about ninety minutes after leaving the gas station.
An aluminum barn sat beside a trashed single-wide mobile home in dis-
repair. The place had been abandoned for years, if not decades. Nobody
lived in the valley of course, since it was one giant military reservation.
Our drivers parked the GMVs beside the barn, and we dismounted to set
up our campsite between the two buildings.

With headlamp on, I set off to explore with the rest of the guys. The
barn was tall, perhaps forty feet high at its peak. The roof was still intact,
as was the siding. But when we pulled open the door, a vile stench poured
out. Rats scurried between the stalls. Animal shit was scattered everywhere. One look was enough. We backed off and went to check out the
mobile home.

The interior looked like the scene of the world's worst domestic fight.
Drawers had been pulled out and smashed. Cabinetry had been yanked
off the wall and now sat splintered in heaps in the kitchen. A foul odor
permeated the air here as well—a combination of rot and the sourness of

neglect. Trash littered the place—broken bottles, wrappers, and shreds of linen or clothing lay intermingled on the dirt-strewn floor. The carpet had rotted away in places, and the linoleum in the bathroom was curled and torn. Part of the roof was gone, too.

George, one of our breachers, whose job it was to blow doors open for the rest of the team to go through, stood inside the place and said, "This looks like something straight out of a horror movie."

We returned to the trucks and began off-loading the food and booze. Not far from where we parked, we found an old campfire site. This was probably a secret party spot for the high school kids in Fallon.

We scrounged around for wood and started our own bonfire. Somebody returned to the mobile home and pulled the grates out of the oven. We put them over the fire and threw the hot dogs on top. Soon, everyone was standing around in small groups, chatting, drinking, and eating.

We hadn't had much of a chance to get to know each other. We'd had some nights out in Reno, but this was our first opportunity to get away from our command and the casino night life and just be together as a team.

I stood alone, drinking a beer and watching the guys. I'd been away from the team for much of the pre-deployment workup. While they'd been together, I'd been off at Joint Terminal Attack Controller (JTAC) course learning how to call in air strikes with pinpoint accuracy. I'd volunteered for the position and had come straight from a Field Artillery unit, so nobody in the Recon community had any idea who I was. Recon Marines are a closed bunch. If you are not one of them, they do not trust you until you prove your worth. That made me the team's question mark. It also made me cautious and quiet.

A sonic boom thundered overhead. More dogfight training. I took a long pull from the can of beer I held and realized Rob was standing next to me.

Dark hair and dark eyes, bushy eyebrows, and broad shoulders, Rob was a Recon guy filling the role of team human intel specialist. He was also one of our senior Recon Marines.

"How you doing, Ski?" As usual, he had a dip in his mouth.

I shrugged. "A lot better now that I am out of that truck."

Since I first came aboard, Rob had been the only one to greet me with any warmth. I'd gotten a good vibe from him right away, and that initial impression proved to be spot-on. As I watched him during our training exercises, he continually impressed me. Smooth and cat-quick in close-quarters combat drills, an excellent shooter, in superb physical shape—he was the consummate Marine. He also had a quiet, thoughtful leadership style that amazed me at times. A few words from Rob could change everything in a heartbeat. He was the kind of alpha male that other alpha males followed.

"You're from Colorado, aren't you?" he asked.

"Now I am. Grew up in Pennsylvania. How about you?"

"Richfield, Ohio. Small town. Just me and my dad."

"Were your folks divorced?" I asked. I never knew my father. He bailed when I was a kid.

Rob shook his head. "No."

The answer seemed like the verbal equivalent of a no trespassing sign, so I changed the subject. "That was a hell of a run you pulled off in Reno."

Rob grinned. "Thanks. Was a long night."

One night, we'd gone out on the town in Reno, and Rob had disappeared throughout the course of the night. The next morning we were supposed to head over to the Reno Police Department SWAT team's rifle range. Rob never made it back to the barracks. We had waited for him as long as we could, then climbed into our trucks and departed. Later that morning, our company's executive officer spotted Rob running on the side of the road, bathed in sweat. He'd woken up someplace in town that morning with his cell phone dead. Instead of calling for help and a ride, he shucked off his shirt and started running the eleven miles uphill back to the Reno-Stead Airport, where we were staying. The temperature couldn't have been under a hundred that morning, and he pulled off this feat without any water.

Our MSOC commander called Andy, our team leader, and asked what the hell Rob was doing running on the side of the highway. Without a thought, Andy covered for him. "He's just doing a little extra PT."

Across the fire from us, George was talking with our team's scout sniper, Mark. The two of them suddenly erupted in laughter at something George had said. Raised in Atlanta, George was a rich kid. I didn't know much about him other than he talked a lot. And by a lot, I mean like non-stop. He was a one-man spectacle of sheer entertainment whose sense of humor was wicked smart and edgy. A few times in Hawthorne and Reno, I'd be sitting near George and the other younger Recon guys, listening to him say things so outrageous that I couldn't help but to bust out laughing. I felt like an eavesdropper and tried to stifle myself. The guys would look over at me like I was the band geek sitting at the next table over from all the jocks.

Rob walked over to grab another beer. Alone again, I sat down in a folding field chair next to our GMV and listened to the conversations around me. Another pair of jets passed overhead. The night grew cold. As the temperature dropped, the team started to gather by the fire. The little knots of friends gave way to a warrior's circle, faces lit red-orange by the flames. Soon they were laughing about Okinawa deployments and a legendary redheaded stripper from Guam.

"Hey, new guy," somebody called to me. "Get over here."

I stood up and carried my chair over and found space between Rob and Pat. A huge bottle of Jameson whiskey materialized. Mark pulled off the cap and took a long swallow, then handed it to George.

Mark had been talking about his first stint in the Corps back in the 90s. He'd had a break in service before rejoining a few years ago.

"Why'd you come back?" George asked him.

Mark said, "I was a cop for a while in Dallas. Then I worked construction. One night, I was in Colorado, watching the movie *Shooter*. Realized that's what I was supposed to be doing. Took a pay cut, reenlisted the next day. Was in uniform a month later. That was in '07."

Pat laughed. "I lasted about two weeks."

George said, "Pat, I have a hard time believing you were ever a civilian. I think you came out of your mother's womb with a KA-BAR in your mouth and wearing cami paint."

"I worked at Home Depot," Pat replied. "Well, that was until I had a misunderstanding with management."

"You got canned from Home Depot?" somebody asked.

"It was a mutual parting of ways," Pat said as he took the bottle of Jameson and drew a mouthful. He stood up, unsteadily, and shouted, "Now, I'm from First Recon, and I'm the best at everything, ever!"

The rest of the team hooted him down as he handed me the Jameson. He sank back into his chair, polished off the dregs of his beer, and suddenly blurted, "Seriously, guys, I love you. There's nothing like the Brotherhood. I never want to be a civilian again."

I took a swallow and passed the bottle to Rob just as Pat added, "Though I gotta tell you, this is the ugliest group of guys I've ever been around. Except for me, of course."

Another round of hoots.

Pat drained a beer and cracked another. He looked over at me and said, "Wish we coulda crashed that prom."

We'd been in Hawthorne, Nevada, for part of our training when we almost did that. Hawthorne was the sort of place survivalists would love should a zombie pandemic ever break out. Out in the middle of the desert near Walker Lake (whose water is toxic), the town is tiny and exists only because of this curious joint Army-Navy base built during the Depression. Row upon row of hardened, semi-underground concrete bunkers stretch for miles. There's something like three thousand of them out there. Originally designed to store thirty days' worth of ammunition for the U.S. military in a global conflict, the place has long since become a weird dumping ground of oddball and cast-off stuff deemed too obsolete to use, but somehow too valuable to destroy. While we were there, we stumbled across a bunch of replacement sixteen-inch gun barrels all neatly stored for use aboard *Iowa*-class battleships. Never mind that they're all floating museums now. I guess the Navy couldn't bear to get rid of its last big guns.

Anyway, Hawthorne was a tiny burg with absolutely nothing to do. That left us bored to tears at night after we finished training for the day. One Friday night, we were unloading our weapons from the trucks after another twelve-hour stint on the ranges. Across the street from us was the house that used to serve as the base commander's quarters. Somebody had put streamers out front, and music was playing inside. Soon, high school kids began rolling up in freshly washed cars. The Hawthorne High School class of 2009 was probably all of a dozen kids, and they all showed up dressed in hand-me-down tuxes with their dates wearing corsages and knee-length dresses. Prom night in the American military's junk-filled attic.

That looked like fun. Besides, what else was there to do? The team discussed this development and made hasty plans to join in the revelry. Hell, I never went to prom.

Before we could finish stowing our heavy weapons, our MSOC com
mander happened by. He watched another carload of kids pull up at the
general's house, looked over at us, and a lightbulb went on.

"Oh hell no!" he muttered. Then, standing between us and the prom,
he said, "I guess I have to say it. The prom is off limits!"

So much for that. The memory conjured all sorts of off-color, filthy
comments, which prompted George to say, "Y'all about the most offensive
bunch of Marines I've ever met."

The team took that as a badge of honor. Stories of leaves in Manila and
Bangkok began spilling out. The guys howled with laughter and set about
topping each other. Gradually, though, the conversation flowed from light
and ribald to something more substantive. It was like we were circling the
real reason we were there, and with each circuit we grew closer to it. A
little at a time, each man brought a bit of himself to the fire. Mark was a
Texan, born to carry a scoped rifle. The team chief, Joe, had been in longer than anyone else. Going on twenty years. He had the gravelly voice
when speaking through the tobacco dip in his mouth and eyes hardened
from years in the field. Andy, our team leader, was soft-spoken and quiet.
He lingered in the background of the conversation, content to watch the
process unfold with a wry smile on his face. Never condoning or condemn-
ing our actions, just letting us be who we are. When I first met him, I got
a frat boy sort of vibe from him. Since then, I'd learned very little about
him other than he always knew how to get the best out of us when needed.
He never yelled, never browbeat. A few words were always good enough
to get whatever results he wanted. He trusted in the skills and talents of
his men.

"Midway through my sophomore year at Auburn, I was majoring in
psychology," George said as he took the bottle from Joe. "Went to go see
what I could do with a bachelor's degree. They told me I could be a school
counselor at a high school."

Another couple of aircraft rumbled in the starry night sky, and George
paused to let them pass. "I said, fuck that. Can you see me telling high
school kids what to do? That's when I realized this was a colossal waste of
time. Went home. Joined the Corps. Was in boot camp nineteen days later.
Next thing I know, some dude's screaming at me, face right in mine, and
there I was thinking, 'Well, this was a fucking mistake.'"

Pat asked him, "What battalion were you in?"

"Went to Okinawa with 2nd Recon. Went to Iraq with 3rd."

Billy, one of our assaulters, was sitting across from George. He was a workout machine, chiseled and huge. He looked like an NFL fullback. In a Florida drawl, he asked, "Where were you in Iraq?"

"Saladin Province."

Billy nodded. The two of them began talking about Iraq, sharing stories as the rest of us listened. Billy had sandy hair and an intensity about him that intimidated the hell out of me. Since coming aboard, he'd given me the cold shoulder even more noticeably than the others. I had made a point to stay out of his way.

Mark interrupted the two and said, "I've never been to combat, but I walked a beat in some shithole neighborhoods in Dallas when I was on the force."

"Hey Mark," Billy replied, "no offense man, but Texas thugs are a lot different than the fifty-year-old hardened assholes we had to fight."

"Yeah, whatever man," Mark said.

"Those guys are warriors, Mark," George said.

Mark ignored him and told a story about Dallas. George and Billy looked unimpressed. Quietly, in a voice so matter-of-fact it could have come from an accountant crunching numbers, Billy spoke of a firefight in Iraq and having to pull a wounded friend out of the line of fire. His brother Marine died of his wounds as he tried to save him. For that, the Corps gave Billy a Silver Star for valor.

George said, "I guess they hand those things out as a consolation prize for bad experiences."

He stood up and walked over to one of the Styrofoam coolers, grabbed a can, and walked back. As he sat down in his folding chair, he added, "Same thing happened to me. Congratulations for a horrible day! Here, take this Bronze Star."

The conversation died away for a moment. The mood had turned serious, and as I watched the circle of men around me by the fire, it dawned on me what was going on here. Only a few knew each other before the team came together. This night had become a way of sounding each other out, learning of the experiences and perspectives we brought to the table. Operators know their lives depend on the men around them. One weak link can get everyone killed. This moment in Dixie Valley became the bridge that led us all toward understanding each other.

The bottle made the circuit again as George said, "August 10, 2008."

We waited for the significance of the date.

"We'd been out searching compounds along the shore of Lake Tharthar. Twelve hours. Kick in doors, nothing. Mount up, go to the next one. Kick in doors. Reset, repeat. Totally smoked by the end of the day. We rolled up on a place we thought was abandoned. An L-shaped building. We were going to stay there for the night.

"The guys stacked up and the team leader gave the word to go. They kicked in the door and ran right into eight insurgents. PKM machine guns. Suicide vests. AKs. They shot the team leader fifteen times. Blew out the back of his head. He died just inside the doorway. Two more guys got hit as they tried to pull him out."

Mark looked on, his eyes never leaving George.

"They fucking assaulted out of the building into us."

"Holy shit," somebody said.

"I dismounted from my truck, came around the fender, and a shithead comes running out the door. He throws a grenade, then charges straight at me. I see he's got a vest on. Twenty feet away he detonates it."

"How are you still here?" Pat asked.

"The vest had only demo. No frag. It vaporized the dude. I was like, stunned. You know? Like wow, that dude was fucking serious. Not even his shoes were left.

"My truck got hit seventy times. That's how much fire they were pouring at us. At one point, another one comes charging out of the building, straight at one of our seven-ton trucks. No shit, the guy climbs up to the driver's door before anyone can shoot him. Our guy in the cab's staring at him as the dude's trying to figure out how to open the door, only he can't find the handle 'cause they're set low on the outside."

A couple of the guys nodded. George went on. "So he gives up and detonates his vest. It goes off, but doesn't hurt the driver. The dude's head, arm, and shoulder helicopter through the air and land between me and one of my guys, who looks over at me in the middle of all this shit and says, 'Whoa! Nigga just blew himself up, dawg!' "

I glanced at Mark. His face was stoic, revealing nothing.

"We ended up ramming the building, collapsing it in on the fuckers. They fought on in the rubble. I shit you not. I tried to run over where the doorway had been, but somebody threw a grenade at me. Thing blew up a few feet in front of me, right between my legs. One of those yellow Chinese fuckers. Blew me off my feet. Was lying there wondering what just happened when another one of my guys came over to me and said, 'You're good. You're good.' So I got up, and we ran to where the doorway had been and started digging through all the crap looking for our team leader. Dudes are shooting at us from inside, but we found him. Started clearing shit off his back. . . ."

His voice grew husky but steady as he delivered what happened next. "I reached down, trying to grab the back of his flak jacket. Put . . . my hand into the back of his head.

"A minute later, the fuckers throw another grenade at us. Me and one of the guys helping me jumped over what was left of a wall and landed on top of each other as it went off. We get back to work. Somebody's screaming, 'Treat him, treat him!' I'm like, 'He's dead.' Our radioman runs up as we got him out of the rubble and starts working on him. Bullets are still smacking all around us. I finally said to our radioman, 'Hey man, he's done. You're good.'"

The bottle reached George again. He took a swig, handed it to the next man, and said, "We backed off, called in air. Dropped a bomb. Blew the place to pieces. When we went back, there were still two dudes alive. They started shooting at us, so we threw C4 in and finished them off. Turned out, we'd stumbled across a cell of foreign fighters. They'd wired the place with propane IEDs. They had cash, a supply of suicide vests, lots of guns, money, and computers full of shit. The intel guys at Camp Fallujah said they hadn't seen anything like it in a long time."

George fell silent, which was rare. Pat stepped in. "It's all about the Brotherhood. It sees you through."

"Yeah. It is. But you know, I learned that you're not out there fighting for the cool story you can tell back home. You're out there for the man on your left and right. If you don't stick together, you're not going to prevail. If you don't throw all your chips on the table, people will have a big problem with you."

Pat nodded. "If you don't give a shit about the people around you, your skills don't mean anything."

"It's almost spiritual," George said quietly.

Nights like these are how that bond is built. Outsiders would see us drinking and saying outrageous things to each other. But that's just the entry point. The alcohol helped break down the alpha male barriers and let us drill into the heart of who we were. I could see it unfold that night as we took measure of each other.

I found the Jameson in my hand. As I took another drink, attention suddenly shifted toward me. It made me uneasy, and I'd been doing my best to stay anonymous within the circle. The guys started asking me about my job as the team's JTAC, their curiosity perhaps triggered by George's story of the bomb drop on that building.

Somebody remarked, "The last JTAC my team had was a lazy shitbag. Deadweight."

I said nothing. Through training, I'd seen all kinds of controllers. Some were conscientious, some were easily overwhelmed. Some were smooth and capable. The good ones were a true force multiplier. They could call in the wrath of God—rockets, bombs, AC-130 gunships, and B-1 Lancers— and vaporize a target with minute accuracy. With a JTAC, a Marine Special Operations Team (MSOT) has access to firepower ground units could only dream of in previous wars. Work the radios and the computer, and the heavens fall on any enemy, no matter how well dug in they were.

Mark asked, "How fast can you get us bombs on a target, Ski?"

I tried to explain the process. Aircraft could be overhead already in direct support in case we needed them. I'd be talking to them as soon as they came into our area of operations (AO) and as they loitered overhead waiting for the word to strike. In that situation, we'd have bombs on target in minutes. If we didn't have air support assigned to us for a particular mission and we got into trouble, I could call over the SAT-COM (satellite communications) radio to higher and they would send us any nearby available aircraft. That could be hit-or-miss, depending on what else was going on around Afghanistan at that time. Sometimes, the well would be dry. In other cases, it might take forty-five minutes for aircraft to scramble from Bagram Airfield or Kandahar and get to wherever our firefight was.

★ ★ ★

I finished by saying, "Trust me, if we get caught in a firefight an aircraft IS coming—just a matter of how long."

"Do you know what kind of aircraft we're going to work with?" somebody else asked.

"Anything from B-1 bombers to unmanned drones. Doesn't matter. JTACs can work with anything and everything. Even other NATO air forces."

"You mean the French could give us air support?"

"French, British, Italians—whoever's available. The airpower support system's universal there."

The questions flowed. They asked me about my radio gear and small laptop computer that I'd been pulling out of my pouch on every patrol. I tried to give straightforward answers. I was new to all this, freshly minted from the JTAC course in Norfolk, Virginia. As an incoming controller, I'd have to be certified in theater and given a call sign once we got to Afghanistan. I knew that this made me an unknown and untested quantity. I tried to project confidence, but the truth was, I felt a lot of anxiety. Being a JTAC requires considerable multitasking. One missed step, one mistake, and a bomb ends up in the wrong place. Usually, that means the wrong people die. I tried not to reveal this to my new team members as they sized me up. Nor did I tell them I was mildly dyslexic and sometimes got numbers mixed up. Not good when you're reading grid coordinates. Because of that, I'd gotten into the habit of triple-checking all my numbers during the training drops I did.

George suddenly looked at me. This was unusual, as he'd basically ignored me since my arrival. Across the fire I caught his eye and could see he was thinking something through.

"Ski, what the fuck is up with that Krishna shit on the back of your neck?"

He was talking about a Hindu tattoo that says, "KRSNA." I'd gotten it in Colorado before I joined the Marines.

This stuff had made others in the Corps uncomfortable too. I'd been in since just after 9/11, but that was the reason I never really felt like I had a place. A lifelong outsider. Outcast as a kid. Definitely not your prototypical Marine.

George asked, "What's your story, Ski? You're like some demented hippie who got lost on his way to spiritual salvation and ended up in the Corps."

"Is Buddha okay with dropping bombs on people?" Billy asked.

If you don't throw all your chips on the table, people will have a big problem with you.

Either I take a leap of faith here, or I never join this Brotherhood.

The alcohol had my head spinning. By now it was well past midnight. The aircraft were still turning and burning in mock dogfights somewhere in the distance.

"Got the tattoo before 9/11," I said. "Was raised Irish Roman Catholic in the Northeast, but organized religion doesn't sit well with me. Constricting, with misleading intentions. When I was a kid, it struck me that going to church was for people who didn't have any morals and needed to be told how to be good. I was around a lot of people who needed that. Then I started learning about Hinduism in the mid-90s. It's spiritual without being rigid. Personal. It recognizes that there isn't one path, and it allows you to see other points of view. Really, I just believe there is a higher power."

Pat asked, "Does your arm really say 'Kill Whitey'?"

I shook my head. "No. 'Peace' in Hindi."

That generated some looks.

Billy asked, "How the fuck did a guy like you end up in the Marines?"

"Look man. I was always self-absorbed. In my own little world, you know? Grew up in a bad neighborhood. Got into drugs, trouble. Didn't give a fuck about school. Mom was an addict. Always on welfare."

"Yeah, and . . . ?" coaxed George.

"I realized after high school, if I didn't get out of Levittown, I'd just end up a shitbag and never escape. Got a job at a dairy. Saved every penny I could until I had enough to move to Colorado. Made a fresh start. Then 9/11 happened. I was working at another dairy, living with my girlfriend, Sabrina. Her folks called from New York. Told us what was going on. Clicked on the TV and watched the second tower fall. Sadness and history was unfolding in real time as the world watched."

I looked up from the fire. The team was staring at me intently. This was their turn to gain the measure of me, their new JTAC. The guy who could be their salvation—or damnation—in a firefight. We are itinerant specialists within MARSOC. We get attached to teams as needed. We're plugged in and pulled out after each deployment, so the team guys never go overseas twice with the same air controller. That makes it even harder for us to gain the team's trust since we're only with them for a single cycle.

"I went outside and placed an American flag on the outside of the studio apartment where I was living. It was the first time I connected to something larger than myself. Does that make sense?"

Nods around the circle.

"You're a 9/11 Marine," Joe muttered.

"I never gave a shit about politics. Never cared about what was going on overseas. But this was different. I didn't want my kid to come home from school and ask me what I did after 9/11 and not be able to tell them that I'd served. I asked for infantry. The Corps sent me to artillery. All I wanted to do was go to Afghanistan and do my part. Got sent to Iraq instead, twice."

"Where were you?" Billy asked.

"Syrian border and Husaybah. Manned checkpoints for what seemed like forever."

"You must have reenlisted," Rob said.

"I did," I admitted. "I extended so I could do this deployment with you guys."

"Why?" asked Pat.

"So I could get to Afghanistan. That's why I joined in the first place."

I'd been holding the bottle of Jameson. I looked down at it, took another swallow, then passed it along to Pat. Only a few more swigs' worth was left at the bottom.

"Took a pay cut when I joined. Just like Mark."

"Yep," he said.

"Sabrina had to move back to New York and live with her folks."

I started to laugh at a memory. "I had long hair and a beard back then. After I joined, I shaved it off and cut my hair short. Sabrina came home from work and saw me in nothing but my boxers. She started screaming. Thought I was a home invader. She'd never seen me with short hair."

"You are a really different kinda dude, Ski," George said after I finished. He said it in a neutral sort of way, as if he wasn't passing judgment. But he hadn't dismissed me either. I wondered if I'd passed the test.

The conversation veered off into more stories from the Philippines,

Thailand, and Okinawa. Mark talked of climbing into an old American concrete fortress in the middle of Manila Bay called Fort Drum. Joe spoke of the old days in Recon Bat—I was probably in grade school when he went to Basic. Mark talked of Dallas and playing football. Billy, a die-hard Florida Gators fan, lit up. Football dominated the conversation for several minutes.

"I played JV at Riverside," George said. "Dudes were huge. Fucking laid me out. That shit hurt!"

"Jesus Christ," Mark exclaimed with an eye roll.

"After that shit, I went out for track. So there I am, running the sixteen-hundred meter at one of my first meets, right? I look over, and there's this blind dude competing with me. He's got a chick tethered—no shit—tethered to him."

"That seems fucked up," said Billy.

"I know, right? So the race starts, and she's running beside him as his guide. Telling him where to go. And they're beating me? And I thought, Oh my God, I'm about to get smoked by a blind guy and his seeing-eye chick."

"What happened?" I asked.

"I poured it on at the last minute, my bitch tits flapping under my shit. Beat 'em by about ten feet. Then I started puking. That's how much he took out of me, right? That's some fucked-up shit. After that, I tried swimming. And lacrosse."

"You better be in better shape now," Joe muttered in a drunken slur.

"Well, I'd be happy to give y'all a full account of the ebb and flow of my man boobs if you'd like," said George.

By now, the night had grown still around us. The Jameson bottle lay empty in the dirt. Dawn was only a few hours away and even the aviators had headed home to bed. One by one, the guys left the circle and went off to find a place to sleep.

★ ★ ★

Looking back, that was the night we started our own Brotherhood. There's always a connection between Marines. The shared experience and train-ing of being in this branch of the service makes us distinct from others in uniform, as well as civilians. But that night was special. We'd come together and opened up in a way difficult for men, warriors, to do. We found respect where once was suspicion and uncertainty.

It did not happen without fallout. A few weeks later, an agent from Naval Criminal Investigative Service (NCIS) showed up looking for Pat. They pulled him into an interview room and grilled him for a few hours. They made him walk them through everything that happened in Dixie Valley that night.

When at last they released him, he burst into our team room and exclaimed, "You're not gonna believe this!"

It turned out that the receipt from the gas station's minimart had fallen out of Pat's pocket while we were exploring the trashed mobile home. Not long after our night out there, the local authorities discovered the body of a murdered prostitute that had been dumped in the crawlspace under the mobile home. When their forensics team picked over the place, they found the receipt and traced it back to the little burg on the edge of Fallon. The security camera footage showed us all in line, free coffee in hand and stacks of dogs and boxes of beer heaped before the cashier.

The girl had been killed and stashed weeks before we were out there. Her decomposing body no doubt contributed to that horrid stench inside the mobile home. The investigation quickly moved on elsewhere, but the incident revealed the extent of our drinking to our chain of command. Every team steals moments like Dixie Valley before a deployment. It is how we knit the unit together. It just usually happens under the radar and away from the flagpole. When our night came to light, our chain of command was outraged. It created such a shit storm that it looked like they'd break our team up and re-form it with new operators. Our fate was thrown up in the air.

Eventually, it all died down. In the adversity, our team closed ranks, which helped strengthen the growing bond we'd forged out in Dixie Valley. I was still regarded as the group's outsider, but the hostility from the younger Recon guys had eased. At least I wasn't the oddball hippie with the peacenik ink anymore, so that was a plus. But the jury was still out, and if I didn't perform I knew I'd lose the ground I'd gained. It made me tense and compulsive about doing my job. I watched everyone around me and tried to surreptitiously learn everything I could from them. Between the pressure of proving myself and the cloud we'd been under as a team for Dixie Valley, our departure for Afghanistan a few weeks later came almost as a relief.

Almost.

I

★ CAMP STONE, AFGHANISTAN ★

OCTOBER 29, 2009
HERAT, WESTERN AFGHANISTAN

The chow hall line moved with interminable slowness. We stood together as a team, waiting with our trays in hand for the Filipino cooks to serve us omelets on Styrofoam plates.

George had been in a foul mood. His humor could be abrasive and sardonic, and he'd been complaining so much that the other day Rob had finally asked him, "Is anything you're saying going to help our situation here?" He quieted down a bit after that. But his mood simmered below the surface.

Truth is, everyone was edgy. Herat was garrison hell. Clean uniforms and M4 carbines being used as accessories abounded. The closer to the flagpole, the more the little shit matters, and Herat was our flagpole. Not only was our MSOC headquarters element here, but the command element from Special Operations Task Force–West (SOTF-W) had set up shop right next door since we were only about a hundred kilometers from the Iranian border.

The chow line began to move. We shuffled forward and made small talk among ourselves. The uniforms around us reflected the diversity of the NATO effort here, which made us feel even more like strangers in a strange land. A sprinkling of Spanish, a few Italians, civilian contractors, a Dane or two mixed in with our Marine SOF (Special Operations Force) team and some Army paratroopers from the 82nd Airborne Division. Each group kept to themselves like little islands in a sea of unfamiliar allies.

Four days in country and we were already sick of the mind-set here. We'd been busting ass to prep for the movement to our permanent home about 180 klicks northeast of Herat. Zeroing weapons, prepping gear, modifying our GMVs with homemade metal side racks so we could carry more gear had dominated the last few days. While we worked to get into combat, the headquarters culture back here was cast straight from the peacetime stateside mold. Officers chastised us about the state of our uniforms and choice of footwear. Paperwork inundated us. The people here seemed out of touch with where they were and what we were supposed to be doing. And while Camp Stone was probably one of the safest places in Afghanistan, all of the personnel here drew combat pay and hazardous duty pay.

Fortunately, this would be our last breakfast in Herat. I'd jumped through all the administrative hoops and had been approved in theater as a JTAC, complete with my own call sign, HALO 14. Our gear was prepped and good to go. We'd be done with our final tasks later today, which included mounting a 7.62mm minigun onto one of our GMVs that would give a significant boost to our team's firepower. Tomorrow morning, we'd be linking up with a convoy from the 82nd Airborne that would make its way to the Bala Murghab Valley, which would be our home for the rest of the deployment.

The chow line inched closer to the Filipino cooks, who seemed to be the only people in the place in a good mood. They chatted and tried to joke with the men they served. The language barrier was a challenge, but a good breakfast is a universal language we all speak.

I stood in line next to Jay, the only black guy on our team. The guys lovingly referred to him as "Token" after the lone black kid in the television series *South Park*. His mood mirrored George's. He'd been grousing on and off all morning as he worked to get the team's radios up and running for tomorrow's departure.

Ahead of us in line, another black soldier, wearing an 82nd Airborne patch, glanced over his shoulder at us. He caught sight of Jay, who was the only other black guy in the chow hall. The soldier looked away quickly and fiddled with his tray.

Jay was a squared-away Marine. Meticulous with his gear, he wore an air of confidence that made him seem a little larger than life. He tolerated no fools, and he had zero social filter. He would have been a disaster in the Diplomatic Corps. As a Marine, he was first-rate, a man you could depend on to get shit done.

During our final weeks in the United States as we finished our train-ing together, I began to watch Jay closely. He was a Recon Marine like Mark, Billy, and George, as well as our team's commo guy. He had a real love-hate relationship with his communication duties. Every down mo-ment we had, I saw him fussing over the radios and comm gear. He also made a point of taking care of everyone's crypto changes. Our radios had encryption codes that were swapped out for new ones every few weeks as a security measure. Jay would hound everyone on the team, reminding them of upcoming crypto changes and telling them to bring their radios to him so he could take care of the swap for them.

Several times back in the States, somebody had forgotten, and I'd seen him sigh in frustration. "Dude, I told you to get your radio to me last night," he'd scold them, but would take the radio and make the changes for him anyway.

The 82nd Airborne soldier glanced back at Jay again. What was going on here?

"Hey Jay?" I asked him.

"Yeah?" he asked. Well spoken and highly intelligent, he had a deep voice that could project like a drill instructor's when he got fired up.

"You think you can show me how to load crypto properly in my radio and how to use TEKs?"—Traffic Encryption Key.

"No problem. I've seen you watching me do it." Like Mark, he hailed from Texas, but you'd never know it by the way he spoke. Both our team's Texans sounded like Yankees.

I'd learned a long time ago in the Corps that it never hurts to bag a new skill. If I could handle this, it'd make Jay's life a little easier. Plus, I was anal about my own gear. I wanted to make sure I knew it inside and out, from the radios to the computer I carried to the M4 I slung over my shoulder. If something was fucked up, I wanted it to be my fault and no one else's.

The 82nd Airborne soldier looked back at Jay a third time. Jay was waiting for that. Their gazes met, and the soldier nodded at him know-ingly.

Jay's eyes widened. His nostrils flared and he suddenly shouted, "Hey, nigger! I don't know you!"

Everyone in earshot froze. The place went dead quiet. The 82nd Airborne soldier appeared stunned. Around Jay, the rest of us wanted to find a fighting position and dive for cover.

The 82nd guy couldn't tear his eyes away.

"Why you nodding at me?" Jay demanded. I swear his voice could have been heard in Kabul.

The man shook his head and turned his back to us. A tense moment passed, then gradually the hubbub usually resident in the chow hall returned.

We got our food and sat down at a table not far from the 82nd Airborne soldier and his buddies.

It took a bit for me to screw up the courage to say, "Jay, I think he was just trying to identify with you a little."

Jay scoffed, then bellowed, "I don't know that fuckin' nigger!"

Ducking, I said, "Okay! Relax man."

"Dude, no need to start a race war with the only other black guy in here," George remarked.

Andy sat down next to me and shook his head. He'd been around Jay enough to know that trying to say anything to him was a waste of time. Besides, Jay did this sort of thing all the time just to fuck with us white guys and make us uncomfortable.

There was also something more significant at play here. Jay had joined the Marines at nineteen back in 2004, and had served with Recon battalions in Iraq and Afghanistan prior to this deployment. The commonalities that exist in civilian life back home meant nothing to him now. Common race or gender, it had no impact. His loyalty, attention, and the friendship he offered came only in the context of his team and fellow Recon guys. That bond transcended all others. He seemed genuinely offended when somebody presumed to be his brother just because their skin color happened to match.

His brothers were Recon Marines, team guys and nobody else. And the scene in the chow hall that morning was a reminder to me to tread carefully. I was still outside the circle. Presume and pay.

We started eating in silence. Gradually, a conversation grew from the favored topic du jour: our future home. We knew little about Bala Murghab, so we pounced on any rumors or scraps of intel that came our way.

Andy took a sip of coffee, then passed along the latest tidbits he'd

picked up. The Spanish army originally established the FOB, the Forward
Operating Base. There'd been some sort of firefight while their engineers
were building a new bridge across the river that ran through the area.
After that, the Spaniards pulled out and turned it over to an Italian mech-
anized infantry unit to take control of the area. NATO politics sucked, and
the word around Herat was that the Spaniards had absolutely no heart
for this fight.

"How about the Italians? Any word on them?" Rob asked Andy.

"Fucking NATO. Pussies," somebody said.

"Not sure yet," Andy told us. "They have different rules of engagement
than we do. We'll find out more when we get up there."

The NATO force in Afghanistan operated under a general set of rules
of engagement. Under those, each nation had its own ROEs. Some coun-
tries were there as a token effort to show unity with the NATO Alliances.
The Poles were like that. Their troops and aircraft were not allowed to
engage unless they personally got shot at by the enemy. Even if other NATO
elements nearby were being shot up, the Poles could not respond as a result of their national ROEs. The Brits were the most aggressive and had
been fighting ferociously in the south for the better part of the decade.

Our own ROEs had undergone a radical revision now that General
Stanley McChrystal had taken over as theater commander (COMISAF).
Where once our troops had flexibility on the battlefield, in my opinion
McChrystal's feel-good tactical directives had clipped the wings of our ag-
gressiveness and ability to effectively kill the enemy in a timely manner.

We'd spent hours talking through them as a team since most of the
limitations he'd placed on American troops struck right at the heart of
what Special Operations units do best. Night raids had to be specially approved at the SOTF commander level now, which was a challenge since
that was when Special Operations units operated. We weren't allowed to
drop bombs on enemy fighters in civilian compounds. We also could not
open fire unless the enemy clearly possessed weapons. We'd heard from
returning teams how all this had affected combat operations. The Taliban
had quickly adapted to the ROEs' restrictions and figured out ways to use
them against us. They'd shoot at American troops, then drop their weapons and run, knowing that since they were no longer armed, our forces
could not return fire. Where would they run? Into compounds, of course.

They used civilian homes as ambush positions, knowing we couldn't bring our superior firepower to bear. McChrystal's new directives were designed to better protect the civilian population, but from what we were hearing, they'd made it easier for the Taliban to infiltrate communities, then terrorize the locals into collaboration.

You practically needed a master's degree to figure out who could shoot at whom and under what circumstances. It was a crazy way to fight a war. Even crazier was the lack of knowledge we had of our assigned AO. Eight years into the war and we were about to go into action as blind as the first SOF units had in 2001.

I asked Andy, "Are we going to get any better maps of the area?"

He shrugged. "So far, no luck."

The only one we had of Bala Murghab was a Soviet Red Army topographical map printed in the 80s during their Afghan war. It had appeared up in our Tactical Operations Center (TOC) one day while we were training at Fort Irwin, California. It showed a valley surrounded by massive, steep hills, accessible by only a couple of dirt tracks, or by helicopter. That quarter-century-old Communist map drafted by a regime long since swept into history's dustbin was the best imagery we could find on Bala Murghab. Needless to say, we all found that a little depressing.

For most of the current war, the valley's sheer remoteness had shielded it from most of the post-9/11 violence that had engulfed the rest of Afghanistan. Until a few months before our arrival, the area had not even been patrolled by NATO forces.

Pat spoke up. "I was talking to a guy in the 82nd Airborne. He said when they first went up there, the people thought they were Russians."

"Russians?" Mark asked.

"Yeah, like they thought the 80s war had never ended. They had no idea what was going on elsewhere in country."

"That's fucking unbelievable," said Jay as he took a bite of scrambled eggs.

Pat added, "The guy told me that they had never heard of bin Laden. He and his unit were the first Americans they'd ever seen."

Heads shook around the table. It sounded like we were rolling into the land that time forgot.

Andy checked his watch. "Rob, Ski—we've got that convoy briefing we need to get to."

We finished up and dumped our trays. The rest of the team headed back to finish loading up the GMVs. Rob, Andy, and I walked over to a large plywood hut to meet the troops we'd roll out with in the morning. The room inside had raised bleachers for seats. We climbed onto them and sat in back, stealing glances at the people gathered for the briefing.

There were too many clean uniforms in this room. Meat eaters can smell their own kind. Andy and Rob—meat eaters. The rest of the room? Not so much. These people had "NOT ESSENTIAL PERSONNEL" practically stamped on their foreheads. Cooks, clerks, headquarters castaways, and slackers, all of whom looked lost and nervous, sat around us. I wondered if they'd even fired their rifles on a range since arriving in country. The bleachers gradually filled up until there were perhaps twenty-five people in the room. I counted three women in the group.

This was not an organic unit from the 82nd. This was a collection of random people thrown together for an ad hoc, temporary assignment to convoy duty. People who haven't worked together before have no common procedures, contingency plans, or tasking. There's no telling what the person next to you will do in a scrap. These people weren't even Marines, so we didn't even have that in common with them.

This didn't bode well. At least the convoy commander would iron out some basic procedures and plans during the brief.

A staff sergeant walked in with a second lieutenant in tow. The lieutenant, a slight kid, looked just as lost as the rest of the crowd. He was so young I wondered if he could even legally drink. Not a meat eater.

This is the guy we're going to have to follow to the middle of nowhere?

The staff sergeant conferred with the lieutenant quietly for a minute, then moved to the front of the room.

"All the way, troopers. This is Lieutenant White," he said as he gestured to the young lieutenant.

The staff sergeant flipped on a projector, connected a laptop, and started a PowerPoint presentation. It lasted all of about five minutes.

The 82nd Airborne had only sent one other convoy to Bala Murghab. It set out a month before and got ambushed on the way up while the vehicles passed through a small village of mud huts in a valley. The staff sergeant showed us the exact location and walked us through what had taken place. The convoy blew through the ambush and made it to Bala Murghab intact, barely.

Our convoy would use the same exact route. In fact, from Herat, there was only one way to get to Bala Murghab, which meant any Taliban look-outs in the area would have a fairly good idea of where we were going.

The staff sergeant said, "We'll stop for the night at Qal-e-naw, a small city about ninety klicks northeast. The Spanish have a PRT site (Provincial Reconstruction Team) there near a small airstrip. We'll fuel up in the morning and make it to FOB Todd by nightfall of day three."

He continued. "We'll be escorting a group of tanker trucks with fuel for the FOB. We'll also have with us some flatbed trucks carrying containers for the MARSOF team"—gesturing toward us. "They'll all be driven by local national contractors."

He finished up the brief, and Lieutenant White stepped before the group. In a reedy voice, he said, "Be ready with your gear. Be ready to execute. See you all in the morning."

As the soldiers got up and headed for the door, Rob and Andy shared worried glances.

"That's it?" Rob said, incredulous. "You hafta be fucking kidding me."

The brief had not included a commo plan, any standard operating procedures, no discussion on what to do if we were attacked, nothing about air cover, Quick Reaction Forces, or even where to go to get help if we needed it. There'd been no intelligence component to go over which villages we'd be passing through were friendly or hostile. There'd been nothing on enemy activity along the route. We hadn't even gone over what our formation would look like. This was no way to do business, especially with the slapped-together crew on this convoy.

At least we'd had our own internal discussion on these things the previous night. No matter what these 82nd Airborne guys ended up doing, at least our team would be on the same page should the situation go to hell. Andy had made sure of that.

We left the briefing room feeling very unsettled. No good can ever come out of lack of preparation and planning. This had all the makings of a first-class disaster. And we had no choice but to be a part of it.

2

★ CONVOY TO NOWHERE ★

Game day. The twenty-three men of Dagger 22, our team's call sign, strapped the last of the gear to the sides of our four GMVs in the predawn darkness. I stood in the back bed of the second GMV in our small column, where I would crew the portside M240 machine gun.

"You ready, Ski?" Andy asked as he opened the GMV's right rear door.

"Ready or not, let's do this."

I settled onto the hard bench seat I'd come to hate so much in Nevada. A moment later, Captain Strom piled in back with me. Strom was Andy's counterpart who commanded the MSOT we would be replacing. He'd come along to help familiarize us with the situation out here.

He shucked off his assault pack and dumped it on the deck. As I introduced myself, Strom unslung a bandolier of 40mm grenades, which he hung from a rack beside the starboard-side M240. Then he stowed an old Vietnam-era M79 grenade launcher by his knees.

He gestured to the bandolier. "I plan on shooting all these before we get to Bala Murghab."

A captain with a grenade launcher and the intent to use it. Not something you see too often these days in the Marine Corps.

Andy gave the word, and our column rolled out of our small compound to a staging area where we linked up with Lieutenant White and his 82nd Airborne element. He assigned us the rear of the convoy, and when the local national trucks began to arrive, we interleaved our four rigs into the last third of the column.

As dawn broke on the eastern horizon, we inched out through the camp's front gate and turned onto Highway 1 (Ring Road), the only paved highway in western Afghanistan. We followed it straight through the heart of downtown Herat and into the bazaar area. Already, the place teemed with people. Cooking fires burned, dead animals dangled from hooks in the tin-shack butcher shops. Men haggled over goods, others wandered around. I noticed some of the shops were built out of metal shipping containers. They'd simply cut windows and doors in the sides of them and opened up for business.

Around us, mopeds buzzed past as garish jingle trucks lumbered along in the opposite lane. A pair of civilians doubled up on a Japanese dirt bike roared by. Traffic slowed, and our column found itself stuck in the middle of a workday morning in metropolitan Herat. A moment later, we came to a standstill as the traffic flow stopped completely. Over the radio, we heard that a jingle truck had caused an accident ahead. We waited for the wreck to be cleared and watched the scene around us for any potential threats.

It did not take long for the kids to discover us. At first, one or two ventured out into the street to coax water or food from us. It was like Iraq all over again. The more timid soon joined their bolder pals. At first, some of our 82nd guys gave them water or scraps of food. Strom saw that and remarked, "That's like spitting on a forest fire."

Sure enough, encouraged by the response, more kids piled into the street. Some tried to climb onto the sides of our rigs.

We're Marines not UNICEF, we don't give out free shit.

We fended them off, but more kept coming. It was like a human wave of seven-year-olds. When they realized we wouldn't give them anything, they brazenly tried to snatch whatever they could off the sides of our GMVs with no luck.

The traffic began moving again, and our column crept forward. Some of the kids paced us, running alongside to beg in broken English. They wore rags for clothes and most had no shoes. I'd seen Third World poverty before on other deployments, but there was something particularly dirty and grim about this place.

It took us a good chunk of the morning just to get through Herat. When we finally broke into open country, the asphalt highway gave way to a rutted dirt road that shook our GMVs violently. Fortunately, our home-made storage racks bolted to the outside of the rigs held up to the abuse, and we didn't lose any personal packs or gear.

Within minutes of leaving the hardball behind, the convoy kicked up a massive dust cloud. I watched it form ahead of us; then like a conveyer belt we drew closer and closer until we were engulfed in the brown fog. I wrapped my shemagh across my face, but that did little good. The dust got into my eyes, mouth, and nose; it coated my machine gun and all our gear around us. A layer of it formed and grew on the trunk floor around our boots. Moving around kicked up little powdery swirls of the stuff.

Hour after hour we bounced and rolled over this shitty road. Occasionally, we came to a village, each one progressively more primitive and impoverished as we traveled farther from Herat. Being in the back of the GMV was like being in a time machine. A customized combat DeLorean, we felt like visitors to the Stone Age.

I stayed quiet for long periods and focused on covering my sector of fire with the machine gun. Every few minutes, I wiped down the M240 and EOTech sight, trying to keep as much dust off them as I could. Lost cause.

At length, I turned to Strom and pointed at the 40mm bandolier beside him. "You seriously plan on using all of those?" I asked.

"I was on the last convoy up to BMG," he replied.

"BMG?"

"Bala Murghab."

"Ah. What's it like up there?" I asked.

"FOB Todd?" he replied. "Well, the Italians are up there. So's an element from the 82nd Airborne. But nobody patrols. The Spanish operated up there at first. They had a deal with the Taliban."

That caught me off guard. "A deal?"

"Yeah. The Taliban would leave them alone as long as they didn't go more than five hundred meters north or south from the FOB. They could go to the Bazaar and the District Center to the east on the other side of the Murghab River, but that was about it."

The column ahead of us lurched to a halt. We'd been making terrible time, barely going more than thirty miles an hour since we left the hardball. The road's condition forced many stops as the tanker trucks bogged down in soft dirt or sand. The brown haze settled around us as we waited to get going again.

"They had a truce with the enemy?"

"The Afghan War's dirty little secret," Strom said. "Not everyone's here to fight. It happens. Anyway, that all broke down last August when some Spanish engineers went out to build a new bridge across the Murghab. The Taliban attacked them. That's when Sergeant Todd (Sergeant First Class David Todd) was killed. He was on the responding QRF. Got hit by small arms fire."

FOB Todd had been named in his honor. That much we'd already learned.

"After that, the Spanish bugged out. Too dangerous for them. Now, there's an Italian unit up there along with an infantillery company from the 82nd."

Infantillery was a new term floating around the U.S. military. Basically, the Army needed more boots on the ground to patrol, but the service was spread so thin and was so short-handed that it had begun converting artillery battalions into makeshift infantry units. In Iraq, a lot of National Guard artillery outfits had been turned into military police companies. Now the Army had taken it a step further here in Afghanistan.

"Now FOB Todd's like an island in a sea of Taliban, smugglers, and criminals. They all jockey for control of the heroin route into Turkmenistan. It's the main line that supplies Europe. Everyone's involved, including the local officials."

"Is anyone trying to do anything about that?" I asked.

Strom shrugged. "Not really. The Italians don't really patrol and the 82nd sticks close to the FOB."

It was hard not to be disheartened by all this. As I mulled it all over, I asked, "Have you spent much time up there?"

"Nah. Just a few days. Part of my team was up there briefly. Got a few guys there now getting your compound set up for your team. Not much there. A few tents, portashitters. Hesco walls. That's about it. You guys will be the first MSOT up there."

"That all sounds pretty shitty."

"No. Not good. But you may as well know."

The convoy started moving again. The road condition deteriorated even further. Water runoff had left it furrowed with mini-trenches. Drifts of dust and sand acted like drag chutes on the tanker trucks. They'd hit those patches and just crawl along, slowing everybody down. Years of conditioning to American highway speeds left all of us frustrated and tense.

To help Andy, I opened up my computer system, called the VideoScout, and booted it up. I connected it to my GPS puck—basically it gave me real-time location on FalconView, the military's version of Google Earth. I wanted to track our position and make sure we stayed on the same route used by the previous convoy. Before we'd left Herat, I'd plotted that into the system. That way, I figured I could be a backup navigation asset to Andy in case he needed it. Given the inexperience of the convoy commander, it made sense to keep tabs on where we were. I had tried to get us air support before we had left, but nothing was available, so this was my way of trying to show I had value to the team besides being a trunk monkey.

We entered another village, this one composed of only a few mud huts. The column wound its way past scenes of utter deprivation. Villagers stood by open doorways and stared at us. Their faces mirrored the landscape around them. Wizened and sunbaked faces lined and pitted from lifetimes of hardship and want, teeth yellowed and rotting—even the young men looked aged beyond their years. They watched us with cold expressions. No one waved. No one spoke.

We passed through the hamlet and broke out into the long and deep valley. The road paralleled a small river with steep banks covered with lush green trees and bushes. The rest of the valley was dead, brown desertscape, so the verdant stripe that flanked the stream stood in welcome contrast. A few hundred meters ahead, the road turned sharply to follow a bend in the river.

Part of the convoy reached the bend. We dragged along behind, Strom and I making small talk as we held security with our machine guns. A minute later, everyone stopped again. I took the opportunity to dust off the M240, then brushed the crud off the VideoScout's keyboard.

"Check that out," Strom said.

I looked up to see a small phalanx of children emerging from the edge of the village. Bare feet slathered in grime, faces filthy, they moved toward us cautiously.

"Not this shit again," I mumbled. By now, we were sick of the begging.

I turned around and spoke to Andy through the large opening between the GMV's bed and the rear seats. "We've got a bunch of kids coming up the road behind us."

The big diesel engine vibrated our rig as we idled in place, waiting for whatever was holding us up to clear.

"Hey, Ski," Strom said. "Can I borrow your binos?"

I handed over my Vector 21s. A powerful set of range-finder binoculars and one of the best pieces of gear I was issued.

Strom stood up and put them to his eyes. He scanned over to the bend in the road, then turned around to observe the kids, who had closed the distance another hundred meters or so.

"Can you see what's going on?"

"No."

Andy grew frustrated. He keyed his headset and called over the team's frequency, "What the hell is going on up there?"

A long pause followed. Finally, George reported from our lead GMV. "One of the tanker trucks just rolled off the road and fell into the river."

"You have got to be joking," Andy said.

"Nope," George replied in a dry and discontent tone. "The truck's upside down sitting in the water, leaking fuel."

That was the village's only source of water. The truck held ten thousand gallons. The people downstream were screwed for drinking water.

"The driver was smoking opium, high as a kite," George added.

Strom just shook his head. Andy laughed in disbelief. So did I.

"Mister! Mister! Biscuit! Biscuit!" I heard a child shout.

The kids had reached us. They flowed around our rig and moved along the convoy, begging for food and water. It did not take them long to discover the tanker truck, and word of it spread like wildfire through the preteen crowd. A few went running back to the village. Soon more followed. As we sat and waited for the shit to hit the fan, wondering how we would placate them for contaminating their water source, adults began coming toward us carrying buckets and water jugs. The kids had grabbed bowls and cups. I saw one hefting a cooking pot. This time, as they passed by our GMV, they ignored us completely.

At the bend, Lieutenant White told the stoned Afghan driver to get his stuff out of the cab of his truck and jump into another rig. He climbed back inside and grabbed his gear, then got into another tanker truck. Not a moment too soon. The villagers reached the wreck site and streamed down the bank to splash into the befouled water.

The convoy started moving again. We edged along, careful not to hit any of the people milling about on either side of us. As our GMV came to the bend in the road, I looked over to see dozens of villagers swarming over the tanker truck. They looked like army ants picking over an animal carcass. Some were already looting what was left in the cab. Others jostled and pushed each other to gain access to the fuel leak, where they filled their bowls, jugs, and cups with gas before sloshing back up the bank toward the hamlet.

No one was mad that the water supply had been compromised. Indeed, the chaos had almost a festive air about it, like this was the biggest windfall they'd had in years.

Ten thousand gallons of free fuel. And they were using their water jugs and cooking pots to poach it. As we departed, the jack-o'-lantern grins on their faces remained stuck in my mind.

We pressed on for the mountains to the north. The only way through them was over the Sabzek Pass, a treacherous, steep road that ascended thousands of feet before dumping into the valley dominated by Qal-e-naw and the Spanish PRT there.

Late that afternoon, we neared the summit of the Sabzek Pass and came to an 82nd Airborne and ANA (Afghan National Army) checkpoint. The soldiers emerged to greet us, almost as if they were castaways. No wonder. They were perhaps ten men dumped in the middle of nowhere dozens of miles from the nearest outpost of humanity. They lived out of their vehicles and had no showers, toilets, or running water. Their uniforms were crusty with sweat and coated with dirt. Their faces layered with moondust and grime. I watched as they unloaded supplies from one of the Army's trucks.

Beside the checkpoint stood a dilapidated building with two walls collapsed. In an effort to gain some protection from the elements, the soldiers had stacked MRE boxes up as makeshift walls.

"Hey Ski," Andy said from inside the GMV.

"What's up, sir?"

"How far are we from Qal-e-naw?"

I looked over at the VideoScout screen and said, "About halfway there. Maybe forty klicks left."

We'd driven all day and covered less than twenty-five miles.

We stayed at the checkpoint long enough to transfer some supplies and fuel. Then we began the final climb to the summit. The road wound along sheer cliffs that stretched vertically above us and dropped precipitously downward only a few feet from the GMV's tires. I couldn't help but wonder how many other Afghan truckers with us were sitting in their cabs smoking dope. One wrong move, and their rigs and our gear would plunge over the side.

The sun dropped lower, setting the sky afire with a crimson glow. A few scattered clouds glowed silver in the distance. The rock-faced mountains towered around us, like something straight out of a fantasy novel. To be honest, the view was breathtaking.

We reached the summit right at sunset. The temperature had dropped and we shivered in the backs of our GMVs. I stood up and looked around. The mountain gave way below us to rolling hills with gentle curves that contrasted with the jagged ridges. Beyond the hills stretched a mountain range as far as the eye could see.

"Wow. How beautiful is this?" I said in wonder.

Strom nodded but said nothing.

"This could be a great vacation destination. Too bad everyone here wants to kill you. This would also make a great spot to put a fucking guardrail," I added.

We began a careful descent along the backside of the pass as darkness fell. The cliff to our right dropped six hundred feet straight down. To our left, the cliff face went vertical into the night sky. The drivers stayed in first gear the whole way down and rode their brakes so much that by the time we reached the valley floor, we had to pause at an ANP (Afghan National Police) checkpoint to let them cool off.

As we waited, the sky darkened and filled with a tapestry of stars. I'd never seen the Milky Way so bright and clear before. The ambient light the stars provided made for perfect conditions for our night vision goggles. Contrary to movies and popular conception, our NVGs don't penetrate total darkness. Instead, they amplify the available light to give us a better view of what's around us. The more star or moonlight, the better they work.

When the convoy began to move again an hour or so later, we hung back and drove blacked out, using only our NVGs. The rest of the convoy turned on their headlights and marched into the valley lit up like a carnival parade for everyone to see.

For two hours, the road zigzagged across the valley floor encased in a cloud of dust of our own making. At times, it got so bad the night sky grew dim and muddy. We crossed and recrossed a dry riverbed that ran through the valley perhaps a dozen times. The road led us into many tiny villages, all composed of mud huts and qalats—walled compounds with metal gates built into them. Each was a mini-fortress and some even had towers at their corners.

Not a soul moved in these villages. We checked the alleyways and darkened footpaths carefully as we slid past them. No lights, no fires visible inside the huts. No power or signs of modern civilization anywhere. Just dark, medieval-like hamlets as empty as if a plague had wiped out their residents.

My hands never left the M240.

At last, we came to a series of low-running, grassy hills. We left the riverbed behind and saw the glow of electric lights over the crests of the hills. A few minutes later, Qal-e-naw came into sight.

We rolled onto a paved road just outside town and saw streetlights illuminating the way ahead. As in the villages, the town seemed utterly deserted. We remained alert and stayed on our guns until we reached the main gate of the Spanish base on the west side of the city.

A few ANP manned the gate. They waved us in, and we discovered that the airfield's runway doubled as part of the road on the base. We drove across it, dropping off the Afghan drivers and their trucks for the night. They set up a little camp near a broken aircraft fuselage that lay in the dirt beside the runway.

The 82nd Airborne's rigs and our four GMVs continued on through the main gate, where a Spanish solider standing guard directed us to a transient parking area that was walled off from the rest of the base by Hesco barriers.

As soon as we stopped, I used a paintbrush to clean the dust off my M240. When I finished up, I put a thin coat of lube on the bolt. Beside me, Strom did the same thing. We swept out the trunk, cleaned off the rest of our gear, and jumped to the ground—and promptly sank into at least a foot of pure, powdery moondust. A brownish cloud billowed up around our legs, covering us in a fresh coat of fine dirt.

I grabbed a collapsible stretcher off our GMV and unfolded it next to the Hesco wall. Strom grabbed one, too.

"Well, that was a shitty day," I said wearily.

As he set up his stretcher not far from mine, he answered, "Yep. But tomorrow is when the fun starts."

3

★ Halloween in Afghanistan ★

OCTOBER 31, 2009

Qal-e-naw was a city on the edge of Forever, the last outpost of "civilization" in this portion of Badghis Province. The city itself bustled with mopeds and small pickup trucks. Throngs of people spilled into the streets in the bazaar area, where goods and animals hung from racks in front of businesses operating from ramshackle tin huts. The Afghans here built their dwellings with anything available, which made the city a checkerboard of brick buildings, mud huts, Conex boxes, and those metal shacks.

The runway looked like modern technology's take on an elephant graveyard. Aircraft carcasses lay in the talcum powder dust in ruined fragments. Here and there, a landing-gear strut poked through the wreckage like aluminum tusks. Stripped carcasses of airliners littered the area, all useful parts long since plucked away. I saw only one intact aircraft—a lone prop plane sitting at the far end of the runway.

The desolation on the horizon only contributed to the malaise and sense of depression this place infused in me. We'd be driving north into it soon, leaving behind this last outpost of "modern" man to trek into a vast and virtually unknown landscape.

Our day started badly, and only got worse. Our Afghan truck drivers apparently thought this was as far north as they were going. When they learned we were driving all the way to BMG, they flat out refused to go. Lieutenant White spent much of the morning in shouting matches with them, reminding them that their contract called for them to drive to Bala Murghab. They would not get paid until they delivered our gear to BMG. Finally, they reluctantly agreed to continue with us.

With the mutiny squashed, Andy sent Strom and me to escort the truckers to a local gas station, so they could top off their tanks for the drive ahead.

But as they filled up, the Afghans refused to pay for the gas. Their contract specifically stated that the trucking company would cover that cost, but it didn't matter. Another logjam ensued as Lieutenant White tried to get them to adhere to the contract.

The impasse dragged on as we pulled security on the busy streets of downtown Qal-e-naw. Gradually, a crowd began to gather around us. Strom and I scanned the people, searching for weapons, our anxiety growing as the size of the crowd grew.

"Dude," Strom said, "we need to get the fuck out of here."

"Agreed," I replied.

The Taliban in the town were known for their drive-bys against the Spanish PRT, which was only a block from here, next to the Badghis governor's building. The walls of the PRT were fifteen feet high, and above them the Spaniards had strung nets to catch or deflect grenades that passing Taliban would throw from motorcycles. And here we were, attracting a lot of attention with very little firepower.

The lieutenant finally noticed the crowds, too. The only way forward was to eat the cost of gas. Using the Army's cash on hand, he paid up, and the Afghan drivers trickled through the gas station. By the time they were finally finished it was late in the afternoon. We returned to the Spanish base, dropping the Afghan truckers off at the runway boneyard, then heading back to the dust bowl.

By the time we got back, it was too late in the day to continue on our journey. We spent another night in the dust bowl, sleeping in the dirt again, coughing and hacking through the night until our predawn wake-up call.

As the sun rose over the eastern hills, we saddled up, organized the vehicles out on the runway, and set out northward. From this point on, we'd be on our own. There were no more gas stations, no more bases, no more cities, towns, just a progressively more primitive road that stretched across a vast and ancient land.

We passed through a bazaar on the outskirts of Qal-e-naw on the only route heading north, which brought us to a Y intersection. The right led to a small 82nd Airborne outpost COP (Combat Outpost), Moqur. Going left would take us to BMG.

Though it was still early, the streets of Qal-e-naw had been full of people. They had watched us roll through the bazaar going in an unusual direction for a large convoy. At this intersection, any Taliban watching us would know we were not going to resupply the COP outside town. Instead, they'd know we were going all the way to FOB Todd. Easy prey.

"Well, this is fucking awesome," I muttered, looking at the people watching us as the convoy took the left fork in the road.

Strom said, "Yeah. They know exactly where we are heading now. No doubt."

Not that the enemy ahead wouldn't have seen us. All these Humvees and GMVs and gigantic Russian-built trucks kicked up an enormous cloud of dust that could be seen for miles. They'd have plenty of time to prepare an ambush, especially if we moved as slowly as we had on our first day out from Herat.

The road ahead was better than we could have expected. Though narrow, it was relatively well traveled in the Qal-e-naw Valley. Once we got to the hills on the north side, we'd be in for slower going and would have to find a flat spot to circle the wagons for the night.

Through the morning, we skirted a dry riverbed, our gunners alert, all our heads on a swivel as we searched for any signs of ambush. The last convoy through had been hit just outside the last village on the north end of the valley. It seemed logical that the cell in the area would want to operate against us, and since they'd surely been alerted to our departure, we expected a fight.

I'd submitted the request before leaving Herat, but didn't know if it had gotten supported until the SOTF air officer contacted Andy over SAT-COM to tell us that we would have a B-1 bomber overhead in about an hour to support our movement through the ambush area.

I manned my machine gun, running through all the communications protocols in my head again. This would be my first time controlling aircraft in country, and I wanted it to go flawlessly. If I failed at my job, people could die. Earning the trust of the team from that point would be impossible.

As we followed the winding route through the valley, I kept checking my watch. We were getting closer to the ambush site, and I had heard nothing from the approaching B-1 Lancer.

Andy looked back at me and said, "Anything yet, Ski?"

"Negative."

"Okay. Let me know when you make contact so I can tell the SOTF."

I glanced down at my PRC-117 radio. The thing looked like a cross between a CB radio and an ammunition box. Though painted olive drab, at the moment my radio was so coated in Afghan dust it appeared almost mustard-colored.

I swiped my hand across its face, sending brown powder wafting into the air. The frequency setting was correct. The VHF/UHF antenna was tightly connected to the base. No issues there.

Restlessly, I checked my watch again. No doubt about it: the bomber should be overhead.

"Any station, this is HALO 14, on White 05, radio check, over?" I said through my headset.

No response.

"Any station, this is HALO 14, on White 05, radio check, over?" I said again.

Andy glanced back at me again. I shook my head.

What next?

The village at the end of the valley was drawing closer. We needed that bird.

"Any station, this is HALO 14, on White 05, radio check, over."

A second later, a voice came through over the din of our GMV's big diesel engine.

"This is HALO 14, Alpha. Got you loud and clear, over."

I recognized the voice right away. Four vehicles in front of us was John, another fire support Marine attached to our team. He was sort of a junior apprentice JTAC, assigned to the team to gain experience before he went to formal schooling as I had.

From his radio check at least I knew now that my radio wasn't malfunctioning.

Where was the bird?

I pulled off my headset and cocked my ear. Sure enough, over the convoy's noises, I could hear jet engines overhead. Our B-1 Lancer, call sign BONE, was on station, but for some reason I couldn't talk to him. If the Taliban attacked us now, the Lancer would be useless. Without comms to me, there was no way to tell them where to place bombs, how to make their run, or even where the enemy was.

The sky overhead was gray over ugly. Solid overcast. Somewhere above the scud layer, the bomber loitered.

Andy asked again, "Ski, you have comms yet?"

I tried to keep the frustration from my voice as I answered, "Negative, Andy. I can hear them overhead, but they are not coming up on the radio."

"Okay, keep trying."

"Roger."

What was I doing wrong?

Stay calm. Work it through, Ski.

The tension grew. I called again on White 05, my assigned frequency, to no avail. If we were attacked now and people got hurt, and I couldn't direct this bomber onto any targets, I'd feel worse than useless. I'd feel responsible.

I was about to call over White 05 again when suddenly a speaker box mounted inside the truck burst to life.

"HALO 14, this is BONE 11, radio check over."

What the hell?

The speaker was plugged into one of the mounted radios in the rig. The voice hadn't come through my headset. In a flash, it registered with me.

"Hey Floyd?" I asked our driver. "What net is that radio on?"

Floyd told me the team freq, and I looked down at my PRC-117, brushed away another half-inch of accumulated dust, and switched frequencies.

"BONE 11, this is HALO 14. Roger, got you five by five."

Relief flooded through me when I heard the pilot reply, "Roger, HALO, same here. Say when ready for check-in."

As a JTAC, my job was to communicate the situation on the ground to the pilots overhead. We had a strict procedure that established all the need-to-knows. I ran through them all carefully with the B-1's crew. By the time I had finished, we were coming to the north end of the valley. A few more klicks and we'd reach the scene of the last attack.

If something did go down, I would not be able to view the video feed from BONE's sensor because of the weather. On a clear day, I could tap into the aircraft's infrared (IR) camera systems and see exactly what the pilots saw. Think of it sort of like an air-and-ground-combat version of Skype between a camera in the sky and my computer screen in the truck. The ability to do this makes putting bombs in the right place significantly easier and more accurate than any other time in our history.

Even as great as our technology was, Mother Nature could still throw a monkey wrench in the works. If we did get hit, because of the cloud cover I'd have to generate grid coordinates from my perspective and pass them up to the aircraft.

One more village before the ambush site. This one was just a small jumble of mud huts clustered around a water source. The people looked even more impoverished and desperate than any other group we'd seen so far. When they heard us coming, some of them came out to see us. They gaped in astonishment, a reminder to us that ISAF Coalition units just did not come out this way, even after nine years of war.

The B-1 Lancer had originally been designed as a strategic bomber in the final years of the Cold War. Now, instead of nuking Soviet cities, these huge, swing-wing birds would launch from Al Udeid Air Base in Qatar and could loiter for hours overhead. This was a huge advantage for us in this area, as we were so far away from Coalition airbases that helicopter support just wasn't available. And fast movers like F-18s and F-16 fighter-bombers also would be fuel-limited in our area and could only spend a short time overhead before needing to aerial refuel.

We passed the last mud hut, sitting squat and ugly beside the dry riverbed. A few barnyard animals wandered about. A chicken or two, a skinny, bedraggled goat. They were the sum total of that family's material possessions.

We drove on, extra alert now. The endless prehistoric landscape played out in every direction. I sat behind my M240, coated in dust, staring out at my sector as we crawled down the narrow route north. My ass hurt. My back was stiff. My exposed skin was caked with layers of sweat and dust until I looked like a brown ghost. Even my eyelashes were gritty with the stuff.

I adjusted my shemagh, but trying to keep the dust out of my mouth and new facial scruff was a lost cause. Afghanistan tastes foul, like you'd just been dumped face-first into a sandbox built atop a landfill. Behind me, Will had been quiet most of the day. Andy had been as well, rarely using the radio and making little small talk. As tired and stiff as we were, I could also feel the tension slowly ratcheting up the closer we got to the last village in the valley, where the ambush happened.

The village appeared in the distance. It reminded me of drawings I'd seen in an illustrated version of the Old Testament. When we rolled through, the people looked even more ragged and pathetic. Men and children, their clothing pockmarked with holes and patches, were unwashed and gaunt. I am pretty sure I saw Moses standing in the doorway of a mud house. Food out here was the only priority, and these people had been flung into a hostile wasteland through circumstances generations old. How they settled here was anyone's guess, but they tried to build a life in the folds of this desolate place. A single water source, little more than a trickling creek, sustained life here. Sustained was the key. They eked out an existence most humans in the modern age would find intolerable, the margin between survival and starvation razor thin. One failed crop, a rash of disease through the village's goats and chickens, and people would die.

We drove through, the people beside their mud-walled dwellings staring at us like we were something beyond conception. No power. No running water. No infrastructure at all. Cell phones seemed like dark magic or a wizard's wand. Television? There was no place to plug one in. Not a single dwelling had a vehicle or a generator.

I saw a boy, his face streaked with grime. Like us, his hair was full of dirt. He looked at me with a hollowed-out expression, an old soul trapped in a child's body, made ancient by this unforgiving place. It was a look of a child who had no future and no hope.

We passed him, and I watched until he disappeared from view. When I turned my eyes forward again, I saw beyond the final sand-colored huts a near vertical wall of massive hills. One row after another like tsunami swells. It was then that I think the full magnitude of Afghanistan struck me.

These people were at war with their environment. There was no hope. There was nothing but a daily struggle for survival lost so frequently that they no longer valued human life. Goats were more important than their women. And if a child died, that meant one less mouth to feed.

America went to war here after 9/11 to destroy al Qaeda. The war aims had evolved and grown. Keeping the Taliban from reengineering their reign of religious terror on these people had become the primary goal. Saving them from this awful existence, made worse by their own government's poverty and corruption, seemed a noble purpose. But how were we Americans supposed to achieve that? As we left the village clouded by our dust trail, I wondered if we were not exceeding our reach. How can one nation fix another that has been so badly broken that people in 2009 still lived as their forefathers had when Alexander the Great marched into their land?

Noble effort. I thought of that kid and wondered if I could even help give him hope.

Two kilometers north of the village, we had not encountered any sign of the enemy. BONE contacted me over the radio, saying they were being pulled off station and directed to support a TIC (troops in contact) that erupted at COP Moqur. From here on out, we'd have no angel above.

Not long after the bird departed, we reached the base of the first steep hill that framed the end of the valley. The road narrowed and rose so steeply up a hillside that the Afghan truckers simply did not have the horsepower to reach the top. Suddenly, after making good progress all day long, we came to a halt. It was like standing at the end of an alleyway staring up the side of a skyscraper's wall.

To get all the vehicles up the first incline, we had to use the winch on the 82nd Airborne's wrecker vehicle. The paratroopers parked it at the top of the massive hill and ran a steel cable down to the first Russian-built truck. Hooking it to the frame of the rig, the vehicle was pulled by the winch up the incline, an interminably slow process made even slower by the Afghan drivers. They were in no hurry to go farther north, so they dragged their feet and made things as difficult as possible for us. Hoping we would rethink our plan and head back.

We moved our gun trucks to the top of the hill, covering the soldiers as they worked to winch each truck up some two hundred feet above the valley floor. The minutes dragged by, then hours passed. The afternoon grew old, and yet not even half the trucks had reached the summit.

About then, we realized we were being watched.

"We have movement," somebody called over our team net.

More calls came in. Several heads had been seen popping up from terrain features to the east of us. We were a good distance—about three klicks—from that last village.

We could not see any weapons, so we could not engage them. Of course, what were the chances that some of the villagers had decided to hike into the hills and do some sightseeing? Zero.

We finished getting the last of the trucks up the hillside, and we rejoined the convoy at the summit. The road from here ran right along a razorback ridge. On either side, the road fell away from the shoulder into a chasm with sheer cliffs. If one of those Afghan drivers was stoned, one sloppy driving error would see them rolling hundreds of feet to the base below.

Once reassembled, we began to move slowly as the last bit of sunlight dipped behind the distant mountain range. The prairie dogging from our sightseers continued on a ridgeline about eight hundred meters from us. Pat traversed his minigun to the right side of the convoy and trained his weapon on the ridgeline. If they revealed any weapons at all, he would be ready for them.

Smart Taliban put one or two terrain features between themselves and their targets to make sure that the Americans they attack cannot assault into their own positions. The gorge between us and those heads served that function perfectly. This was really starting to smell bad. The hairs were standing up on the back of my neck and an empty feeling filled my gut.

"Way to put your dick in the wind and wait for it to get slapped," Strom muttered. I'd hardly heard a word from him all day. His frustration mirrored my own. We were a string of sitting ducks, just waiting to be hit.

The sun hit the hilltops, dyeing the sky bloodred as it surrendered to the night. We drove on under watchful eyes, bathed in that crimson glow. Everyone's thumbs gently tapping the sides of their weapons.

4

★ LET THE BURNING BEGIN ★

NOVEMBER 1, 2009
EIGHT KILOMETERS SOUTH OF THE TURKMENISTAN BORDER

The night's darkness devoured the last fading streaks of light on the ridge of the western mountain range. We donned our night vision goggles and rolled on, encased in our moving cloud of dust. We needed to find a good stretch of flat ground so we could RON (remain overnight). Problem was, flat ground looked to be in short supply up here.

The local national truckers didn't have night vision. So they turned their running lights on, which ruined our attempt at staying blacked out as a convoy. The orange and yellow lights also played havoc with our night vision goggles.

Dark, running lights on, big, slow, loud, fucking easy targets. Dudes following us. We are being served a shit sandwich and everyone is going to have to take a bite.

No need to rework the equation, the answer was simple. My gut began to tingle even worse now, like some sort of primitive part of me was setting off alarm bells. All at once my senses were suddenly heightened. I could smell, breathe, and see better. The fatigue vanished.

We were moving at perhaps two miles an hour when two rocket-propelled grenades lanced across the valley, their motors glowing bright orange in the darkness. They streaked overhead and exploded above us in midair.

"Contact right! Contact right!"

The sudden volley stopped the convoy dead in its tracks.

The warning hadn't even finished coming over our radio when Pat laid on his trigger. His minigun spun and spewed bullets at four thousand rounds a minute.

Brrrrrrr . . . Brrrrr . . . Brrrrr . . .

The minigun has a sound like no other weapon, like a low-pitched drill boring through hardwood.

Behind me, Strom let loose with a long burst from his machine gun. A split second later, Jamie, our turret gunner, opened up with the Ma Deuce, his .50 cal. The M240 sounded like a giant zipper being ripped open. Jamie's .50 was its bass line, its slower rate of fire echoing across the hills.

I pressed my shoulder into the butt stock of my M240 and stayed on my sector—which was directly opposite from where the enemy lay. After years of counterinsurgency warfare, we'd learned that the enemy would sometimes initiate an ambush from one point to draw our attention. Then, as our guys were focused on the initiators, another enemy element would pop up on a flank and hammer us. To combat that, we'd been trained to maintain 360 degree security, even in the midst of a firefight.

I sat there, back to the firefight, watching Taliban tracer rounds streak overhead. A moment later, another RPG soared high and wide. It exploded a few dozen meters beyond the convoy right in my sector of fire.

Stay in your sector and wait for it.

The enemy poured fire at us. We poured it back. The fight raged behind me, but I had no role to play. I was like a spectator with the worst seat in the house. I felt exposed and useless, fear welling as I saw more tracers shoot past our convoy.

I will not turn around. I will not take my eyes off my area.

Our Afghan truck drivers lost their minds. As gunfire laced the convoy, they flipped on their headlights, stomped on their gas pedals, and tried to blow past our gun trucks to escape the bullets. Their headlights swung left and right, raking across us and washing out our night vision. The road was too narrow for this, and our GMVs ahead of us found themselves in a hopeless snarl, giant fuel trucks in front, behind, and to either side. They were surrounded by thousands of gallons of gasoline.

Joe, whose truck was Tail-end Charlie, called over the radio, "We're just sitting here! We need to push through!"

There was no place to go.

"Push! Push! Push! If one of those fuel trucks gets hit, the whole convoy will go up in flames!" Joe urged.

In all the chaos, Andy was a picture of calm. He called up the engagement situation to the SOTF, then asked me, "Hey Ski, do we need air?"

I thought it through quickly. "No," I replied. Even if we did have a bird overhead right now, I wouldn't be able to use the aircraft's sensor to scan the ground for the enemy. The blanket of clouds above us was solid. Right now, Joe was right, we just needed to get out of their kill zone and keep heading north.

I explained my reasoning, and Andy answered, "Yeah, good call. Just wanted to make sure."

Suddenly, an RPG skipped into the road and sizzled under the fuel truck directly behind our GMV. Trailing a short red tail of flame, it bounced across the opposite shoulder, got airborne again, and exploded a few dozen meters out. A few feet higher, and that rocket would have ended us.

In Joe's truck, Mark's Ma Deuce went down. He furiously went to work trying to get it unjammed, to no avail.

The enemy stayed in the fight, even as Pat's minigun tore chunks out of the rocky hillside that served as their cover. At the same time, Strom unslung his M79 and started lobbing 40mm grenades over the ridge. They exploded with a dull thump every few seconds.

"Push!" Joe's gravel voice shouted over the radio.

Ahead, the 82nd Airborne trucks finally started to move. The tanker truck in front of us surged forward and we followed it as Pat's minigun spun and whined. The volume of incoming diminished. We were gaining the upper hand—or the enemy was breaking contact.

Four minutes after the fight began, we inched clear of the enemy's kill zone. The convoy limped to a patch of open ground about two kilometers farther down the road and stopped to consider our next move. We wanted to chase the enemy down. Lieutenant White wanted to keep going until we reached an ABP (Afghan Border Police) outpost a few more klicks to the north. The Afghan truckers just wanted to go home.

We knew the priority: get to BMG. We were not on a hunting mission, though with the firepower we had, none of us had any doubt that we could crush the Taliban cell that just attacked us. Lieutenant White decided we'd keep going to an ABP outpost.

We crawled forward, the Afghan drivers so spooked that trying to keep order in the convoy became impossible. The truckers sped up, shined their brights, stopped suddenly and caused such chaos that we accordioned our way along the road. Finally, we reached the ABP outpost, little more than a one-high Hesco barrier wall surrounding a tiny building atop a hill that overlooked the road north. The Border Police looked like a motley group of castaways. Rough beards, weather-beaten faces, they eyed us warily as the convoy reached their perimeter. Most lacked complete uniforms. Instead, they wore whatever was at hand—blue-green slacks, old-style American forest-green camo jackets, a weird assortment of foreign uniform parts, too, including beat-up Chinese helmets that looked like they'd been discarded after Vietnam. Some of these men didn't even have combat boots. A few even wore loafers.

The Afghan government had put these men in a terrible situation. Thrown out on a walled box in the middle of nowhere, resupply infrequent and help far, far away, they had been left to fend for themselves. To survive, they had to cut a deal with the Taliban. The enemy would show up at their gate and demand ammunition or weapons. The ABP had two options: fight, get overwhelmed, and die or give the Taliban bullets, guns, and live.

Not surprisingly, these outposts became resupply depots for the enemy. Every few months, the Taliban would come to collect, then the ABP would beg the Coalition for more ammo and weapons. Once delivered, the enemy would simply come by to take it again. They were just as bad as Afghan National Police.

If the American taxpayer only knew.

The ANP in general were a despicable lot. Perhaps we could have some sympathy for the way this group had to survive, but the truth was the local population hated the ANP and ABP more than they hated the Taliban. Cruel, corrupt, officious, they ran rackets and extorted local leaders. They took part in the drug trade and had absolutely no stomach for a fight. The Afghan National Army soldiers hated the police with frightening intensity—so much so that we'd heard of fights breaking out between the two groups. The ANP were recruited from the community they worked in, while the ANA come from different regions and are stationed anywhere in Afghanistan. Needless to say, local politics and nepotism clashed with the ANA's attempt at nation building. The relationship between them became corrosive.

The convoy's main element bedded down close to the compound with the ABP. Andy decided he didn't want our rigs all crammed together with them, just in case the local Taliban decided to lob mortars or rockets at the post. Instead, we set up a perimeter on a flat stretch of ground not far below the outpost. I climbed out of the rig and walked around to Andy's door. He piled out, shucked his helmet, and looked at me with a wry smile.

"Well, Ski, that sure got out of hand quick, didn't it?"

I shook my head. "Fucking clown show."

Pat showed up a minute later while I was pulling my sleeping bag off the side rack of our GMV.

"Wanna smoke?" he asked, handing me a cigarette.

"Thanks."

I lit it and took a long drag. Pat looked wired and intense, his eyes wide.

"That could have gone bad. Real bad," he said.

I thought of the fuel trucks. The headlights.

"Yep."

"The Humvee in front of us . . ." Pat said, then paused.

"What about it?"

He exhaled a lungful of smoke. "Jesus Christ. They had a girl up there on the .50. When we took contact, she didn't even have the strength to rack the bolt."

"You're shitting me?"

"Nope."

We stood there, both in disbelief, staring out into the black Afghan night.

At length, Pat finally said, "Can you believe that? Those 82nd guys put a girl in a turret that didn't even have enough ass on her to charge the weapon."

"Fucked up," I agreed.

"One of the guys inside their truck had to get up in the turret and take over."

A .50 caliber machine gun is one of the best and most effective casualty-producing weapons a convoy possesses. This wasn't a trivial mistake.

We thought about that in silence for a while. This scratch force from the 82nd was jacked up, plain and simple. Inexperienced lieutenant, patched-together outfit pulled from a bunch of FOB dwellers. I thought of the convoy brief, the lack of identified contingency plans, no real effort to explain any procedures to the team.

"Keep your eyes open tomorrow, Ski. They're still out there."

"Roger that."

He took another drag on his smoke and flicked it away. "Could have gone real bad tonight," he mused almost to himself as he headed back to his GMV.

"Get some rest, brother," I called after him.

He waved a hand as he vanished into the darkness.

I finished my cigarette alone, wondering if we weren't about to get into even more trouble as we followed our lost shepherd to nowhere. As for now, there were only two things in my future, sleep and turret watch.

5

★ Welcome to FOB Todd ★

NOVEMBER 2, 2009
ABP OUTPOST

It took all morning to get back under way. Just before noon, the convoy reassembled and stretched out on the dirt track through those mammoth hills, looking like a great metal centipede from a distance. We inched around breakneck turns and hairpin curves that looked cut straight from the marrow of the rock hillsides. The progress we made was maddening. The terrain dictated our speed, which remained below five miles an hour through much of it. At the same time it became evident that the Afghan truck drivers were doing everything they could to hinder our progress. Their rigs got stuck in soft parts of the road; at every major slope they could not seem to coax their rigs forward, forcing the 82nd Airborne's wrecker to winch them up, one vehicle at a time.

Hours passed. We stayed on our guns and slow burned through it all. Stop. Go. Stop. Go. We crawled along this rat trail, wondering when the enemy would strike again. Whoever attacked us the night before had to be close. Given our speed and the fact that there was only one possible route for us to use, they could easily get ahead of us to lay another ambush. It felt like something out of World War II's Battle of the Atlantic. Beyond our little convoy lane, the wolves lurked.

"I don't think I can handle another day of this shit," I muttered as we lurched to a halt again.

"Suck it up, Marine," Strom said with a chuckle.

"Fuck you," I responded.

"You stink like wet ass."

In the cab, I heard Andy laugh.

"How we looking, Ski?" he asked a minute later.

I checked the VideoScout. We were only about ten kilometers from where we started. We still had plenty of ground to cover to get to a village called Mangan, the only other village between here and BMG. Lieutenant White wanted to stop there for the night. The place had been friendly to Coalition forces before, so it seemed like a good place to RON. After that, we'd have one more day's drive to get to FOB Todd.

"We have a long fuckin' way to go, Andy," I reported.

About half an hour later, we came to a large and distinct Y intersection. I checked my laptop again. The map included the previous convoy's path. "Andy, we'll be turning right here."

The convoy came to a halt. We sat for several minutes, waiting and wondering what was going on. I double-checked FalconView again. No question, we were supposed to go right.

We went left.

"Um, Andy, we're supposed to be going right. This is not the way."

Andy looked back and said, "Lieutenant White says he's found a shorter way to Mangan."

"Uh, okay," I said, totally unsure about this.

"He's in charge. We gotta go with his call," Andy said reluctantly.

We looked uneasily at each other. Who diverts a convoy onto an unknown route in the middle of fucking nowhere? A second lieutenant.

God, I hope he knows what he's doing.

The convoy cleared the Y, and I kept a careful watch on our location. The road stretched even farther north toward the Turkmenistan border, edging us farther away from the last convoy's route with every minute. My mind kept throwing warning flags. This wasn't right. But I was just a trunk monkey, how could I influence things?

We came to another series of hills. Each one grew progressively steeper, and it did not take long for our progress to falter again. The trucks carrying our gear in cargo containers did just fine. They made it up each slope without any help. But the tanker trucks got stuck, even when the inclines didn't seem that significant. Each time it happened, Lieutenant White had to send the wrecker back to drag them up the hills. After another couple hours of this sort of progress, it grew obvious that the Afghan drivers were trying to force us to give up and turn around.

Inside our GMV, Andy got a radio call over SATCOM from the SOTF.

After a short conversation, he turned back to Strom and me and said, "Intel guys are tracking Taliban moving on us. They're going to try and hit us at sundown again."

"Same guys as last night?" Strom asked.

"Unknown."

Andy reported what he'd learned to Lieutenant White, who decided we'd try to get to a plateau just outside Mangan, and then circle the wagons for the night on the high ground.

We hit another steep hill about an hour before sunset. Once again, the fuel trucks all got stuck. The wrecker busily winched them up to the crest, while we kept watch on the surrounding ridges.

"This is a bad fucking spot," Pat said over the radio.

He was right. If we got hit here, we'd be split up between elements on top of the hill and those on the base. We were in a bad situation and only getting worse.

This is crazy terrain to fight a war in. Now I know how the Russians must have felt.

By now, the wrecker crew had their job down to an art form. They worked feverishly, doing what they could to minimize our exposure to ambush as we waited. Still, every second preyed on us, and the tension became unbearable.

"Movement in the hills at our three o'clock," Rob reported over the radio.

The enemy had found us.

The fuel trucks were pulled to the top of the hill, and we began the bumpy ride to the last plateau before Mangan. The route narrowed even more until it looked like little more than a goat trail. Our wheels sank into a foot of powdery dust, and several more times we had to stop and pull out a fuel truck that got bogged down in the soft ground.

All the while, heads bobbed up and down on the ridges beside us. We saw no weapons and could not engage as a result, but we knew who was watching us.

"Wonder why they haven't hit us yet," I mused.

"Maybe they have something bigger planned for us down the road," Strom answered.

"Cheerful thought," I said.

"Here to help."

Rob jumped out of his GMV to come talk to Andy.

"We need to put some overwatch up here," he said, gesturing to either side of our position.

"Agreed," Andy said.

"I could see some of them in and out of ditches on that far ridgeline," Rob added.

When I heard that, I started bringing up satellite imagery of our surroundings on my laptop. When I zoomed in, I saw what looked like old trenches zigzagging across the ridges on either side of us.

"Hey, Andy," I said slowly, "this is a really bad spot."

The trenches scarred the hilltops for kilometers.

Pat's voice came over the radio. "If we're going to be here for a while, we need to cover those hilltops."

In the GMV ahead of ours, I could see him pulling an M240 machine gun off its scissor mount in preparation to hump it onto higher ground.

"Hold up, Pat," Andy said, thinking all this through. He looked out his side window, then asked, "Rob, do you think we can get the GMVs up that hill to our left over there?"

Andy pointed, and Rob studied it. "Sure, I think so. We'll just need to ground guide them up there."

"Okay, let's try it."

We managed to get two GMVs up on the high ground west of the road. The Army took care of the other flank. The wrecker finished winching the last fuel truck, completing the convoy again.

We reached the plateau just outside Mangan at sunset. Once again, the sky turned to fire, casting contrasting shadows across the Mars-like landscape. As we finished getting the fuel trucks to the RON site, the shadows lengthened, then joined while dusk settled over us.

After we parked along the perimeter, I walked over to Pat's GMV. His 7.62mm minigun system had been paired with a high-tech thermal imaging system called a MARFLIR (Maritime Forward Looking Infrared) system. Basically it was an aircraft FLIR (Forward Looking Infrared) ball mounted on a telescoping twenty-foot mast that fed a thermal video feed to a flat screen monitor inside the cab of the truck. It was up now, sweeping the darkness for human heat signatures. Anything moved out there, Pat and his crew would know it in seconds.

He saw me and made a sweeping gesture with one hand. "Check this shit out, Ski."

"What?" I asked.

"We're a klick from the Turkmenistan border," he said with awe in his voice. "I bet we're the first Americans to ever stand on this hill."

We thought about that in silence. What would all those Cold Warriors who came before us think of us out here so close to the former Soviet Union's Asiatic frontier?

"All those fighting positions around us . . . I bet some of them were dug by the mujahideen back in the 80s," Pat continued. "They used them to ambush Red Army convoys crossing the border."

The thought hadn't occurred to me.

"Same battlefield. Different players," he said.

"Dude, you sound like one of those narrators on the History Channel," I told him.

"Well, that would sure beat the fuck out of working at Home Depot if the Corps and I ever part ways."

"That it would, Pat."

I returned to my GMV and climbed in the trunk, settling down for another stint behind the M240. A cold wind was blowing across the hilltops as the temperature started to drop. Hot as fuck during the day, bone-chillingly cold at night. Afghanistan existed in the extremes, a place as bipolar as a girl I once dated.

Sometime after midnight, Floyd swapped out with me, and I sought refuge from the howling wind behind my tarp lean-to.

★ ★ ★

The next morning, we awoke before dawn to prepare for the drive out of the hills and into the Alkazai Valley. The village of Mangan was on the valley floor only a few kilometers from our position, so I think we all felt like the worst was now behind us. We'd be going downhill today, so the Afghan truckers wouldn't have the opportunity to delay us with their antics.

Andy left for the morning brief with Lieutenant White and the rest of the vehicle commanders. I watched them out of the corner of my eye as we loaded our gear back onto the GMVs. A few minutes later, when Andy returned I could see he was struggling to keep his impassive expression intact on his face.

"What's up?" I asked, feeling the optimism I'd had slipping away.

"Well, Ski," he began. "You want the bad news or the bad news?"

"Oh, fuck it. Let's hear the bad news," I said.

"Well, you know that Y intersection yesterday?"

"Yeah."

"The one you said we needed to go right?"

"Yeah."

"Well, we should've gone right."

I stared at him.

"Yep. Shoulda gone right."

"You're shitting me."

"Nope. The Army sent a Humvee out this morning to check the road to Mangan, just to make sure the trucks wouldn't have any more issues."

"Okay."

Andy shook his head. "Yeah. Well, the road is washed out. There's a big wadi going right through it. No way the trucks can make it."

I couldn't believe it. "You mean we have to go back?"

"The soldiers could see Mangan from the wash-out. That's how close we are."

I wanted to punch something or someone. I supposed Andy did, too, but he kept his cool. As our team leader he needed to be self-possessed. He stayed low-key as he gathered the team and explained the situation. We would have to backtrack through those hills again, return to the Y, then take the right turn.

"We'll be driving into the enemy, winching those fucking fuel trucks over every goddamned hill," Joe fumed.

The team piled on that. All the frustration from the last few days poured out. The Army had blown this. Now, we were either going to fix it, or continue to suffer. At length, we decided to take charge.

Joe said, "Look, we can't waste all fucking day with those goddamn fuel trucks. The first one that gets stuck, we pull the driver out and light it up with a .50 cal."

"I'll volunteer for that!" George said.

Andy agreed. He went and had a talk with Lieutenant White. Dagger 22 was taking over tactical control of the convoy from here on out. From there Lieutenant White told the Afghan drivers that we would abandon and destroy the next truck that bogged down. Make it up the hill, or you lose your ride. They didn't look like they took him seriously. I think they'd grown used to empty threats from the 82nd Airborne ever since the dust bowl.

We turned around and headed back the way we'd come the day before. We'd only gone two kilometers when, sure enough, one of the Afghan drivers got his fuel truck stuck in some soft powder. Lieutenant White went to talk to the driver, who stood beside his rig looking flustered.

The lieutenant was not suffering fools that morning. "Get your shit out of the cab and get in another truck, or we'll leave you here for the Taliban."

Reluctantly, he did so, then watched in disbelief as the lieutenant called over the radio for our EOD (Explosive Ordnance Disposal) tech, Licon, to blow the vehicle up.

Andy nixed that idea, instead telling the lieutenant we'd just destroy it with a machine gun. The Afghan driver caught another ride, and the convoy rolled out, easing past the abandoned truck. George, in the convoy's Tail-end Charlie GMV, trained his M240 on it. A short burst, and the bullets tore into the fuel truck's belly. Instead of blowing up, a sudden jet of flame spewed from the holes like World War II flamethrowers.

"That was unexpected," George reported over the radio.

We stared at the spectacle of thousands of gallons of gasoline burning in the middle of nowhere, a $50,000 truck melting down at the same time. It was something out of a Joseph Heller novel.

"Well, one down. Nine to go," Joe said over the radio. I chuckled inside.

"Do you think they know we're serious now?" Andy asked.

"Amazing what a little motivation will do," Floyd said when we passed one Afghan on his hands and knees, digging a half-sunken wheel out of the pliant earth.

"Yeah, shoulda lit one up yesterday," Andy said.

Behind us, a cloud of oily black smoke rose over the ridgelines, a good indicator that George's target was still burning. This must have really thrown the Taliban off as they wondered what the hell we were doing. Plus, it was always good to warm up your heavy guns early in the morning. It lets everyone in earshot know that you are ready to play.

Later that morning, George scored his second fuel truck kill. I think the Afghan driver earnestly tried to free his rig after he bogged down, but nothing he did could free it in time. George put a burst into it, and flames jetted out of the holes again. Now we had two vehicular funeral pyres rising in our wake.

A third one got stuck going up an incline. No time for the wrecker. George burned it, too. The convoy was down five trucks when we finally made it to the Y intersection in the early afternoon. We made record progress after that. Each time one of the fuel trucks got bogged down, the driver would bail out and frantically work to get it clear before George came into view. Columns of black smoke dotted our route back to the intersection.

I'd submitted a JTAR (Joint Tactical Air Request) last night before racking out, and as we finally got back on the right route, a section of A-10s, call sign HAWG, arrived on station overhead to support us. This time everything went smoothly; the lead aircraft checked in on my assigned frequency and I brought them up to speed on our fucked-up situation. At the same time, the SOTF was talking to Andy over SATCOM to warn us that they were picking up SIGINT (signals intelligence—this time communications chatter) that the enemy was trying to set up another ambush near Mangan, complete with a PPIED (pressure plate IED).

The A-10s could only hang out with us for forty minutes at most, so I wanted to use them as aggressively as I could. The clear blue sky was our friend today. At first, I had them run visual and sensor scans on the route in front of us so they could see anything unusual waiting for us down the road. With their thermal sensors, they could see the distinction between a cold IED against the warm ground around it.

The A-10 was designed to destroy Soviet tanks in case World War III broke out in Europe. Armed with a powerful 30mm Gatling gun cannon, the twin-ruddered aircraft could pack a massive load of bombs, rockets, and missiles. Heavily armored, they were very difficult to bring down.

As the two birds ran interference for us, the convoy slowly began to make its descent into Alkazai Valley. The A-10s reported that the way ahead was clear. No signs of enemy activity or any "cold spots" along the route.

It was about that time when the last of the fuel trucks got hopelessly bogged down. The Afghan driver climbed aboard one of the Russian-built rigs carrying our cargo containers, and George set fire to it with his machine gun. The last of the fuel we had with us jetted from the truck's ruptured hull, immolating everything in its path. Now there was none.

The A-10s only had a few more minutes left on station due to fuel limitations. I didn't want to let them go without doing something more. I asked them for a show of force along the road that lay ahead of us.

I passed the word to Andy, who warned the convoy that things were about to get loud.

"HAWG in from the south," the lead aircraft reported a few minutes later.

The two A-10s fell out of the blue sky in a row, engines throttled all the way forward. The pilots pulled out less than two hundred feet over the road and blasted over us, their four huge turbofan engines thundering. They shot ahead of us, going perhaps 450 miles an hour, and followed the road the six more kilometers down the valley.

Hoots and hollering came over our team's radio net. After all the frustration of the past several days, seeing those two magnificent aircraft served as an adrenaline shot to our morale.

"That was fucking awesome!" Strom shouted over the din.

"The Taliban will think twice about fucking with us now," I said.

Once complete, the A-10s pulled up, each leaving twin tails of white condensed water vapor until they disappeared into the vast sky over the valley.

"HAWG, complete with show of force, checking out at this time," called the pilot.

"Thanks for the good work, guys, have a safe flight back. HALO 14, out," I responded.

"You guys stay safe out here, HAWG switching station."

The A-10s spooked the enemy away for us. Instead of risking bombs and gun runs, they simply melted away into the surrounding hills.

The village of Mangan appeared off to our left as we reached the valley floor. No pit stop today, we were pushing all the way for FOB Todd. The convoy whined slowly but steadily through the Alkazai Valley for the rest of the afternoon. Near vertical two-hundred-foot hills flanked the valley and gave us no room to maneuver had the Taliban decided to attack us. Fortunately, this area of Afghanistan was remote even for the Taliban. We were officially in Nowhere.

The convoy reached the end of Alkazai Valley just after sundown. We paused briefly before making the final jump to FOB Todd. We were just outside of Bala Murghab, a twenty-four-kilometer-long valley that was oriented north–south and split right down the middle by the Murghab River. We regrouped the convoy near an ABP outpost that sat atop a massive hill to put our night vision devices on. From there, we slowly poured into the BMG valley itself. We entered into the northernmost village called Alkazai, go figure. It was a maze of mud walls and huts with a single driv-able road straight down the middle. There must have been a hundred dogs barking at us, their barks echoed in the cold night air. We were on high alert, ready for anything to come at us from the darkness.

After passing through the village proper, the road continued parallel to the river. On the left side of the convoy was a steep drop-off into its rush-ing waters, to our right, hillsides rising straight up two hundred feet. Sev-eral times, the roadbed narrowed so much that to keep from flipping the GMV into the water, Floyd had to scrape the right side of the rig against the hill.

We eased around a sharp turn and somebody reported, "I see it."

Through my night vision, I stood up in the trunk of the GMV and looked out over the front of the convoy and saw a guard tower, Hesco walls, Italian and American flags fluttering in the evening's breeze. FOB Todd in all its glory.

"Wow, it really does exist," I muttered.

"Don't get your hopes up," Strom replied. "Nothing there worth smiling about."

The guard in the tower waved us inside. Our convoy split; the 82nd Airborne went to their portion of the FOB, leaving what remained of their contracted trucks just outside the front wall to setup camp. Meanwhile, another soldier led our cargo trucks and GMVs to what would be our home area for the next six months.

Just before midnight, we shut our engines off and dismounted. Our new home consisted of a large and empty extension of the FOB's Hesco perimeter. Two lone khaki-colored GP (general purpose) tents and a few portashitters sat in the middle. Farther away sat two massive MRAP (Mine Resistant Ambush Protected) vehicles, RG-31 and RG-33 models. This was the sum total of the preparations to receive us. At least the Italians who ran the chow tent were nice enough to save us some cold cuts and bread from dinner. They understood what we had just gone through to get here and knew we needed it.

Four days and 180 kilometers to get to this. We shook our heads and went to work, getting our cargo containers off the trucks with a portable crane and pulling our gear out of the GMVs. The work took hours. When finally we finished, the team discovered our living tent had only a dirt floor. Some cots had been tossed in one corner. No interior walls, no floor, no heat, no nothing.

I grabbed a cot, set it up, and fell onto it, boots still on and my gear scattered around me. In seconds, I was out cold.

It seemed like I'd just closed my eyes when the roar of turboprop engines jarred me awake. In the darkness of the tent, I recognized the distinctive sound of a C-130 passing overhead.

Must be an airdrop or something.

I closed my eyes again and drifted.

"Get up! Everyone up! Now! Grab your weapons!"

My eyes jerked open. Had I dreamed that?

A rash of gunfire bloomed from somewhere nearby. I could hear the bark of AK-47s intermingled with the sharper cracks of M4s.

"GRAB YOUR WEAPONS!" Joe yelled into the tents.

Another flurry of gunfire. People shouting. The guys around me jumped from their cots and grabbed their gear.

"Let's go! NOW!"

A machine gun tore off a long burst in the distance.

Day one at FOB Todd, and the shit was hitting the fan.

Welcome to BMG.

6

★ OPERATION HERO RECOVERY ★

"Grab your shit and let's go. Now!" Joe shouted again. Around me, the guys began to stir. Mark, wearing only his BDU pants and a T-shirt, grabbed the gun box containing his M107 Barrett .50 caliber sniper rifle. Ignoring his kit and helmet, he scooped up a couple extra magazines, then dashed out of the tent with Paddy, one of our other snipers.

I'd slept with my boots on. Now I was glad that I'd done so, as it saved me a couple of heartbeats. I threw my kit on, reached for my rifle, and stepped out into the late morning sunlight just as another volley of gunfire racked the air.

"Let's go! Let's go!" Joe's voice rose over the commotion. He was standing by the RGs. I moved toward him just as I caught sight of Mark and Paddy running for an empty guard tower at the corner of our compound. They scurried up the makeshift ladder and set up the Barrett. Soon, they were scanning for targets somewhere off to what I thought was to the north of the FOB.

Jesus Christ. I don't even know which way is north.

"Load up! Come on!" Joe yelled.

I got to the RG-33 and stuffed myself inside. The last time I was in one of these vehicles was during a road trip from Camp Al Qaim to COP Rawah in Iraq, and it instantly made me feel like I was inside an armored coffin. The other guys piled in around me until we were squashed so closely together none of us could move.

The rig began to roll. The RG-33 had only one window located in the rear door. It was thick, blast-resistant glass that had been smeared with grime and coated with Afghan moondust, making it all but impossible to see out of it. The RG turned sharply, and we leaned into each other. A few other turns, and I'd lost all sense of where we were or which way we were going. The rig bounced and jerked over the hardscrabble terrain, tossing us around violently.

Joe finished strapping on his helmet and told us, "Two 82nd Airborne soldiers just drowned in the river. We're going out as QRF."

"Drowned? How the fuck did that happen?" somebody asked.

"The bundles from the CDS drop drifted out of the drop zone. Some landed in the water and the east side of the river. Two paratroopers went into the river and tried to secure one of the bundle chutes. One fell into the water and the other went in to grab him. They both went under with all of their gear on."

"Holy shit," I muttered.

We'd rolled out with only part of the team. The rest of the guys would follow us in the other RG when they finished getting into full battle rattle. In the meantime, we were heading straight into a fight.

I wanted to see what we were getting into, but the window was useless. I turned slightly and looked over at the gunner's station. Jay manned the remote-controlled .50 cal on the roof. A camera was mounted next to the machine gun, so Jay could see whatever the weapon was pointed at from a flat screen monitor at his station. I tried to peer over his shoulder to see what the terrain ahead looked like, hoping to get some idea of the situation we'd face when our boots hit the ground. I caught glimpses of a rugged dirt track, a few mud huts, and some trees, but it was like trying to make sense of a painting by looking at parts of it through a toilet paper roll.

"Get ready."

The RG lurched to a halt. Joe said, "Dismount here."

The hatch in the rear hull eased open and the team filtered out. I pushed through the doorway to discover we'd stopped at the edge of a small village. An irrigation canal skirted the first row of mud huts, and the road we were on continued down toward the river. Sporadic gunfire played out just across in the air. Above it, I could hear the occasional boom of Mark's Barrett. He and Paddy had obviously found some targets.

I moved for the village, but as I crossed the canal I sank up to my knees in brackish water and mud. My feet got soaked. I uttered a curse as

I took up a position behind a compound's mud wall. My boots were soaked through.

A few Italian soldiers milled around by the road we'd used. Joe spotted them and went to find out what was going on. A few moments later, he called to us to mount back up. We climbed back into the RG and lurched down the road, through the heart of the village and out toward the river another hundred meters or so, before halting again.

We dismounted right into the middle of a gun battle raging across the river. Around us, 82nd Airborne soldiers sprinted past carrying loads of gear down to the riverbank. Some of them were actually in the water, holding on to parachute suspension lines as they eased out into the rushing current. The opposite bank was high enough that it seemed to protect them from the incoming fire, but if any of the Taliban shooting at us maneuvered closer, the men in the water would be trapped in the open.

While the 82nd Airborne soldiers dashed about, ANA troops lay behind walls and huts, occasionally exposing themselves to trigger off full-auto bursts from their AKs. Spraying at whatever. No fire discipline. Several Italian armored vehicles had parked on this side of the village, guns manned but silent. Bullets smacked into compound walls as the Taliban raked our positions with machine guns and AKs.

I took cover behind a compound wall just as a burst of automatic fire tore into nearby trees, sending bits of branches and leaves showering around me. Our other RG arrived and took up position across the road from me. Pat was on the gun, and he unleashed the remote-operated Ma Deuce with cold vengeance. The heavy machine gun boomed, and the incoming diminished, at least for the moment.

Rob came running down the road in a crouch, weapon up. He moved with grace through all the chaos, a man born to be a warrior.

"Rob! Hey, over here," I shouted to him. He looked up and saw me behind cover.

"Where's Andy?" he called back to me as he splashed through that same canal on his way over to me.

"Don't know."

In the distance, Mark's sniper rifle thundered. He'd found another target.

"Why are the Italians just standing around?" I asked.

"They aren't allowed to engage unless they are personally being shot at. Personally," Rob said.

"Well, that's useful."

I glanced over at the nearest Italian armored car. Sure enough, the gunner was on his weapon, staring across the river—finger off the trigger. A few meters away, bullets sprang off a compound wall being used as cover by some Afghan troops.

"Joe and Rob, we need you down at the river," Andy's voice said over our radios. Rob slapped my shoulder and bolted down to the river.

"See ya later, brother," he said as he left.

A moment later, I heard George swear. He'd come down with the second half of the team and had set up on the rooftop of the hut nearest me.

"Can't see shit from up here," George said as he shifted around, trying to get a better view of the village on the other side of the river.

The Barrett roared twice in quick succession, like a distant cannon. Over the radio, Mark reported dropping two men carrying a mortar about a thousand meters from his tower.

"Fuck me! There's trenches and ratlines in front of that village," George reported. "Dudes are running all over the place."

His M4 cracked. The enemy retaliated swiftly. A Taliban gunner a few hundred meters away swung his PKM our way and tore off a long burst. The 7.62mm rounds sawed right through the tree between George's hut and my position on the wall. Another blizzard of trunk, branches, and leaves rained down on me.

"Jesus fucking Christ!" I shouted, leaning into the wall as the debris storm continued.

"Ski, you okay?" George asked.

"Fanfuckingtastic."

"That was some good shit right there."

His M4 cracked again. Somebody else was up on the roof with him, and he opened fire as well.

A throng of confused ANA ran by on the road, weapons held at every angle. I had no idea where they were going, or what they thought they were doing, other than exposing themselves. I doubt they had any idea either.

We'd been sent here in part to train those guys. It was going to be a long deployment.

"Ski, what's your location?" Andy's voice asked over my radio.

I keyed my mic. "Edge of the village, near the intersection."

"We've got air en route. We're gonna need you down here at the river. The 82nd Airborne guys don't have a JTAC."

"Roger that, on my way."

I said good-bye to George and dashed along the wall, breaking cover only when I had no choice. A quick sprint down the bank, and I reached the river. A small mud shack stood along the rocky beach there, and I made my way over to it. Gunfire rattled and popped, but down in the riverbed it was safe—for now. All the rounds were passing overhead, as the Taliban hadn't been able to get eyes on the river itself yet.

"Who's the senior man here?" I asked a group of 82nd Airborne guys holding positions along a reedy group of trees.

"First Sergeant Zappala," said one of the men, pointing to a rugged figure down the riverbank a ways.

I ran over and introduced myself. We talked for a brief moment, then I went back to the shack and shucked off my gear. We were going to be out here for a long while. Might as well settle in.

I looked around. Which way was north? No idea. I was going to need to orient myself fast before the aircraft arrived.

"Hey! Are you a JTAC?" I turned away from my assault pack and saw a young-looking soldier running toward me. At first glance I could tell he was no 82nd Airborne regular. He wore Air Force–style cami pants, only a T-shirt under his body armor, and a black sweatband that kept his long hair out of his eyes. He had a scraggly, trailer trash sort of beard struggling to grow. He looked like a cross between Joe Dirt and John McEnroe.

"You a JTAC?" he asked again as he took a knee beside me.

"Yeah. I'm with the MARSOC team."

We stood up and shook hands.

"I'm Ski. HALO 14," I said.

"Ben. TRIBUTE," he replied, giving me his JTAC call sign.

He had all sorts of high-speed gear dangling on his body armor. I was told there was no other JTAC here. All of this made me suspicious and guarded right off the bat.

"Okay," he said. "I've got a Predator en route along with a pair of F-16s."

"Excellent," I replied.

"Do you want to control the aircraft, or do you want me to do it?" he asked.

I stared at him briefly. The question confused me.

He'd called in the air? What the hell is he talking about?

"Wait, are you JTAC qualified?" I asked bluntly.

He looked uncomfortable. He dodged the question and started off on some line of bullshit that made no sense. Warning lights went off in my head as rounds continued piercing the tree limbs above us.

I cut him off. "Look, are you a JTAC or not?"

"I'm a ROMAD," he finally said. A ROMAD was sort of like a JTAC-in-training who was supposed to be working in conjunction with a qualified JTAC.

"Why'd you give me a call sign?" I asked him. Call signs are only given to qualified controllers. He'd lied to me right out of the gate.

"Well, it's my JTAC's call sign," he replied.

"Where's he at?"

He looked uncomfortable again. "Herat."

This was fucked up. I may not have known which way was north, but there was no way this guy was going to be dropping bombs anywhere near my team.

"Okay. Listen," I said pointedly. "I am the only qualified guy here. I'm taking the air. What's the freq?"

The wind went out of his sails. Grudgingly, he said, "Beige 44."

"Roger, Beige 44. Thanks."

That's all I needed from him. I set to work assembling what amounted to my battlefield work station: radio and VideoScout. Then I got ready to check in on Beige 44. Ben watched for a few minutes, then slipped away.

I put my headset on just in time to hear a calm, clear voice say, "Any station, this is Barbarian Fires on Beige 44."

"HALO 14, send it," I replied. Barbarian Fires was the fire support NCO, who was back on the FOB in the 82nd Airborne's Command Operations Center (COC). Basically, his job was to coordinate all fire support in the BMG area—artillery, mortars, air.

"HALO, this is Barbarian Fires. Do you want me to stack air, or do you want to do it?"

"Thanks, brother, but I got this," I said.

"Roger. Here if you need me."

"Thanks," I said. The calm voice in the middle of all this chaos settled me. I took a deep breath and looked around. Rob, Billy, another assaulter and former Recon instructor named Jack, and Joe had stripped down to their black silkies and had waded into the river. The current was absolutely fierce, and the guys relied on ropes strung into the water to keep from being swept away like the two lost 82nd Airborne soldiers.

The gunfire had slackened a bit, but I could still hear Mark's and Paddy's massive .50 caliber Barretts' report over the occasional AK and M4 shot.

I memorized everything I could see, committing the images to my brain like snapshots assembled in an album. When the birds got here, I'd have to see from their perspective as well as mine while still maintaining my own situational awareness to what was going down around me. Knowing the ground in sight would be critical for that.

I knelt down. The VideoScout booted, and I started scanning signal bands for video feeds.

Two F-16s and a Predator drone. That was a lot of firepower. This is the real deal. No rest for the weary.

I wasn't going to fuck this up.

I keyed my handset microphone.

Here we go.

7

BALA MURGHAB RIVERBANK

"HALO 14, VIPER 21, in from the south for show of force," came a voice over the radio.

"Continue," I replied.

Above us, an F-16 streaked down out of the cloud layer, afterburners searing the sky with a cone of blue-red flame like a comet's tail. At first, it was nothing but a dot in the sky, no sound to accompany its five-hundred-mile-an-hour approach. Then it resolved into a flat gray bird. Single tail fin, pointed nose, its big air intake nestled under the fuselage giving it a deadly sleek look. VIPER 21 followed a straight course over the east side of the river where the enemy was entrenched, dropping ever lower until its jet wash ruffled the scattered trees around the Taliban positions.

The firing stopped. The Taliban on the far side of the river saw what was coming their way. The Taliban know all too well the destructive power that can be delivered on call by U.S. aircraft. One trigger pull and in seconds the Vulcan cannon would unload a hundred explosive shells, raking a target area. Only the supremely lucky survive.

A gun run was the least of the Taliban worries. The F-16 carried JDAMs, GPS-guided bombs. Punch in the exact coordinates down to a few meters, and the JDAM will pulverize with a precision never seen in any other war.

A single F-16 thundered past us in a fury, burning hell across the valley. I watched it, my heart beating faster. Such power and beauty never ceased to leave me in awe. And I hoped the display would scare the shit out of the enemy and send them scurrying for whatever nooks and crannies they lived in around here.

The aircraft crossed over the villages on the far side of the river. I imagined that if there were any windows over there, they're all broken now. The sound of the General Electric F-110 engine was simply deafening. Down this low, the earth trembled as if the rolling shock waves of an earthquake were fast approaching.

The single aircraft pulled up into a steep climb to avoid crossing into Turkmenistan airspace. Near vertical now, the gray bird vanished into the cloud deck.

It was over in a matter of seconds. The sound of the engine diminished until they were lost to the afternoon breeze. But they were up there, loitering. And the enemy knew it now.

A few minutes passed with the valley still and silent until a few shots echoed across the riverbanks. Ignoring this, Rob and Joe waded farther into the water in search of our lost troopers. I stayed beside the shack, working the radio. The Predator drone arrived on station twenty minutes after the F-16s. Must have been close by to get here so fast.

Strange how the pilot was a world away from here, controlling the aircraft somewhere stateside in a building, flying the drone like some gamer freak, hopped up on caffeine at the keyboard of a computer playing a flight simulator program. I had near instant communication with the drone's pilot, thanks to the voodoo of satellite technology.

The Predator had the sole mission of scanning the river downstream from our search area. If either body surfaced, we'd see it from the drone's sensor. Meanwhile, VIPER orbited far above, out of sight but still audible.

The frantic search continued. The cloud layer began to break up, and bolts of sunlight pierced through. The temperature rose quickly. Soon, we were all bathed in sweat, the sun beating down on us with all the intensity we experienced in the Nevada desert.

Forty-five minutes passed. VIPER flight went "bingo" on fuel, meaning the F-16s had just enough gas to get back to base and land. They turned for home. As they pulled off target, two more birds arrived. This time, we'd been pushed a HAWG flight—another pair of A-10 Thunderbolts, known affectionately to their pilots as Warthogs due to their hideously ugly appearance. The A-10 violates every rule of aviation aesthetics. Twin tails, 30mm chain gun designed to blow away Soviet tanks. Wingloads of bombs slung underneath each rectangular wing. They were glorious eyesores for us.

They circled like raptors, waiting for the mice to make their move.

Meanwhile, the team guys in the water discovered how the two troopers had fallen. A rock ledge stretched out from the riverbank to about mid-river. The current was pure fury, and on the ledge the men could just barely keep their footing against it. Then it dropped away without any warning. The water was moving too fast, was too muddy, and too turbulent to see that precipice. One minute the 82nd Airborne soldiers had boots on solid rock. The next, they'd fallen into an underwater chasm at least sixty feet deep. No human could have survived the raging current and the depth when wearing full combat gear. Our guys were having trouble staying afloat in their silkies (running shorts), and they were Recon Marines with plenty of water training.

Midday approached and HAWG pulled off station. I checked in with their replacements. Operation Hero Recovery, as this was being called now, was the top-priority mission in all of Afghanistan. Our higher commands made sure we had all the air support we could handle, and we were never without those protective birds overhead.

A lot of them and just one of me.

My voice grew scratchy and raw. I drank water out of my Nalgene bottle, which I kept next to the radio. Whoever Barbarian Fires was back at the FOB proved to be a huge help to me. We fell into a rhythm, each helping the other and making sure the load never got too heavy for one man. I made a mental note to track him down and thank him later.

With the weather clear, I could use my VideoScout to link into the aircraft sensors overhead. The Predator carried a sophisticated color camera suite, which I used to keep scanning the river downstream. We also used its infrared system to see if we could locate the heat signatures of either body, however faint it may be by now. The day wore on with no luck at all. Through it, while working with the other aircraft, giving updates to Barbarian Fires and Andy, I kept in constant contact with the Predator crew. As the fast movers came and went, the Predator loitered overhead. It could stay on station for upward of ten hours, making it an incredibly useful asset for us.

Following the afternoon call to prayer, the Taliban grew restless. Mark, who had hitched a ride out to the recovery site, was on the roof of the shack providing overwatch with his SASR (Special Application Scoped

Rifle). His search effort spotted movement along the trenches and ratlines again. Soon, another firefight broke out, and tracers arced back and forth across the river above us. I put an end to that with another show of force. This time, a single A-10 came down and buzzed the battlefield. The Taliban went to ground, and the firing abruptly stopped. Perhaps twenty minutes passed, and sporadic gunfire resumed.

Using his high-power scope, Mark began to give me a steady stream of updates. I used his info to talk HAWG's sensors onto a series of three compounds on the edge of the village across the river, where Mark had spotted a lot of activity. I was oriented now and growing more familiar with the terrain. The village was called Ludina, and every time we had a lull in the fighting, the people in it would try to get out into the field where the trenches were to loot the pallets of supplies dropped there by accident earlier this morning. At times, we'd be exchanging gunfire with the Taliban, and the villagers would still be out there, digging through our stuff. Then, when it got too hot for them, they'd scurry back into their qalats and hunker down. To our astonishment, a few minutes would pass and they would send their children—boys and girls—out to continue the looting. Bullets and tracers whizzed by as swarms of six- and seven-year-old kids picked away at the pallets. Every so often, one would score a case of Gatorade, or some other treasure, and go bounding back for the village clutching it like a football. It was a miracle none of them got killed.

As Mark gave me a running commentary on this, I couldn't help but think of my own little girl. What if my home back in Colorado got engulfed in such violence? What would Sabrina and I do?

Well, the last thing on the list would be to send her out into the street.

"What the fuck kind of parent makes their kid run into a firefight?" I asked Mark. It was hard not to keep the disgust out of my voice.

"Don't know. Desperate ones, I suppose. These people have less than nothing."

A few bottles of Gatorade versus losing another mouth to feed—the equation of life in Afghanistan.

Every time the fighting flared up significantly, I called in the aerial cavalry. The show-of-force flybys were very dramatic, and good for morale. Plus, they'd shut the Taliban up for a few minutes each time, though they were becoming used to them by now and perhaps were feeling safer since we hadn't hit them with bombs or strafing runs yet.

I tried to pick and choose the moments for maximum effect. Each run burned a lot of fuel, curtailing the time each pair of aircraft could support us. Yet for the moment it was all I could do. I wanted to do more, and it was frustrating not to have a firm target within our rules of engagement that I could take out with all the firepower hovering overhead. I couldn't drop on the village—too many civilians. The compounds Mark had identified could have noncombatants in them, as well as the men shooting at us. In most wars, it'd be a tough-shit moment for those civilians. We'd have flattened their homes with bombs or artillery. Not now. We had to risk taking casualties from the Taliban exploiting these safe havens to protect the lives of the "innocent." What did our command call it? Heroic restraint. I still have no idea what that means.

If I went ahead and called in a target, that bomb and whatever it destroyed was on me, no one else. If I killed civilians, the military would likely prosecute me—especially if the incident became a news story, plastered across the major networks.

The work continued, the men in the river trying to drag the bottom with grapnel hooks attached to parachute lines. They'd found a lot of debris, but the bodies of our fallen eluded them. We'd need more than hooks. A call was made for divers, and toward the end of the day, an Air Force Pararescue team was airlifted to FOB Todd. The 82nd Airborne brought them out to the recovery site, and as I watched them break out their SCUBA equipment, I realized we were going to be in place for a long time.

As they were gearing up, a platoon from the 82nd joined up with a gaggle of ANA and swung upriver to the old bridge that had been built by the Russians back in the 80s, just east of the FOB. They crossed it, then moved along the far bank out of sight of the enemy until they were beside the field where the pallets lay.

There was a scattering of adults out with the kids rifling through our supplies at that point. The 82nd and ANA stormed over the bank and pushed into the field, sending the villagers bolting for their homes. They secured what was left of our supplies, but before they could do anything else, the Taliban counterattacked. Coalition forces had rarely been on that side of the river, and from the enemy handheld radio chatter we picked up back at FOB Todd from our SIGINT Marine, James, it was clear they thought we were assaulting their positions.

From trading shots across the river, the fight morphed into a furious battle on the edge of the village. Now the civilians there were in significant jeopardy, as the Taliban were using their homes and buildings to fire at our men at close range. Once again, I felt helpless. We couldn't hit them in these circumstances without killing women and children. All I could do was observe, and send the attack aircraft down on more show-of-force flybys.

At evening prayer, the enemy broke contact and the battlefield grew still.

"I guess praising Allah comes before killing infidels," Mark said.

The sun went down as the Pararescue diver entered the water. The 82nd and some of our men continued to drag sections of the river with the parachute shrouds and grapnels. The search had yielded no sign of the missing men. The longer we were out here, the longer we risked losing more Americans, but nobody budged. This was personal to all of us. Everyone comes home, everyone. For our warriors to be left in this hellhole was simply unacceptable. In truth, there was a part of me that was eased by all the effort, firepower, and assets brought to this tragic scene. It reminded me that if I died out here, my brothers would move heaven and earth to make sure my remains returned to Colorado. There'd be closure for Sabrina and my little girl.

Losing a loved one in combat is bad enough. But losing their remains as well leaves so many unanswered questions. The mind plays out all sorts of one-in-a-million scenarios that give false hope, and keep the warrior's loved ones from moving on and finding their new sense of normalcy after such a terrible blow. Plenty of nations, plenty of militaries and Monday-morning quarterbacks criticize the risks we Americans take on the battlefield to recover our fallen. This is why. We do it for our families. Everybody comes home.

"Hey, I think I see something," Mark reported from the shack's roof.

I glanced up at him. By now, we were in that hazy gray twilight just before full dark.

"ACUs in the river," Mark said. "I'm almost positive. We've got a body floating."

ACU's were the standard issue uniforms worn by the 82nd Airborne and most of the Army in Afghanistan at that time.

A group of our teammates—our medic, Ryan, and Jack, Billy, Rob, and George—joined some 82nd soldiers and rushed into the water. Hanging on to the parachute lines, they eased out in chains across the underwater ledge, trying to intercept what Mark had seen. George was at the end of the chain, the farthest out. He could see the soldier's ACUs as the current swept him downstream a few feet from his grasp. George lunged for him—and fell off the ledge into the chasm.

Rob was next in the chain, and he saw George go under, only a few fingers remaining in view above the turbulent water. He grabbed George's hand and yanked him back onto the ledge. Soaked and shivering, water pouring down the sides of his head and face, George stared at Rob knowing that he'd probably just saved his life.

"You good?" Rob asked.

"Yeah. Maybe this isn't such a good idea though," George replied.

A moment later, the current caught Jack, another seasoned Recon Marine, and flipped him on his back. Someone snagged him before he could be carried away. Enough was enough. In the darkness, we ran too great a risk for further loss of life. First Sergeant Zappala ordered everyone out of the river for the night. The search would have to continue at first light.

The site still needed to be secured. The worst-case scenario we faced was the Taliban getting ahold of our fallen. They'd defile the bodies, take photos and video, and post them victoriously on the Net—an agony for the families, and a PR victory for evil. That was not going to happen on our watch.

The 82nd Airborne rotated their men out and brought fresh troops to the scene. They took up positions along the banks and settled down for a long night. With the 82nd handling security, Andy called the team back to FOB Todd to get some rest. Tomorrow was going to be an even busier day.

Being the only JTAC, I remained behind. We'd have air support all through the night, and somebody had to control it.

Mark and George approached me, absorbed in conversation. George had to be freezing at this point, as the temperature was dropping as the night grew black. If he was, though, he showed no signs of it.

"Did you see Ryan out there all day?" George asked.

"Yeah. He had more shit on his back than anyone out there," Mark replied, referring to Ryan's medical pack and additional gear, on top of his already heavy combat loadout. Ryan was our team's SARC (Special Amphibious Reconnaissance Corpsman) and a damn good one.

George nodded. "Gotta say, it is damn good to know we've got a medic who comes prepared for anything. Dude'll take care of us."

Mark nodded, then stopped beside me. He looked me over and cocked his head a bit.

"How you doing, Ski?" he asked.

"I'm good."

Barely. How long had I been doing this? Fourteen hours? Maybe more. My brain was getting foggy.

"You sound hoarse, you sure you're okay?" George said.

"Yeah. Thanks. Tired is all."

"You going back?" Mark asked.

"Can't. Gotta coordinate air for the 82nd."

George and Mark glanced at each other. Then George said, "Well, we're not leaving you out here alone. Fuck that."

"Yeah, fuck that," Mark echoed.

For just that moment, all the day's exhaustion drained away. The night's chill breeze couldn't touch me, and the hunger pangs growling in my stomach vanished. I don't remember if I ever thanked them or not, but that gesture was the first real sign that the door to the Brotherhood had been opened to me.

8

★ Cleared Hot ★

All night long, Mark and George stayed with me, keeping watch from the roof of that little shack while I talked to the pilots overhead. My throat grew raw, then gravelly as the hours passed. By 0200, I was hoarse and losing steam. More Rip Its were needed, and First Sergeant Zappala made sure the recovery site was well supplied.

The enemy had gone to bed. Once nightfall came, the stray shots diminished, and movement on the far bank ceased. Before midnight, there wasn't a sign of another human toward the village. Our rescue teams at the river worked on through the night, dragging the channel and searching for the bodies through the darkest hours.

At 0300, my last set of batteries began to fade. I told Mark and George I needed to get back to our compound and grab spares. They clambered off the roof, and the three of us caught a ride back to the FOB. As I walked into our compound, I saw Andy was still up.

"How ya holding up, Ski?" he asked.

"Good as I can be, I guess."

He slapped me on the shoulder, and I dove into the tent to dig through my gear in search of MBITR and BA-5590 batteries I needed until my patrol pack was weighted with them. God knows how long I'd be out there, so I loaded up with everything of use. I put the dead ones on chargers, snagged a pack of cigarettes, and headed back out into the night. An hour later, I got back to the river, just in time to check in with the next set of fast movers coming to support.

Dawn broke and the birds arrived. Another Predator rotated out, too, and I set it up to search the waters downstream again. The 82nd worked closely with the Pararescue team, but through the morning they had no luck finding our two fallen soldiers. Meanwhile, the Taliban, still unsure of what we were doing, took occasional potshots at the men pulling security over the recovery site. Each time it started to flare, I called in the fighter-bombers overhead, and they filled the valley with the thunder of their engines.

Captain Perry, the 82nd Airborne's battery commander, came out and joined First Sergeant Zappala at the PR (Personnel Recovery) site. He'd been at their operations center through all of yesterday, trying to coordinate the response and reinforcements. But Perry's battalion commander (Task Force Professional), call sign PRO 6, flew in from Herat this morning and took over control of the situation. I'd heard him over the radio a couple of times this morning and noticed his blunt, sometimes ignorant way of giving orders.

The rescue turned into an international effort. The Italians had been involved on the periphery the day before, but now Afghan Commandos arrived with an Army Special Forces team via helicopters. A Chinook delivered a group of specialized British divers to FOB Todd, and soon after dawn they were out in the river with the Pararescue team. ISAF command was sparing nothing; those men would be found at any cost.

As I worked with the aircraft overhead, my teammates departed FOB Todd to meet some ANA soldiers living at the Alkazai School; the building had been turned into an outpost and road checkpoint. We'd passed their small outpost coming into the valley two days before, and their training would be our primary mission while we were in the valley. Andy and the others wanted to get started right away, but be close enough to the FOB to help out if something should happen at the river that would require reinforcements.

The day wore on and the sun cooked me in my gear. I had no shade, no respite from the heat, and no matter how much water I drank from my Nalgene bottle, my mouth felt like cotton. I rasped like Joe Cocker until the pilots overhead couldn't help but notice how bad I sounded.

Toward evening, after being on the radio for over thirty hours, a pair of fighter-bombers arrived. I gave them a ten-minute-long check-in brief and went over every significant event that had happened during the course of the day. When I finished, there was a long pause on the radio. Then the lead pilot said, "Wow. That was the most detailed brief I've ever heard. You doing okay?"

"It's rough, but we are doing good."

"No, I mean are *you* doing all right? You sound worn the fuck out," he added.

"I am okay, just a little tired. Thanks for asking," I responded.

As the aircraft and drones came and went, helicopters buzzed over the hills and down into the valley in a continuous stream, bringing in more men and supplies to assist the operation. At times, they would appear with no warning, popping over the ridgelines behind us with surprising speed and agility. Even the venerable, Vietnam-era Chinooks used these terrain-hugging tactics. Eighty feet long, capable of carrying a platoon of infantry or thirteen tons of supplies, the CH-47 was the aerial workhorse of the Afghan War. I once heard a Black Hawk pilot describe a Chinook as looking like "two palm trees fucking a Dumpster." For all their size, the crews got the absolute most out of them in the air. None were hit as they hugged the ridges and flitted in and out of our FOB.

As it got dark, First Sergeant Zappala sought me out. "Hey Ski," he said as I looked up at him. He cut an imposing figure in the dusk with broad shoulders and square jaw—a soldier's soldier.

"PRO 6 has a new tasking for us."

"What's that?" I asked.

"He's afraid the bodies might be washed farther downstream. He wants us to take ten men and two Humvees to a bend in the river about two klicks north and set up a blocking position."

"Has anyone been out there before, do we know exactly where we are going?"

Zappala shook his head.

"That's why I need you to come with us. You're controlling a Predator right now, correct?"

"Yes."

"We may need it."

"Roger that," I said.

"We're going to overwatch the river there to make sure the bodies don't leave the country."

"Understood."

I started to gather my gear, noticing that Zappala didn't seem too thrilled with this plan. Neither did I. Ten men, two Humvees out in the middle of unknown, unexplored country at night? In Iraq, Coalition forces never left the FOB with fewer than four gun trucks. This seemed a little sketchy to me.

I finished packing up and followed Zappala to his Humvee. We climbed in and drove back to the FOB. I'd been gone twenty hours since the last time I'd dashed back to get batteries.

"Meet back here in twenty minutes," Zappala said, then vanished into the night as he went off to round up some soldiers for the mission.

I rushed over to the tent to grab fresh batteries for my radio and computer. When I got there, I discovered the compound was virtually empty. John, my JFO (Joint Fires Observer), was the only one from our team left in the area not on radio or gear watch. "Where is everyone?" I asked.

"Still out at Alkazai School with the ANA," he replied. "Should be back soon."

I told him what PRO 6 had ordered us to do, then asked if he wanted to come along.

John jumped at the opportunity to get back outside the wire. Sitting back on the FOB was driving him stir-crazy. This was his chance to get back into the game, and he wasted no time. Grabbing his weapon and several extra magazines of ammunition, he followed me out into the night to link back up with Zappala.

When we got back to the Humvees, we discovered that PRO 6's blocking force consisted of a ragtag bunch of rear-echelon types. I am pretty sure some of them were with us on the convoy up here. With all the front-line soldiers already out at the river, Zappala was left with a collection of cooks, techs, and clerks. They did not look happy.

"Where's First Sergeant Z?" I asked one of the young soldiers.

He pointed a finger over at the brick shell of an old Russian textile factory. A large olive drab tent that looked like it had come straight out of an episode of M*A*S*H was set up inside the roofless structure. "In there. Talking with PRO 6," the soldier added.

I looked over the assembled crew. Ten nonshooters. Two Humvees. This had "fuck-up" written all over it.

I walked over to the tent and pulled the makeshift plywood door open.

It turned out to be Captain Perry's Command Operations Center. The place bustled with activity. Radios crackled. Soldiers busily moved about between plywood desks and shelves. Two-by-four benches were pushed in around a conference table, and video monitors took up the main wall of the tent. In the middle of the chaos stood PRO 6 with his hands on his hips with a very "Dad is here now" posture. This was their battalion commander and all eyes were on him.

In the middle of the ops center, surrounded by a bank of computers and radios, I saw a staff sergeant hard at work. I'd presumed him to be Barbarian Fires. Short in stature, hair a mess with empty cans of Coke and notepads filled with grids surrounding him. He looked as exhausted as I felt, but I went over to him anyway and stuck out my hand. He looked up at me as I told him my name and said, "Hey, I'm the guy on the other end of the radio. Just wanted to introduce myself and put a face to the voice."

He shook my hand and said, "Danny. You've been awake for like thirty hours. Damn, man. Welcome to BMG."

"Thanks for all the help. Been great working with you," I said.

Danny's unflappable voice had helped keep me calm more than once over the last two days. It had become a reassurance to hear it.

"Anytime. You need anything, just let me know."

"You, too."

I started to walk away, but Danny called out after me. "Ski, be careful out there tonight. I'll be right here if you need anything." He glanced over at PRO 6, then back to me. "We'll have whatever you need on tap."

That was a relief. We'd become a good team. "Roger. Thanks, brother. Will talk to you when we get set up out there."

Ten minutes later, John and I loaded up with Zappala, and our two-vehicle element headed north from the FOB. We hadn't gone far when headlights appeared down the road in front of us. It turned out to be Andy and the rest of the team's column of two RGs coming back from the Alkazai School.

We stopped and I dismounted, meeting up with Andy between the two patrols. I wanted to make my case before Zappala arrived. In the glow of the headlights, he greeted me and I realized I hadn't seen him all day. This was unusual. Since coming aboard, I'd been Andy's constant shadow. Where the team leader went, the JTAC always followed.

"Hey Ski, where you going?" Andy asked.

I told him what PRO 6 had in mind. When I finished, Andy blinked and cocked his head. "Ski, that's fucking ridiculous. Two Humvees? You don't have the ass for that kind of mission."

"No. We could really use your help, Andy. We're gonna get smacked otherwise."

He thought it over, staring out into the darkness. At length, he whispered, "This is not a good idea."

He shook his head as Zappala walked up to discuss a new course of action to skin this retarded potato. "Okay, let's turn around, go back to the FOB, and regroup. We'll go out together."

"Sounds good," Andy said.

Relief fell over me.

Zappala and I returned to the lead Humvee, and he told the driver to turn around and head back to the FOB.

"Thank God for that," I thought to myself as we drove back.

Ten minutes later, we had consolidated back in our compound. Andy needed to get permission to head out with the 82nd from the SOTF, so he went off to explain the situation over one of the SVoIP (Secure Voice over Internet Protocol) phones in our TOC. Meanwhile, the rest of the team grabbed ammunition and gear. We'd take the two RGs and about half the team. George and Rob were part of the element we were leaving behind, and they were not happy with it.

As I stood beside Andy's RG, Pat walked over to talk to me. We made small talk and smoked a cigarette, chatting about the events of the day. Then I asked about the team's trip to Alkazai School.

"Well Ski, we met the ANA commander today. Colonel Ali."

"Oh yeah? What did you think of him?"

Pat took off his helmet, ran his fingers through his greasy hair, and sighed. "Piece of shit, Ski. He's a fat fucking joke. Like a bloated reject from the Red Army, circa 1982."

I started to laugh, then realized Pat was bitter about it.

"He shows no concern for his soldiers. He doesn't even seem to know how many he has out here. We asked him and he just shrugged his shoulders. His headquarters element has a total of six men. Complete shambles."

"Guess we have a lot of work ahead," I offered.

"He doesn't care about anything but himself, Ski. You'll see that the first time you meet him. Dude's got like early onset Alzheimer's, too. Either that or he's been hit in the head too many times."

"Jesus. Are the ANA any good at least?"

"Hard to tell. I suppose a few of them will turn out to be okay. But with leadership like that . . ."

Pat let that hang, but I knew what he meant. The Taliban and their insurgent allies were well organized and led. The Afghan army somehow got the dregs of the nation's leadership gene pool. It was the same all over the country. It was one of the main reasons why, after nine years of fighting, we couldn't disengage and hand the keys over to the Kabul government. The ANA would simply dissolve.

Andy returned to the RG and announced, "Okay, we're good to go. They just needed an updated kill roster. SOTF gave us the green light."

We did a quick game plan, talked about the order of march for our vehicles, then all mounted up to drive north again. We stopped at the Alkazai School to get an element of ANA. One of the rules here in country is the necessity to have Afghan forces embedded on every mission outside the wire. Colonel Ali chose not to go out with us, but he did offer up a pickup truck with about six or seven men. It was a Toyota Hilux, just as unarmored and vulnerable as any civilian rig seen on highways across the globe. We put it in the center of our convoy in hopes of keeping the ANA safe from rockets and roadside bombs.

Andy and Zappala took a minute before we left to give everyone a final brief. "Okay," Andy said, "the village here is relatively safe. The ANA are here, and there's an ABP outpost on a hill on the other side of the village. But once we push north into the fields beyond Alkazai, we're going into Taliban-controlled territory. Keep your eyes open."

I sat in the back of the lead RG next to the rear door, feeling like I was inside an armored sardine can again. Back at the FOB, Danny monitored the Predator's feed for me, so I could set up when we got to our overwatch position. The RG armor shielded my VideoScout antenna from the FMV (Full Motion Video) signal emitted by the drone. He gave me periodic updates over the radio. Still no sight of our soldiers.

Floyd manned the MK19 40mm grenade launcher mounted in our

turret—it was weird not seeing him in the driver's seat—while Pat manned the M2 .50 cal in the RG behind us. I always felt safer knowing Pat was behind a heavy gun. Big bad Billy sat across from me, cradling his M4. Up front, beside Jamie, who was driving, I could see Andy's left shoulder. He gave the word to Jamie, and we moved out again.

Blacked out, our little column drove down the main dirt road of Alkazai village. The place looked like a ghost town. A few minutes later, we broke out into open countryside to the north. The valley floor was flat and covered with empty farming fields. As we drove, Andy studied the satellite imagery of the area he had on a Toughbook laptop. He reached for the radio handset and called over to Zappala. "There's a spot about fifty meters from that bend in the river that looks good for an OP (observation post). Why don't we go firm there?"

"Sounds good."

We made our way to the area Andy selected and eased off the roads. The RG lurched and bucked as we rolled over the rough ground. I tried to see where we were by peering through the window in the rear door, but all I could make out was the green glow of the instrument panels in the cockpit reflecting on the ballistic glass. I looked forward between Jamie and Andy and managed to catch a quick glimpse of the river. Other than that, I had no idea where we were. I hated feeling that disoriented.

The RG jarred to a halt, Jamie popped its air brakes. Andy called out to us, "Okay, this is it. Go ahead and dismount."

Billy opened the rear hatch and stepped into the night. Floyd used the remote gun's thermal imaging sensor to scan for human heat signatures on the far side of the river. I watched his flat panel monitor for a bit, hoping to get the lay of the land over there. Then I, too, dismounted into the cold night.

Once outside, I flipped my night vision goggles down to my eyes and switched them on. The scene around us resolved in shades of green and black—a stand of trees growing on the riverbank, a few compounds on the far side, nothing but open ground around our rigs. At least we'd have good fields of fire if somebody decided to light us up.

We'd positioned the vehicles about thirty meters apart, with each gunner covering a compass point, ensuring we had 360 degree security. I stood on the back steps of the RG, flipped up my night vision, and got to work on my computer and radio that I had pulled down onto the floor of the vehicle. The Predator was still downriver from us, scanning the water with its thermal sight in hopes of locating our fallen. I quickly checked in with the crew operating the drone from back in the States. Our drivers had shut off their engines, and the silence made using the radio much easier. Beyond a few words spoken by the men around me, all I could hear was the soft babble of the river coursing by.

A flash erupted from the far bank. A split second later, an RPG sliced the darkness with its red-orange exhaust. The rocket whooshed overhead and impacted against a hill behind us. Before any of us could react, the trees lining the river flared with muzzle flashes. The men around me dropped flat to the ground and brought their own weapons to bear.

"Contact! Across the river!" I heard someone yell.

The enemy AKs and PKMs cracked and rattled. They were so close it sounded like I was inside a popcorn machine loaded with ball bearings. They'd caught us in a point-blank ambush from concealed positions less than a hundred meters away behind compound walls.

We needed all guns in this fight. I dropped to a shooter's crouch and swung my M4 up underneath the RG's rear door. The treeline sparkled with orange flares from all the muzzle flashes. I began triggering off rounds. Movement to my right caused me to pause; I took my eye out of my weapon's sight long enough to see Mark and an ANA soldier run by toward the river. The Afghan carried an RPG launcher. Mark used his NVGs to orientate him toward the trees. A few steps later, both men stopped. The ANA soldier took a stance and fired. The rocket sparked and spewed flames but did not leave the launcher. In an instant, the whole front of the weapon was sheathed in flames. The ANA dropped the weapon and began to back away. Mark grabbed him, and together they ran back for the Toyota pickup.

I kept firing, waiting to hear our heavy guns engage. Floyd's MK19 was silent. So was Pat's .50 caliber machine gun on the other RG. The Humvee gunners hadn't opened fire either.

Come on guys. Get the heavy weapons going!

"Floyd! What's going on? Get that MK19 up," I heard Andy shout through the cab of the RG.

"Can't. Jammed!" he called back.

What are the odds of having all four heavy guns malfunction at the same time?

Pat suddenly appeared out of the other RG and began climbing up the side of it. The remote-controlled turret with the .50 cal in it had malfunctioned, and he couldn't get it to traverse. Bullets pinged off the rigs as the Taliban shooters walked full-auto fire back and forth across our position, but Pat seemed unfazed. He climbed atop the massive rig, disconnected the .50 cal from the automatic turret, and swung it manually toward the enemy. He stood high above the vehicle's roof, completely exposed to the incoming fusillade. But he never flinched. He lowered the barrel level to the treeline and uncorked a long burst. The Ma Deuce bucked and boomed, its muzzle belching flame.

Mark reappeared, wielding an AT4 rocket launcher that Pat had tossed down to him before he got to the M2. He let it fly toward the trees. The rocket exploded with such force that the ground beneath us shook. A moment later, the enemy responded with another RPG. It landed long, exploding beyond one of our vehicles.

I drained my M4's magazine and reloaded while Mark dashed back toward the ANA pickup truck. After casting the empty AT4 launcher aside, he'd recovered the malfunctioning RPG and managed to somehow clear it. He brought the launcher back to the ANA, who quickly reloaded it and got it into the fight. Meanwhile, the two Humvee gunners struggled to clear the malfunctions on their weapons. Without them, we were going to have a tough time gaining the upper hand. No luck, they remained silent.

It was time for me to be more than just another rifle on the ground. Things were getting desperate, and it was a miracle nobody had been hit yet. I scampered back into the back of the RG and grabbed the radio headset.

"OLDS 4-5, OLDS 4-5, troops in contact, troops in contact," I said as calmly as I could manage. It didn't sound calm to me.

On the other side of the world, the Predator crew operating out of Hancock Field in the suburbs of Syracuse, New York, heard my distress call.

"Stand by to copy grid," I added.

I checked my map and plotted our position. Where was the enemy? I looked across the river on the imagery and made my best guess. I passed the grid over the radio, and the Predator crew moved the drone our way.

A minute later, I linked up with the aircraft's FMV feed and saw through its thermal eye four men between the trees and a compound wall not far from the edge of the river.

Two men scampered along the back side of the nearest compound. I called them out to Andy, who was on the radio directly to the SOTF. I heard him repeat into his handset, "Our JTAC has communication with the drone and is tracking multiple PAX."

PAX is military slang for personnel or people.

I looked back down at the video feed I was receiving from the Predator just in time to see three men bolt from the main building in the compound. They moved swiftly through the gate, swung along the wall, and ran into the treeline, where they joined two other men.

"I've got five in the treeline, Andy."

"Do they have weapons?"

"Can't tell," I replied. Our rules of engagement prohibited us from dropping any ordnance on humans unless we could positively identify that they were a threat and carried weapons.

Right then, Floyd was able to get the MK19 working. He triggered off several grenades, which sailed across the river and exploded long. I turned my laptop toward him so he could see where the enemy was hiding. He fired another burst as I began walking his fire onto the enemy's position, using the Predator's view to do so. They were well protected by something, though, and Floyd couldn't hit them. Perhaps they'd gone to ground in a trench hidden in the treeline, or perhaps there was a natural fold in the terrain. Whatever the case, they were in defilade.

I keyed my radio and called back to the OLDS. "I'm going to pass you a 9-line right now, just to get it out of the way. Our team leader is working to get ordnance-release authority. As soon as we have positive ID on weapons, we're going to kill these fuckers."

It took a few seconds for the transmission to beam to the satellite orbiting overhead, then get bounced down to the crew in Syracuse. A few more seconds passed and I received their 9-line read-back, "Good read-back! Standing by."

A 9-line consists of all the basic information the flight crew needs to know in order to drop a bomb on a target. It includes the location of the target, the location of the nearest friendlies, the direction of flight the JTAC wants the aircraft to be going at the moment of release, and a number of other details.

From the Predator's feed, I saw a man stand up and spray a long burst of full-auto fire at us with an AK. His muzzle flash illuminated the area around him, and I could see he was using a wall for cover.

"Positive ID, Andy! AK! Got him!"

Floyd launched a few 40mm grenades at the guy. They impacted on the wall, spraying the area with chunks of mud and shrapnel. The man recoiled, then crawled into a culvert built into the wall. I could see part of him sticking out as he huddled low against Floyd's fusillade.

"What do you want me to do, Andy?" I asked.

No answer.

"Andy, I can have a Hellfire on these guys in under a minute. Just tell me when."

Still no reply. Dropping ordnance was one of the surest ways to destroy a career. One wrong number in the 9-line, friendlies die. One wrong judgment, civilians die. We would be hitting Taliban near a compound, so we were skirting the edges of General McChrystal's new tactical guidance. If we screwed this up, Andy or I—or both of us—could end up in a court-martial. Welcome to modern warfare.

"Andy?" I said calmly. I needed him to trust me. "I can drop the Hellfire, and we can use it to break contact. I can do it now, and we'll kill these guys. But I need you to say yes. We have positive ID on their weapons. This is legal, we are in the right."

Andy confidently said, "Okay, Ski. Do it."

I called back to New York. "OLDS 45, we have approval, execute 9-line, time now."

"Roger."

I could see five, all clustered together now down by the treeline, most of them using that wall for cover. If we could keep them there, the one Hellfire the Predator carried would take them all out.

The operator called, "OLDS 45, IN from the south."

"OLDS 45 from HALO 14, Cleared Hot."

"One away. Fifty seconds."

The Hellfire was on its way. I hoped to God I'd done everything right. All of the schooling and training had led me to this point. Nothing could stop the missile from impacting now. There was no fail-safe. Only death at the end of its flight.

My eyes flicked from my wristwatch to the video feed. The seconds ticked down. The enemy stayed hunkered down. Outside, our men kept up a steady fire. Mark was beside the ANA rig, triggering off rounds from his M4 carbine side by side with our Afghan allies. Pat stayed atop the other RG, walking the M2's barrel back and forth and scything the trees with short, accurate bursts.

The volume of fire we kept up pinned them in place.

We might just have them.

"Twenty seconds," I said aloud.

Don't move you motherfuckers. Don't move.

I checked my watch again, the same one I used during my first and second combat deployments to Iraq. Fifteen seconds.

Eyes back on the feed now. Suddenly, one of the fighters stood up and began walking away from the group. He reached the nearest compound and ducked inside it.

"Shit! Andy, one of the PAX just bugged out. Still got four."

Suddenly, the video feed went completely white. Outside, an orange glow and sparks tore away the blackness on the far side of the river. A moment later, the shock wave rattled through us.

"Target!" I called back to OLDS.

They zoomed out with their sensor. As the smoke cleared, the thermal sensor picked up a large, circular hotspot in the ground that glowed white in my monitor. That was the impact site. The Hellfire had landed right in the laps of the four remaining guys. Not even a finger or a foot was left.

Outside, the gunfire ceased. The night went silent again. Then a voice somewhere close by called out in awe, "What. The. Fuck. Was. That?"

"Whoa."

A plume of smoke rose over the trees. The lone surviving enemy fighter slipped away, wanting no part of martyrdom that night. As the patrol mounted up, I put the Predator on him and followed his progress as he went from compound to compound farther east of the engagement area. At each stop, he emerged with several more individuals. Keeping them around him, he herded the people to the next compound, where he gathered up several more. By the fourth compound, he had surrounded himself with at least fifteen men, women, and children. I could tell by the height of the individuals in relation to each other and their outlines.

What kind of man turns kids into human shields?

"That is one cowardly son of a bitch," Andy said as I reported what our lone survivor was doing. He vanished with his shields into a mosque in the next village east—alive but surely without his dignity intact.

We moved the patrol back over to the hill where the ABP outpost was. Pat helped to clear the malfunctions on the 82nd's heavy guns while Andy and Zappala discussed our next move. The call was made to fall back to the FOB. Zappala wanted to regroup his men, weapons, and reassess the options on how to hold a blocking position there. PRO 6's plan was not going to cut it in this neck of the woods. Enough was enough. It was 0200, nothing more could be done tonight. We'd continue the search for the fallen 82nd Airborne soldiers at first light. We drove back to FOB Todd, dropping off the ANA pickup at Alkazai School. When we got to our compound, I was at my emotional and physical end. I'd been up for days trying to manage all the air overhead through multiple firefights. Danny took control of the oncoming B-1 bomber that was replacing OLDS.

"Wake me up if you need to drop a bomb," I said.

All I could do was stagger into the tent and collapse on my cot. I didn't even have the energy to take my boots off.

It seemed like I had just closed my eyes when a noise jarred me awake. Daylight streamed into the tent. It disoriented me for a minute. Was it still nighttime? I checked my watch: 1432. I'd been asleep for almost twelve hours without even a twitch. I couldn't believe it.

I sat up. My head ached. My mind still felt fuzzy. As I tried to stand, a sharp pain shot up my legs from my feet. I sat back down on the edge of my cot and took my boots off. I'd not changed my socks in two days since I ran through that canal at the onset of Operation Hero Recovery. Now, as I peeled them off my flesh, I could see the dampness had caused lesions to form on my feet and between my toes.

Trench foot. The bane of every ground pounder.

I swapped out socks and laced my boots back up, thinking about all the things that had happened over the past two days. The memories came in a disconnected jumble. A radio conversation here, a fragment of a firefight there. Mark and George on the rooftop next to the river. That Air Force guy impersonating a JTAC. None of it made any sense.

Then with a jolt, I saw in my mind's eye the video feed go stark white on my computer screen.

Had that happened?

I got up and walked over to the tent that housed our TOC, where I found Andy busily working on a computer at a folding plastic table. He looked up at me and smiled. "Hey! Ski balls! Get some sleep?"

Ski balls. I fucking hated that nickname. Ugh.

"Yeah. Looks like it," I managed.

"How ya feeling?" Andy asked.

"Better. But still groggy, you know? Can I ask you something?"

"Sure."

I approached the table and stopped, leaning against it. "Andy, I have this vague memory of dropping a Hellfire last night. Did I drop a bomb?"

Andy let out a long, low laugh. "Oh fucking-yeah you did."

9

★ AFGHAN COMMANDOS ★

NOVEMBER 6, 2009

Andy looked back down at his computer. He had finally gotten access to his SIPRNet e-mail account, and as he stared at the screen, his smile vanished. I stood and watched the humor of the moment drain away as whatever he was looking at had evoked a baffling expression.

"What's up, Andy?" I asked.

Eyes still on the screen, he said, "SOTF sent up a mixed team of ODA"— Operational Detachment Alpha—"and MSOT, along with the Afghan Commandos. They're about to go hit some compounds east of the Bazaar."

The news surprised me. Why would the SOTF send up an Army Special Forces team to our base, when we're already here? What the hell? Like we weren't capable of doing whatever mission they'd come up to do? It felt like a rebuke, especially after what we'd been through since leaving Herat.

"Yeah, I know," said Andy, reading my face.

"Why didn't they just use us?"

Andy shrugged. "I guess they already had a mission package for the area. We're new, and they've been in country for a couple of months. They flew up last night. We're going to be on standby as QRF for them. Joe is already telling the guys to start getting the rigs ready to roll if needed."

"Wait. They're going out in the middle of the day?" I asked.

Andy nodded.

This was unusual. ODA, like MARSOC and SEAL teams, almost always operated in dark because the night optics we carried gave us such a tremendous advantage. We own the night.

"Do they have a JTAC?"

Andy replied, "Yeah, they do. They've got an ODA one and a backup MARSOC JTAC, too. You'll be number three today."

I'd been in the game since we got here. Now I'd been sidelined. It felt unsettling.

"Where they at? I'll go see if they need anything from me."

Andy pointed to the wall behind him and said, "They've got two tents set up against the Hesco wall."

"Okay. I'll go introduce myself."

I turned to leave. As I did, Andy added, "We're going to brief the mission here in about an hour, Ski."

"Roger that."

I stepped out into the sunlight. Somewhere above us, I could hear the distant rumble of jet engines—reminders that since the two 82nd Airborne soldiers went missing, BMG was the highest priority for Coalition forces in Afghanistan. This happened whenever there was a Duty Status Whereabouts Unknown (DUSTWUN) situation in country. We will do whatever it takes to find our fallen. Everyone makes it home, everyone.

Fighters, bombers, rotary-wing, and drones had been tasked to our valley in such numbers that the sky above us was already stacked with assets. At the same time, reinforcements flooded into FOB Todd. A few days before when we had arrived, there were perhaps about 250 Coalition troops at our base. I awoke on November 6 to find helo lifts had brought in almost six hundred 82nd Airborne troops, along with the ODA, another MARSOC element, and the Afghan Commandos.

I walked over to the two large olive drab tents the Commandos had set up in the corner of our compound. In the first tent, I found the Commandos lounging around, their gear scattered around them as they waited for word to roll. One glance and I could see these guys were no regular Afghan army. They'd been equipped with body armor, helmets, and American-made weapons, including M4 carbines and M240 machine guns. The squad leaders carried night vision goggles. A few smiled or nodded as I entered, but most looked impassive. They sat or lay near their packs, a few quiet conversations going on here and there among small knots of the men. They carried themselves differently from the ANA we had seen so far. Maybe part of it was the fact that they all wore old-school camouflage uniforms (BDUs) when most Afghan platoons looked like military refugees clothed in anything they could find. *Well, they looked squared away. Hope they can fight. The ODA is going to need all the ass they can get.*

In the second tent, I found the MARSOC JTAC who was acting as the secondary controller for this operation. He was short and sinewy and scowled at me like I was beneath him after I introduced myself.

"Browski," he said, briefly shaking the hand I'd offered him.

"Do you need anything?" I asked.

"No."

I pointed to his makeshift workspace inside the tent and said, "You gonna set a Rover or something up in here," unaware that he was going out with the team.

"No, I don't need that."

"No?" I asked, surprised. Why would you not want access to the aircraft's video feed, I thought to myself. It would give him eyes on the target area in case he needed to take control or help out the lead JTAC.

"Didn't bring one," he grunted.

I brightened, figuring I could help out here after all. "Oh, well I've got an extra one you can borrow. I also have an MVR III that I'm not using. I can go pull it out of the Conex box."

The MVR III was a small handheld device used to view the video from the aircraft's sensor. It was called a "Mover" for short.

"No. I don't need that."

I stepped back from him, thoroughly put off by his attitude. It went beyond a veteran's dismissal of a new guy. He was just pompous and full of himself.

"All right," I said as I started to leave. "I'll be at our TOC if you need anything."

He ignored me. I left feeling like a fool. Maybe I was new around here and things were done differently in country than back in the States. But who wouldn't want to see what's going on if a firefight should break out? Having a way to view FMV had already proven to be a godsend to me on more than one occasion so far. But then again, maybe I was just a rookie.

I headed back to the TOC to link up with the rest of the team before the mission brief. As I did, my mind kept going back to the fact that he didn't have a way to see the video feed. If Browski didn't have any device, chances were that the ODA JTAC didn't have one either.

Maybe it's just me. I like the feed. Maybe I'm too dependent on it, and these guys are as badass as they act.

At the TOC, Andy gathered the team together. I stood with Pat, Rob, Mark, and George as he laid out the plan. The ODA, MARSOC element, and the Afghan Commandos are going to depart on foot from the FOB in about an hour. They'll make their way through the Bazaar and use the ANP checkpoint on the east side as their jump-off point for a sweep through the compounds that abutted a stretch of the road dubbed the Bowling Alley. The Bowling Alley was flanked by two long, twelve-foot-high walls for several hundred meters, creating a channel that made the road particularly dangerous. Anyone on it who took fire from the east end would be trapped in the open, unable to move out of the line of fire thanks to the walls on either side. It was a deadly obstacle, a rattrap.

Andy handed us the ODA's Grid Reference Graphic. Known as a GRG, it's an essential piece to any sort of combat mission where multiple units are involved. Usually, it is a single sheet of paper with an overhead image of the target area. It is usually just a piece of satellite imagery, like Google Earth, an image that shows terrain, which is far better than a traditional map in this type of situation because it shows the area as it is in real life. The only drawback is you can't plot a grid on it.

On each GRG, the mission planners number every single structure in the target area. That way, in the heat of battle you can quickly relay your position to aircrew overhead, or to other forces operating around you. If they are taking fire, they can simply reference the building or terrain feature's number and have an aircraft drop a bomb on it. Calling out, "Building 3-5" in the middle of a firefight is significantly easier and more direct than a nine-digit grid. Thus, GRGs are among the most important pieces of pre-mission prep work. They make sure everyone is operating on the same sheet of music.

I looked down at the GRG that was given to our team, and my heart sank. Only a handful of the buildings east of the Bazaar had been numbered. They were the ones the ODA were interested in, but none of the surrounding ones were even marked.

"What the fuck is this?" I heard somebody say.

"This is a goddamned joke."

"Looks like a goddamned kid put this together," I muttered.

Somebody asked, "Andy, which compounds are they going to clear?"

Andy looked frustrated. "They're going to hit Building 20, the compound closest to the ANP checkpoint on the north side of the road. From there, I really don't know what they plan to do."

"Andy," I said, "there are only a few buildings labeled on this GRG."

"I know, Ski."

"I am pretty sure that neither of the JTACs has any way to view video feed," I said.

Andy shook his head slightly.

"What's in Building 20?" Rob asked.

"I don't know," Andy said.

We all looked around at each other. This valley already showed us that anything could happen. The Taliban were spoiling for a fight. That much we knew.

"What about our piece of the pie?" I heard Pat ask Andy.

"We're going to be the QRF and ground medevac. If anyone gets injured, they'll call us and we'll transport them out of the engagement area."

Andy turned to Joe, who was standing on the other side of a folding table being used as a desk, looking thoroughly pissed off. "Joe will be going over the trucks one more time. Make sure we've got everything we need."

"We're going to stage at the ANP Castle when they call for us."

I looked at the GRG. The Castle was just on the west end of the Bazaar and had been built on a flatiron-shaped hill. From the Castle to the Bowling Alley's entrance was only about a hundred meters, so we'd be very close to the action instead of being at the FOB on the other side of the river.

Andy went on to explain the rest of the day's operations. Fortunately, the 82nd had kept us updated on everything, so at least we had the big picture. The search had continued all along the river. U.S. Navy and British dive teams had arrived in BMG. The Air Force Pararescue team that was first on the scene was still working as well. A sonar-equipped aircraft had been dispatched to help map the river bottom and see if it could detect our fallen brothers, but it had not yet arrived.

In the meantime, the additional men who had arrived had established overwatch positions at key points along the river. From these, the search teams in the river could be protected from any Taliban attack.

To keep the enemy from pulling off a repeat of day one at the initial site, several platoons from the 508th Parachute Infantry had been tasked to assault across the river into the compounds the Taliban had been using as firing positions. Once they captured the area, they were to establish a combat outpost there by strongpointing one of the compounds. The 82nd planned to use a pincers attack to pull this off. One platoon would cross the river at the search site and attack northeast. The other element would drive gun trucks through the Bazaar, and then follow Ring Road north right into the objective area. That platoon would protect the east flank and create a buffer area for the PR site, while the ODA and Commandos put pressure on the east side of the Bazaar.

The ODA/Commando operation was supposed to help keep the heat off the 82nd as they established the new COP, but so far it looked like they were going to do their own thing with little coordination between them and anyone else. Throughout the war, there had been times where SOF units arrived in a local area, conducted a mission, and left without much interaction with the conventional forces assigned to the area. Without working with the boots already on the ground, their mission could have unintended consequences. It is a delicate balance.

The ODA team that came to FOB Todd virtually ignored everyone else. As a result, PRO 6, the 82nd Airborne, and our own team had little idea what they would be doing, only that they would be operating around the Bowling Alley area.

Andy gave us what little information he had, then we filed out of the TOC and walked to our waiting rigs. We'd go out with two GMVs and two MRAPs if the ODA called up QRF. They were warmed up and ready to go, gear stowed aboard for every contingency we could conceive.

It was a lonely moment for me. The situation made everyone quiet and frustrated. The team kept it professional, sharing words only when necessary while I stood off to one side stealing glances and making sure I had all my gear. I think all of us had that bad vibe we'd felt just before we'd been ambushed on our way up to BMG. None of this felt right, and it made us edgy.

I had just slung my last piece of gear into the MRAP when the ODA, their MARSOC element, and the Afghan Commandos formed up and streamed for the east gate. Roughly fifty strong, they left the safety of FOB Todd as we watched their departure in silence. When the last man exited the compound, the tension within the team rose palpably.

The force crossed the old bridge and patrolled into the Bazaar. This was friendly territory with little chance of any contact, but we stood by our vehicles and hung on every radio transmission to the SOTF. No hiding it now, the Taliban knew that the Commandos were on the move.

"Why didn't they go in at night?" Rob asked.

"I have no fucking idea," I replied.

Rob shook his head and leaned against the side of the MRAP. "The Taliban here are not just going to cut and run, they are going to hold their ground."

We'd seen enough to get an idea of that over the past few days.

I have to believe they know what they're doing. They've been in country for months.

The ODA team leader radioed that they'd reached the ANP checkpoint. Next stop: cutting through the Bowling Alley to Building 20.

I checked my watch. They'd been out for less than twenty minutes. They'd be in position to hit the compound about now.

A Russian-made PKM machine gun cut the silence with a ripping burst. It echoed across the valley like a series of thunderclaps. A second later, the all too familiar sounds of AK-47s joined in. An M249 SAW light machine gun barked back, so did a few metallic-sounding cracks of M4s and M16s. The ODA leader came over the SATCOM radio. He reported heavy contact as soon as they stepped out into the Bowling Alley. Not that we didn't know. In seconds, the firefight grew from that first PKM to an intense cacophony of overlapping machine gun bursts, steady hammer blows of assault rifles, and the staccato *tick-tick-tick* of American-made M249s.

Joe listened to the battle develop and growled, "Jesus fucking Christ! This is all rushed! Twenty minutes. They've been out twenty fucking minutes and they're already in a fight? You gotta be shitting me."

The SATCOM squawked in our MRAP. Andy could hear the ODA asking the SOTF to stand up the QRF. The Commandos were in a hell of a fight. It was time to stage at the Castle and be ready to assist.

Andy passed the word to Joe, who shouted at the others, "Mount up, we're going."

The sound of all that gunfire? Yeah. That's where we're going.

Time to go play. I climbed into the back of the MRAP and swung into my seat. I put my headset back on and continued to monitor the air net. DOOM, the ODA JTAC, was talking to a pair of A-10s orbiting overhead like metal vultures.

The drivers shifted into gear. Engines revved and our four gun trucks rolled out of FOB toward the new bridge. I sat in back as our rig swayed and pitched over the lumpy dirt road, focused on the radio traffic. With a start, I realized DOOM was passing a 9-line to the aircraft. At first, I thought I'd misunderstood what was going down; I got clued in quickly. My stomach clenched.

What the fuck? Joe's right. This is happening way too fast.

"Andy," I said with more calm than I felt. "They're getting ready to drop a bomb."

"On what?" he asked.

I was trying to piece together the situation by listening to the radio traffic. "I think on Building 20."

They were about to put a JDAM on their initial objective.

I closed my eyes, tilted my head, and placed both hands over my headset, focusing on the chatter. The enemy had ambushed the ODA and Commandos less than four hundred meters from the FOB.

Heading blindly into another firefight. This shit is getting old real fast.

Ski's JTAC workspace in the trunk of the team leader's GMV during the convoy from Herat to FOB Todd in Bala Murghab. *(Courtesy of Michael Golembesky, BMG Archive photo)*

MSOT 8222 members conducting training and test firing of the vehicle-mounted M134 minigun, with the capability of firing 2,000 to 6,000 rounds of 7.62mm per minute. *(Courtesy of Michael Golembesky, BMG Archive photo)*

Aerial view of MSOT 8222's compound on the north end of FOB Todd, it was commonly referred to as the "SOF compound." *(Courtesy of Robert Chicvara, BMG Archive photo)*

Photo was taken moments before Sherman and Islip slipped into the Murghab River trying to secure airdrop pallets that had gone off course from the drop zone. *(Courtesy of Chris Hesse, BMG Archive photo)*

Team members from Dagger 22 bobbing in the frigid Murghab River looking for any sign of the two paratroopers while a firefight raged overhead. *(Courtesy of Chris Hesse, BMG Archive photo)*

An 82nd Airborne soldier holds his head in his hands along the far side of the Murghab River, grieving and in shock over the loss of his two brothers. *(Courtesy of Chris Hesse, BMG Archive photo)*

The Entourage standing in front of a memorial to honor Sherman and Islip, (left to right) BMG District Governor Shawa Ali, ANP Chief Leval, village elder Haji Wakil, PRO 6's interpreter, Badghis Province ABP chief, village elder, and ANA Colonel Ali. (*Courtesy of Chris Hesse, BMG Archive photo*)

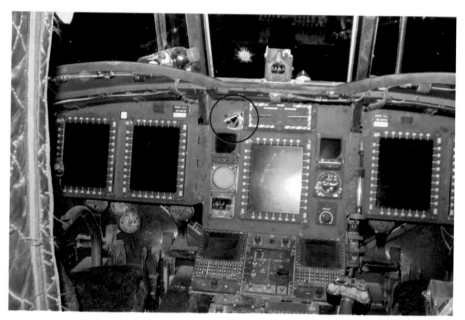

A view inside of the medevac CH-47 after landing at the north end of FOB Todd, showing the puncture hole left by the failing RPG. (*Courtesy of Licon Isven, BMG Archive photo*)

Medical staff members treating the incoming wounded during a mass-casualty situation following the A-10 blue-on-blue incident. *(Courtesy of Chris Hesse, BMG Archive photo)*

James, Pat, Paddy, and Rob stand kitted-up and ready for the team's first combat-reconnaissance patrol into the village of Daneh Pasab. *(Courtesy of Michael Golembesky, BMG Archive photo)*

Rob *(right)* and Easy, our team interpreter, talk with an elderly man before the team patrols into the village of Daneh Pasab for the first time. *(Courtesy of Michael Golembesky, BMG Archive photo)*

Dagger 22 shooting and moving under enemy fire while egressing out of the village of Daneh Pasab after a Taliban ambush. *(Courtesy of Michael Golembesky, BMG Archive photo)*

George, providing covering fire during the teams egress out of the village of Daneh Pasab after being ambushed by an entrenched Taliban force. *(Courtesy of Michael Golembesky, BMG Archive photo)*

Pat and Ski having a smoke and sharing a candid moment outside of the living tents in the SOF compound portion of FOB Todd. *(Courtesy of Michael Golembesky, BMG Archive photo)*

Andy and Ski *(far left)* during a battle-update brief given inside of the 82nd Airborne COC at FOB Todd, PRO 6 *(far right)* looks on as the Afghan soldier speaks through an interpreter. *(Courtesy of Chris Hesse, BMG Archive photo)*

Members of Dagger 22, 82nd Airborne, and Afghan National Army conducting walk-through rehearsals of their assault on Objective Pathfinder during Operation Buongior-no. *(Courtesy of Michael Golembesky, BMG Archive photo)*

Mark on his M107 SASR "Elvis" engaging targets just after dawn of Day 1 on Objective Pathfinder. *(Courtesy of Michael Golembesky, BMG Archive photo)*

The Entourage study a satellite imagery map at the ANP Castle during Operation Buongiorno, (clockwise) ANA Colonel Ali, ANP Chief Leval, PRO 6, Colonel Bruno, NDS chief, and BMG Sub-Governor Shawa Ali on his cell phone. *(Courtesy of Chris Hesse, BMG Archive photo)*

The view of Pathfinder Hill as seen from Objective Prius during the complex assault on Day 2 of Operation Buongiorno. *(Courtesy of Michael Golembesky, BMG Archive photo)*

Team Prius holding the line, American and Italian forces working together, fighting from makeshift positions atop buildings within the compound. *(Courtesy of Michael Golembesky, BMG Archive photo)*

Mark holds up "Elvis," his .50 caliber sniper rifle after the conclusion of the complex assault launched on Team Pathfinder on Day 2 of Operation Buongiorno. A single bullet can be seen, lodged in the center of the magazine well of the weapon. *(Courtesy of Michael Golembesky, BMG Archive photo)*

SPC Cory Ballinger looks on from atop Pathfinder Hill at the aftermath of a 2,000-pound JDAM dropped on an enemy position at the end of Day 2 of Operation Buongiorno. *(Courtesy of Michael Golembesky, BMG Archive photo)*

The view from Pathfinder Hill, looking south to the village of Kapeh Baba and beyond. *(Courtesy of Michael Golembesky, BMG Archive photo)*

The aftermath of a 2,000–pound JDAM that was detonated in the village of Kapeh Baba in response to the Taliban's last-ditch effort to escape from the battlefield on Day 2 of Operation Buongiorno. *(Courtesy of Michael Golembesky, BMG Archive photo)*

Day 3 of Operation Buongiorno, paratroopers from Objective Prius stepping out on foot-patrol to conduct a battle damage assessment of the area and to search out any remaining Taliban fighters. *(Courtesy of Michael Golembesky, BMG Archive photo)*

Bear, a Central-Asian Sheppard puppy is safe and sound on Pathfinder Hill after being rescued during a village sweep for surviving Taliban fighters. *(Courtesy of Michael Golembesky, BMG Archive photo)*

The Entourage poses for a picture after touring Objective Pathfinder. (From left to right) Major Grissom (OPSO), NDS chief, PRO 6's interpreter, ANP Chief Leval, ANA Colonel Ali, BMG District Governor Shawa Ali (kneeling), Andy, Colonel Bruno, and PRO 6. *(Courtesy of Michael Golembesky, BMG Archive photo)*

Dagger 22 stop to pose for a *Red Dawn*-style photo after finishing a foot patrol through the BMG Bazaar. The abandoned Russian T-62 tank outside of the FOB's parameter wall served as a reminder to the history of the Bala Murghab Valley. *(Courtesy of Michael Golembesky, BMG Archive photo)*

A small building made of plywood atop Pathfinder Hill displays the names of the men who fought for five days to capture and hold this key piece of terrain in order to limit the Taliban's freedom of movement throughout the valley. (*Courtesy of Michael Golembesky, BMG Archive photo*)

A sign bearing the name of SFC David J. Todd hanging above the entryway of the old Russian textiles factory, providing overwatch to all who passed under it as they stepped out on missions in the valley. *(Courtesy of Michael Golembesky, BMG Archive photo)*

10

★ FURTHER DOWN THE RABBIT HOLE ★

NOVEMBER 6, 2009
IN THE BOWLING ALLEY

The GBU-38 five-hundred-pound JDAM fell out of the sky at over six hundred miles an hour. Plunging toward Building 20 at a near vertical angle of attack, its fins made tiny course adjustments based on data fed to its computer brain from Air Force global positioning satellites orbiting some twenty thousand kilometers overhead.

The ODA assault was pinned down at the ANP checkpoint by incoming fire from the other end of the Bowling Alley. Dropping Building 20 would give them a foothold into the kill zone and signal to the Taliban that they were not fucking around this time. No more shows of force.

Game on, assholes.

The bomb passed two thousand feet, closing in on the target at the edge of the sound barrier now. As it fell, a roaring *phoooooossshhhh* echoed through the valley. To the uninitiated, it sounded like a jet making a low-altitude pass. But to those of us who had heard it before, we knew it was the sound of impending DOOM for those unlucky enough to be standing near the Desired Mean Point of Impact (DMPI)—"Dimpy."

The JDAM penetrated the building's roof and detonated five milliseconds later inside the structure. The blast sent tentacles of smoke and flames shooting skyward as debris rained down for hundreds of meters. The shock wave pushed through the area, rattling everyone's bones but doing no damage to any other building. The GBU-38's precision, combined with the slight delay set on the fuse, ensured the damage remained localized within Building 20's thick compound walls.

The enemy fire ceased. The assault force swept into the compound, clearing what little remained. The bomb had paved their way. Once they secured a foothold in that first compound, the assault force split into two elements and kept going. They flowed back out into the Bowling Alley and struck the next two qalats at the far end simultaneously. A storm of gunfire greeted them. The fight was on again.

As they battled the enemy, Dagger 22 rolled into the ANP headquarters at the Castle. I have no idea when the fortress was built, but it looked like something straight out of Middle Earth with its rounded towers and massive walls. The towers were studded with old firing ports, probably for archers and crossbowmen back in the day. The walls had walkways that the Castle's defenders could access via ladders. From there, the occupants could fight any attacking force while exposing only a small portion of themselves above the wall's parapet.

It was built entirely from dried mud blocks, centuries old. Say what you will about the Afghan people, they knew how to build something from virtually nothing.

We dismounted and waited. Farther to the north, a huge firefight erupted as the 82nd Airborne assault went in against Ludina, the village at the edge of the recovery site. Back at the FOB, Danny coordinated fire missions with the 81mm mortars on base. When that proved insufficient, he started calling in air strikes with the help of Ben, the ROMAD with the 82nd, who acted as Danny's eyes on the ground. In the distance, we could hear the bombs detonating.

Eight years into the war and we are in a full-on fight. Fuck.

"Hey Ski, let's get some eyes up on the wall," Mark said to me. I grabbed my radio and followed him. Pat, Paddy, and George came with us. We climbed the ladders onto the parapet's walkway. We peered over the chest-high wall, perhaps four or five feet thick. Even though its ancient blocks were crumbling in places, this historic place would have been hell to assault. I was glad the ANP owned this place, dubious as their loyalty was in most cases. Clearly, tackling the private compounds was difficult enough. If we had to hit something like this, we'd need heavy artillery or two-thousand-pound bombs to breach the walls and kill the defenders. It would have been easier to just wait and starve them out, modern-day siege-style. Technology may have evolved, but the basic elements of warfare remained timeless.

Feeling secure atop the thirty-foot wall, we looked west over green treetops that had defied the autumn's cold. Beyond the trees stretched the Bowling Alley's walls, and while we couldn't see anyone, we could track the progress of the firefight by the smoke coiling up over the compound walls in that direction.

Mark rested the bipod of his MK11 rifle on the wall and stuck his eye into the scope in hopes of finding the Taliban currently shooting at our brothers. I had my radio with me, tuned to the air net to keep tabs on their progress. For the moment, all was silent there on the net. DOOM wasn't talking; neither was the MARSOC JTAC, Browski.

The Taliban fought hard, but the pressure proved too much. They fell back into a mazelike series of compounds just south of the Bowling Alley in the village of Khasadar. Now, the assault force was adapting on the move to the situation. They pursued their retreating enemy, kicking in doors and clearing compounds one after the other, deeper into the maze. I rolled my radio to the assault force's net. The transmissions were fast and sporadic. We couldn't keep track of where each element was. The fight was evolving too fast.

I looked back at the rest of our team. Andy had the guys by the vehicles in the Castle bailey. A fat, sloppy-looking Afghan National Police officer stood a short distance away, holding a radio while a few of his men sat at a table beside him. The ANP were dressed in blue-gray uniforms and bad shoes. One had an ancient pair of combat boots, as did the ANP chief, Lewal. The others had a mix of loafers and tennis shoes. Their weapons looked just as shabby and old as their footwear.

The SATCOM radio in Andy's GMV came to life. The ODA team leader reported they'd just taken a casualty. Their interpreter had been shot in the face. The bullet had torn most of his lower jaw away.

"We are requesting ground medevac for the wounded," said the voice on the radio. That was the call for us to roll.

Andy looked up and yelled to the team to load up. But now we had a problem. A wounded man would take up a lot of space inside an MRAP. We had to make room to get him back to the FOB, so some of us would have to stay behind. Andy glanced around and told Mark and Paddy to stay behind with the long guns. Mark ran for the GMV and grabbed the gun box housing his M107 .50 caliber sniper rifle, which we called the SASR. Mark called it "Elvis," which puzzled us, though nobody had had the temerity to ask him why.

"Where do you want me, Andy?" I asked.

"Stay here with them. Make sure you're talking to me over the radio," he said as he climbed into the front passenger seat of the MRAP.

Fuck. Being left behind sucked. I watched as George dashed down the ladder and dove into one of the rigs. The doors closed a moment later, and our four vehicles sped out of the bailey, through the gate, and down the steep slope, bound for the Bazaar and the Bowling Alley.

The ODA had pushed into a compound perhaps 150 meters south of the Bowling Alley. One element maneuvered and assaulted forward while the other supported from the compound just captured. They'd been leap-frogging south like that, clearing each qalat and searching the Taliban dead while the enemy harassed them with sporadic fire. Now, with the terp wounded, the element supporting the maneuver force hunkered down as their medic went to work.

As they did, the other element—about ten ODA and thirty Commandos strong—assaulted toward the next qalat in line. They ran headlong into a Taliban ambush. Rocket-propelled grenades and machine gun fire swept the area. The supporting element got onto the rooftop and walls of the compound they'd just taken, and a furious point-blank gun battle erupted.

The team SARC (medic), Eddie, had been directing the placement and fire of about fifteen Commandos when a single, deep report echoed over the valley above the din of PKM and AK-47 fire. From the rooftop, he heard a team guy call out for help.

"I'm hit," he yelled to Eddie. "Single shot. I think it was a sniper."

Eddie got on the roof anyway, where he found himself fully exposed, with no available cover. One look, and he realized the situation was bad. Two of the Commandos lay sprawled, face-down, each man struck by a single well-placed round. Eugene, an ODA team member, was lying on his back, unable to move. The sniper's round had caught him in the upper thigh, breaking his femur before embedding in his pelvis.

"Eddie, there's a sniper!" he called out again.

Hefting an M249 PARA-SAW, Eddie sprinted to Eugene. Movement

Back at the Castle, Mark, Paddy, and I tried to get a handle on what was going on at the Bowling Alley. Mark and Paddy scanned the landscape through their scopes, looking for targets. We could hear the fighting, see clouds of black and gray smoke rising above the treetops and walls, but the situation remained unclear. We couldn't see any Taliban, and the assault force had all taken cover. If we'd been able to get a little higher, perhaps we could have had a better view of the battlefield, but the parapet walk was the highest point on the east side of the Castle. We were frustrated—stuck and useless.

A whining engine sound rose in the distance behind us. I glanced over my shoulder to see an overcast sky of dreary gray. Here and there, soft blue highlights exposed holes in the layers of clouds. A single dark silhouette dove out of the overcast. Another followed a few seconds later. Though they were just specks, I knew instantly what they were.

A-10 Warthogs. Their engines spooled up to a metallic scream as they swept toward the battlefield at more than four hundred miles an hour. This was no show of force, and nobody dropped a bomb like this. The dive angle, the severity of the situation, and the intensity of their approach made it clear:

Gun run.

The A-10's six-barreled 30mm Avenger Gatling gun is like no other weapon ever built. As long as a Cadillac, its ammunition loadout includes over thirteen hundred shells that can be fired in less than seventeen seconds. Those seventeen seconds cost the American taxpayer about $94,000.

But the damage inflicted is beyond all cost. The A-10 carries a mix of depleted uranium armor-piercing shells, each one of which strikes its target with two hundred tons of force. It is such a devastating blow that one of these AP rounds can cave in the side of even the heaviest armored vehicle. But they never fire one shell. Behind that first one comes over seventy more each second the pilot holds his trigger down. The AP rounds are mixed with high-explosive ones that throw thousands of slivers of shrapnel around a target area upon impact.

The lead A-10 had a deadly beautiful grace as it flattened out its dive and the pilot made the final corrections to get on target. Before I could utter a word, the pilot squeezed the trigger on his control column. Black smoke belched from the nose and streaked back along the fuselage. A tongue of flame, like dragon's breath, frothed out from the Avenger's barrels.

BRRRRRRRRRRRRRRRRRR, the sound of the Gatling gun sent a warm wave of fear through my body.

In two seconds, over 120 shells smothered the target area. Those two seconds felt like an eternity. Explosions engulfed a compound south of the Bowling Alley. Showers of red-orange sparks erupted from the impacts. The detonations piled one atop another in a deafening sound like strings of gigantic, crackling fireworks.

"Holy fucking shit," I heard Mark say in awe of this display of unrivaled firepower.

The lead A-10 pulled off target. Nearly every shell fired struck within the walls of the target compound.

A small plume of green smoke rose from the impact area. I saw it immediately, and my stomach lurched.

"Oh no," I whispered, full of dread.

Over the radio, somebody screamed, "ABORT! ABORT! ABORT!"

The second A-10 was already ramping down to engage. The pilot saw the smoke and heard the desperate calls and suddenly lifted his aircraft's nose. The twin-ruddered attack aircraft swept upward, clawing for altitude, its weapon unfired. An eerie silence engulfed the battlefield. The Taliban's weapons ceased firing. The American M4s no longer barked their metallic reports. Smoke drifted above the stricken compound, the black and gray mingling with the single plume of green. I stared out at it. We all knew what that color meant.

Green smoke was for friendlies.

We had just chewed up our own guys.

II

★ MASS CASUALTY ★

EN ROUTE

Dagger 22 barreled down the Bowling Alley in a column of armor and heavy guns, setting up a fortified blocking position outside the last breaching entrance. The team dismounted and flooded into the maze, leaving only the drivers and gunners behind.

George stacked up behind Rob as bullets cracked and whined overhead. They hugged the compound wall, unsure if this was the one held by the assault force or not. Heath, our other SARC medic, was close behind George. Jack, Andy, and Joe fell in behind, everyone waiting to go through the rusty metal door set in the compound's wall. Since dismounting, they'd been running through the alleys between identical-looking compounds. The place was a rabbit warren, and the Taliban seemed to be everywhere at once.

A slight push from the back of the stack telegraphed its way forward to Rob. When he felt the nudge, Rob rushed forward and kicked open the door. George stayed hard on his heels, stepping through the entryway into the compound's courtyard. The sight inside stopped him cold.

A Commando limped by, his face torn and bloody. George saw that his lower jaw was gone. Another Commando lay nearby, one hand missing, his eyes wide with horror. Blood splatters dried on the compound walls. Men screamed. Two Commandos knelt by a motionless comrade. Both were sobbing. Others sat slumped against the building in the center of the compound, eyes wide and vacant.

George saw a team guy, part of the MARSOC element with the ODA that day. "Hey? HEY!" George called to him. "Is whatever the fuck did this, still here?"

Being inside the metal hull of the MRAP, George had no idea the A-10 had caused the carnage, and he couldn't think of anything that could have done it short of a Taliban suicide bomber. His eyes swept the courtyard. Dozens of men lay bleeding in the dirt. A few walking wounded moved here and there, some in a daze, some trying to help where they could.

"Hey!" George said again, "is whatever caused this still here?"

The operator just looked at him for a moment, expression blank, then turned away.

The magnitude of the moment played out slowly in George's mind. The level of human misery and pain everywhere he looked seemed almost too much to comprehend. Virtually the whole element was wounded. And by the looks of it, there were several dead as well.

Andy pushed through the doorway and sucked in a deep breath as the scene assailed him as well. For a second, he said nothing as his eyes wandered from one side of the courtyard to the other. Yet he never lost his composure. At length, he leaned over to George and said, "Okay, look. We gotta get a handle on what we've got here medically."

"On it."

George moved for the building in the center of the compound, intent on clearing it to make sure whoever caused this was not still lurking inside. Heath followed him as Joe, Jack, and the others began to triage the wounded. There were Afghan National Police among the wounded—a bad thing for community relations in the valley. The ANP were recruited straight from the local population. When they died, especially at the hands of Americans in accidents on the battlefield, their communities usually reacted harshly. At times elsewhere in Afghanistan, such moments destroyed trust and turned villages against the Coalition.

George saw the ANP wounded and wished they hadn't been in here. This place already had enough hate and discontent to go around.

As Joe, Andy, and Jack went to work on the wounded, they discovered several of the MARSOC operators with the ODA had been hit, including their team chief. Shrapnel from one of the 30mm shells had struck him in the leg. His pants were shredded, and he was staggering around using a shovel as a crutch. He was a huge, towering man with a massive upper body and legs like steel girders. George saw him just before he reached the doorway to the building.

Turning to Heath he said, "Holy shit, I think I'm looking at Odin himself."

Heath glanced over his shoulder, then plunged into the building. George followed.

"Eddie!" he yelled as he saw the wounded MARSOC medic lying on a pile of hay in the building's first room. Eugene lay beside him, and Eddie was trying to talk a team guy through stabilizing Eugene's thigh and pelvis wound.

Eddie looked up and recognized George. "Hey man," he said weakly. "I haven't seen you in forever."

George and Eddie had served in a Recon battalion together before they both joined MARSOC.

"I know, it's been like five years," George said, kneeling beside his friend.

"This is fucking crazy. Running into you here."

"I know man. Listen, hold tight. We'll be right back," George said. He and Heath quickly cleared the rest of the dwelling. By the time they returned to Eddie and Eugene, the Taliban had started firing at the compound again. Outside, the ODA and Marines who could still fight were trying to suppress the enemy. A few Commandos had joined them, but most remained in the courtyard with no fight left in them.

George and Heath went to work. Eddie's wounds were serious—all three of them. He needed immediate evacuation. So did Eugene, who was drifting in and out of consciousness and going into shock. But how were they going to get them—and all the others—out of there? They didn't have room in the vehicles for all the wounded. There had to be two dozen or more guys down. And those who were left standing would have to carry them 150 yards back to the edge of the Bowling Alley under fire the whole time. There weren't enough able bodies to carry the wounded and provide security.

It was a nightmare come true.

DOOM, the ODA JTAC, recognized the problem and realized there was only one option. He got on the radio and requested an immediate medevac by one of the massive CH-47 Chinook helicopters standing by at FOB Todd.

Chinooks are a Cold War–era design. Most of the airframes are older than their pilots and have survived repeated rebuilds and upgrades over the decades. They're fussy and complicated aircraft with so many systems that things on them break all the time. Yet the pilots have a reputation for being easygoing, laid-back in a crisis, and highly skilled. They are also some of the most unheralded and courageous aviators in the American military.

A Chinook was the only way out for the wounded. The big cargo bay could hold over forty men or 26,000 pounds of supplies. Even on stretchers, they could get everyone aboard.

The launch approval came back over the radio to DOOM. The bird would land in a field beside the compound and the wounded would be carried aboard. Everyone else would extract on foot under the cover of Dagger 22's vehicles.

The Chinook lifted off the FOB's landing pad and sped east across the river, taking less than a minute to reach the HLZ, the hasty landing zone. Meanwhile, one of the ODA engineers went over to the double metal doors in the compound's outer wall and tried to get them open. They were stuck, or jammed, or locked—or something. He pulled and tugged furiously at it as the firefight raged around him. No luck. The door opened right onto the field the Chinook would use for a HLZ, and they were running out of time before the aircraft set down.

The wounded were placed on stretchers, and the able-bodied men waited for the bird to touch down. George, Joe, Jack, and Heath carried Eugene out into the courtyard. They went back and got Eddie a moment later, returning in time to see the engineer slap a charge on the door.

They put Eddie down with the other wounded, then hunkered down to await the blast. The engineer detonated the charge, and the door blew outward just as automatic weapons fire raked the top of the compound's wall.

A moment later, the sound of the Chinook's twin rotors drowned out the sound of the gunfire. Few things are louder than a CH-47 on a battlefield. When they touch down, their six blades generate hurricane-force winds so severe they've been known to blow goats and other livestock clear off landing zones. Urban legend among Chinook pilots has it that one unfortunate goat was blown clear off a cliff during the fighting in the Hindu Kush back in 2005.

The owner was duly compensated by the American taxpayer, of course. That's the nature of our war.

"You guys ready?" Andy asked. The door was open, and the men could see the field stretching beyond. It was flanked by compounds perhaps two hundred yards away. They had four dead Commandos, two wounded ANP, and five Marines down. One of the element's terps was dead, too. Another fifteen commandos and five ANA soldiers had also been hit. Several of them were urgent surgical cases. The aid station at FOB Todd was going to be overwhelmed.

But just getting them to the bird would be a challenge. The casualties outnumbered the non-wounded.

The Chinook hopscotched over the Castle, where I was providing rear security for Mark and Paddy while they scanned with their long guns. We had no idea whose side the ANP were really on, and we weren't about to trust them. So I sat facing the rear, between the two snipers, back against the parapet, and watching Chief Lewal, the fat ANP commander, and his minions while they ran back and forth. They looked busy, but so far I had yet to see them actually doing anything.

I looked up as the Chinook went by, its rotor wash rocking trees and kicking up swirls of dust. It made a short half-circuit over the HLZ, looking for obstructions, and dropped to the ground.

As it did, the team guys and remaining Commandos willing to fight poured through the doorway and out into the open. The Chinook sat in the field some fifty yards away with nothing but open space between the bird and the door.

George, Joe, Jack, and Heath grabbed Eugene's stretcher and made a break for it. They got him through the doorway, but as they ran into the field, they discovered it had been plowed. Not recently, but the ground was so uneven the men kept tripping. Down went Joe. The stretcher dipped. He regained his feet and they kept going, each man holding his weapon with one hand, the other gripping the stretcher. George stumbled next, fell forward onto his knees into the soft Afghan soil. He cursed, got up, and started running again. Around them other operators carried men out on stretchers or helped them along with arms around their shoulders. The walking wounded limped and hobbled along as fast as they could go, holding their rifles at the ready. A few had set up security, weapons up, suppressing the compounds the Taliban had been using.

The MARSOC team leader with the assault force was one of the most badly wounded. His leg was almost completely severed below the knee. He'd initially treated himself. Now the other operators carried him to the bird, his face a mask of pain and the despair of realization that his life had been forever altered this day.

An AK-47 barked. A PKM followed. More guns opened up. In seconds, the landing zone became a killing field for the Taliban. Bullets swept overhead; others struck the ground and kicked up plumes of dirt around the men like miniature explosions.

"Oh for fuck's sake!" Joe snarled as rounds cracked past.

"Run!" somebody bellowed.

The MARSOC team chief howled with rage as he saw how vulnerable his men were. Exposed, with nowhere to hide, all they could do was run the gauntlet and get to the helicopter. Except the Chinook offered no safety at all. It was a gigantic target, a bullet magnet. One shot in the wrong place and it would explode. Out of the frying pan into the fire.

The team chief staggered to the Chinook's ramp, spun around uneasily, and flung the shovel-crutch as far as he could into the field in an act of furious defiance. He climbed into the bird and started grabbing stretchers to pull the wounded men aboard. Others joined in. Soon, the aisle between the long line of seats mounted against the fuselage walls was filled with wounded. Others laid stretchers across the seats until the wounded were criss-crossed within the cargo bay.

Ahead of George and the other Dagger 22 men, the ODA's radio operator took a knee and opened fire at a Taliban PKM gunner. He drained his magazine, reached for another, and realized he was out.

More incoming stitched the landing zone. The Chinook crew stayed in place, rotors churning, waiting helplessly as the wounded were pulled aboard. Eighty feet long, filled with fuel, and lacking any sort of armor plating, a Chinook presented an easy target for the enemy. The longer it stayed on the ground, the more vulnerable it would be. But the men were working as fast as they could to get everyone inside.

The pilots gritted their teeth and rode out the storm. They had no other choice: they would not abandon the bleeding men. Everyone goes home. But Jesus, that interminable wait must have felt like a lifetime, as they were the epicenter of the firefight raging around them.

George, Joe, Heath, and Jack reached the ramp. They passed Eugene up to the crew chief and a few team guys. Jack stayed on the ramp to help with the others, while George spun and took a knee beside the radio operator, who had run out of ammunition.

"I got this," George told him. He leveled his M4 and started searching for targets among the trees and the compounds on the far end of the field.

The Chinook carried three machine guns. One on the ramp, and one in each door on either side of the fuselage. It did not have any forward-firing armament, a fact the Taliban had long since learned to exploit.

The pilots sat strapped in the cockpit, their eyes on the compounds flanking the landing zone. Suddenly, a figure darted onto a rooftop, armed with an RPG. The aviators watched as he swung his rocket launcher and pointed it their way. The RPG was a Chinook crew's worst nightmare—a hit would be catastrophic and ignite the thousands of gallons of jet fuel the aircraft carried in tanks above the cargo bay. It had happened several times before and always with heavy loss of life.

The RPG man took a knee, aimed, and fired. The rocket shot off the launcher. On the ramp, Jack heard the weapon's dull *thunk* and just had time to glance at George. The men knew exactly what that sound meant.

The rocket streaked straight toward the Chinook's cockpit.

12

★ ONE WAY OUT ★

HOT LANDING ZONE

From the Castle, we saw the Chinook's rotors spinning above the treetops, but we had no line of sight to the field around it. The RPG flashed in
the late afternoon haze.

A downed aircraft? How bad can this shit get?

The rocket arrowed across the open space, punctured through the
Chinook's nose, a foot below the windscreen. It tore through the center
console just above the nav system's computer screen, nicked the pilot's
upper body, and blasted heat through the cockpit as it penetrated the
bulkhead into the cargo bay. It went clean through and dropped at the
feet of the crew chief, who was standing next to one of the door guns.
Fully expecting to die, he looked down at the ugly projectile, vibrating on
the floor from the rattle of the propellers, its metal fins extended, sizzling
hot and dribbling smoke from the tailpipe.

The RPG failed to detonate.

At the back of the Chinook, George and Jack heard a chaos as everyone tried to figure out what to do with a piece of live and potentially
deadly ordnance now sitting on the cargo deck next to dozens of wounded
men. In a normal situation, everyone would get the fuck out of the aircraft as fast as they could. But this was no normal situation. The bird could
not be abandoned and the wounded could not be dragged off into the
middle of a firefight with no cover.

"On board, or get off now!" one of the helo trunk monkeys shouted
over the engine noise. Jack bailed off the ramp, George laid down more
suppressing fire. Joe launched himself off the bird and ran clear, weapon
blazing.

A moment later, the CH-47 jumped aloft and shot skyward like an elevator. This was an old Chinook pilot trick to throw off enemy gunners. Normally, a helo rises and moves forward simultaneously, gaining altitude gradually at a relatively low angle of climb. Not this time. The crew went straight up, making the most difficult possible target. Once above the fight, the pilots dipped the nose and thundered toward FOB Todd and the waiting medical team.

When the bird landed at the far north end of the FOB, everyone bailed out the moment the wheels touched the soft dirt. Licon, our EOD tech, went the opposite direction and climbed aboard. The RPG was just lying there on the deck between a box of MREs and some loose linked 7.62 machine gun rounds for the door gunner's M240. He picked up the still warm ordnance and carried it off the helicopter. Later, after X-raying the projectile, he determined it had not been fully armed after it had been fired.

RPG 101: The grenade is instantly armed from the inertia of firing, locking together the internal mechanism that makes the impact tip active, detonating once crushed.

The RPG man was dead-on with his aim. The rocket should have detonated, killing at least forty men with a single shot. Thanks to some internal malfunction, probably created during its construction in a Russian arms factory, everyone in the Chinook survived the attack. It was a one-in-a-million fluke.

Meanwhile, Dagger 22 remained behind in the hot HLZ. Without the Chinook, they were hopelessly exposed in the field, and the Taliban poured fire at them. Everyone began a mad dash back to the compound's doorway fifty meters away. George stumbled and tripped, picked himself up, and saw Joe ahead of him, running flat out with his M4 in one hand. He suddenly spun, aimed his carbine at the Taliban, and unloaded. His weapon cracked, his feet still moving backward as he triggered off the rounds. It was something straight out of Hollywood—or a measure of the desperation of the moment.

The men made it into the compound, consolidated, and pushed back out into the maze of compounds. They ran through another gauntlet of fire, shooting and moving the entire way back to the vehicles. When they reached the blocking position, they used the vehicles to escort those that were able to walk back through the Bowling Alley. As they tried to withdraw back toward the ANP checkpoint, they came under heavy fire again, pouring salt on the wound one last time.

DOOM, the ODA JTAC, wasted no time in calling in another air strike. As the men sought cover, he put a JDAM right onto the enemy-held compound. The blast took out enough of the enemy that they lost heart in the fight. The firing drained away, and the column passed through the checkpoint without further incident.

Paddy, Mark, and I had spent the entire time at the ANP Castle, frustrated and despondent over what we had just witnessed. We were unable to intervene in any way. Hell, we never even saw the enemy.

Now Andy called on the radio and told us to meet the column on the road and we would all head back to the FOB together. Paddy and Mark grabbed their gear, I packed up mine, and the three of us shuffled down to the road and found the rest of our team and what remained of the assault force.

It was a depressing sight, really. I'll never forget the looks of complete despair on the faces of the Afghan Commandos. I got the sense that they weren't used to a full-on fight, they were more accustomed to helo inserts, quick rushes into houses in the dead of night to capture an HVT (high-value target). But today, they'd taken a beating in a stand-up fight made infinitely worse by the A-10's blue-on-blue fratricide. They sat along the roadside with slumped shoulders and faces wrenched with grief over their lost comrades.

The ODA were still doing their jobs. A few of the senior NCOs were working to get a head count to see who was still with the column, who had gone back on the Chinook, and account for gear and weapons. It was taking time to figure all that out.

As I passed by, I overheard one say, "What the fuck happened, man?"

"Dunno," the other one answered. "But you bet your ass we'll have to explain it."

The sun dipped below the western mountains, and in the dusk there was little talking among the men. A few smoked. The ODA moved about taking care of business. I spotted Jay and walked his way.

He gave me a sullen, hard glance, then nodded to the Commandos standing nearby. "Those guys got fucked up," he said under his breath.

"How bad?"

Jay shrugged. He'd been gunning in one of the vehicles.

"Bad," George said, coming up to us.

George's face was covered with grime and dirt. His kit was spotted with blood.

Rob joined us. He sketched out what had gone down in the compound. George added a few details. When they finished, we all fell silent, as if we were sharing the same thought.

Finally, George voiced it. "At this rate, there is no fucking way we're going to last seven months of this shit. Some of us are not gonna make it."

"We've been here less than a week," Jay said.

Multiple firefights. JDAMS being dropped daily. Ambushes. Tangos—Taliban—shooting at us from every compass point and the shooter sniping guys from afar. The U.S. had been at war in Afghanistan for eight years.

Seriously? Wasn't the fucking president just extolling our progress on the ground a few weeks ago, saying the Taliban is on the ropes?

Rob agreed—we all did. George was right.

We loaded up and slow-walked the rest of the way back to the FOB. In my entire time in the military, I'd never seen an American force as utterly dispirited. When we finally reached our compound, the Commandos and ODA headed for their corner and disappeared inside their tents without another word to us. Our team started to unload the gear off the rigs, and we made the ritualistic post-mission hikes back and forth from the vehicles to our tents to stow our shit.

Mark and George and a few of the other guys gathered up the weapons, magazines, and vests taken from the wounded and the dead. As Andy and Joe went into the TOC to have a very difficult conversation with the SOTF, they sorted, cleaned, and bagged those items for transport back to Herat. It was a sobering task, made all the more sobering by the bloodstains on the chest rigs and other pieces of equipment. When they finished up, they carried their bundles over to the ODA and turned the items over to them.

As the rest of us worked around the vehicles, the valley continued to echo with gunshots. The 82nd Airborne was still in a fight northeast of the FOB in the village of Ludina. Gradually, the fighting lost momentum. The firing turned sporadic instead of sustained. Finally, only a few shots here and there broke the silence of the night.

The FOB was blacked out. In the darkness, we squared away the gun trucks and prepped them for whatever mission awaited us next using our red-lens headlamps to see. We shared few words; I think we were all still trying to process the magnitude of the disaster.

I stepped into the TOC briefly and saw Andy and Joe. Joe looked exhausted and furious. For him, none of this had been done right from the beginning. The planning, the prep work, the execution—riddled with holes like Swiss cheese, and now Marines were down because of it. Nothing affected Joe more than that, especially when he felt that the losses could have been avoided.

At the folding table next to him, Andy held his trademark composure as he spoke to the SOTF while sitting in front of his laptop, simultaneously sending our MSOC more information over SIPR Net. The conversation clearly was not going well. But what the hell could Andy have done differently? In my mind, not a damn thing. Andy saved the situation when he got to that compound. He provided leadership when everyone else was still in shock from the A-10's deadly effectiveness.

This was not our fuck-up. But the fallout would no doubt land on everyone's plate after something like this.

I returned to the rigs, grabbed the last pieces of my gear, and lugged them back to my cot. My feet ached from the mild case of trench foot I'd developed. So did my head. All I wanted was a smoke.

We didn't have access to American cigarettes anymore. Camp Stone in Herat had a PX where you could get almost anything you wanted, from energy drinks to Marlboros and laptops. Not here. FOB Todd was so far from the ass end of the supply line that the only smokes we had available were from the Bazaar. "Pleasure Lights" from South Korea. They were shitty excuses for coffin nails.

I grabbed a pack, pulled a cigarette from it, and stepped outside to light up. As I did, I noticed a new sound filling our valley. I cocked my head and listened.

What the hell is that?

The sound pulsed from far overhead, a deep bass *WaaarroomWarroom-Warroom* that echoed rhythmically off the valley floor. That was definitely no fast-mover or helo.

Those are turboprop engines.

That can't be what I think it is. Not all the way up here in BMG? There are only a handful of AC-130 gunships in all of Afghanistan at any given time. Did they really send us one?

"Ski?"

The voice caught me by surprise.

"Hey, Pat," I replied.

"Got a smoke?" he said in a flat, exhausted voice.

"Yeah," I said, handing him one from my pack of Korean crap.

He lit up, and took a deep drag. Overhead, the sound grew in intensity. It could only be one thing: a gunship.

"What happened today, Ski? Everyone's wondering the same thing."

I shook my head. "I don't know."

"Did you hear anything on the JTAC net?"

I shook my head. "Whatever was said, I missed. I heard the A-10s on approach, turned, and saw it. After the first one opened up, someone screamed, 'Abort.'"

Pat stood in silence for a while, considering this. He'd been a gunner in one of the rigs, hadn't been in the compound. But he was deeply affected by the day, just like we all were.

Was there something we could have done, could have said?

"The whole thing seemed to be executed from the hip."

"Yeah. Their GRG really worried me. It was a complete piece of shit."

Pat exhaled sharply. "Well, one thing's for sure, shit is going to roll downhill. They're going to investigate the hell out of us until they get the answer they want."

"They are going to find someone to pin this on," I said.

"You know it, someone's career is over," Pat replied.

Friendly fire incidents happen in every war. As bad as this was, it was not the worst. During the Normandy campaign, a USAAF bombing attack accidentally killed about five hundred GIs waiting to launch an attack against the German lines. One of the Army's top generals died with those men in that attack.

I wonder what became of the bombardier whose mistake cost all those lives.

Pat rethought what he had just said. "Career, hell. This is the sort of fuck-up you don't recover from, Ski."

This was why I was so anal about my procedures and gear. I did not want to live with a mistake on my conscience for the rest of my life. That sort of weight would destroy everything waiting for me at home. Sabrina, our daughter—if I fucked up like this, they would live in its shadow.

Careers were the least of it. That sort of guilt will kill a man's spirit, wreck his family, leave his life in tatters.

"How do you forgive yourself for something like this?" I mused.

"You can't," Pat said softly. "All you can do is your best to make sure it never happens."

"When it does, you're fucked."

"Yeah."

BRRRRRRRRRRRRRRRRRRTTTTTT! BRRRRRRRRRRTTTT!

"What the fuck now?" Pat exclaimed as we heard the zipperlike sound of an AC-130's Equalizer five-barreled Gatling gun tearing off a long burst.

A moment later, we heard the shells impact like a series of distant crackles.

"There's a gunship on station," I said.

"This shit just won't end."

"I wonder who's controlling it?" I said.

BRRRRRRRRRRTTTTTT! BRRRRRRRRRRRRRT!

The AC-130 was the American version of Thor's Hammer. From ten thousand feet, it could orbit the battlefield and smother any Taliban force in high-explosive firepower with pinpoint accuracy. Need to take out a single bad guy close to friendly forces? Use the Equalizer. If the 25mm spewing seventy cannon shells a second is not enough, the AC-130 carries a 40mm weapon system as well as a 105mm howitzer. It is the ultimate fire support platform in the sky.

And somebody was dropping the hammer right now.

"I better go see what's going on," I told Pat.

"Good luck," he said as I turned and headed toward the 82nd Airborne COC.

BRRRRRRRRRRRRRRRRRRRRRRRRRRRRT!

"Jesus Christ. They're pounding the shit out of somebody," I said aloud.

I hustled over to our compound's wall that separated the SOF area from the 82nd Airborne. Nobody had bothered to make a doorway or a gate yet in the Hesco wall, so the only way to get from our section of the FOB to the rest of the base was by climbing a makeshift ladder built out of a wooden pallet, walking along the top of the wall, passing through a guard tower, then down another ladder.

As I got there, I heard a faint voice in the darkness talking over a radio. It sounded like an aircraft's crew.

I passed through the guard tower, where two Italians stood watch. They looked impassive and only offered a nod as I slipped past them.

Fifteen feet farther down the wall on the other side of the tower, I saw a figure hunched over a radio.

What. The. Fuck.

The figure spoke into his microphone.

I stepped closer.

BRRRRRRRRRRRRRT!

"Hey man, are you controlling that gunship?" I asked.

The figure's head turned. Slow motion, almost unearthly slowly, I saw it was DOOM.

He stared at me with an expression I'd never seen before. I didn't know what to make of it, but the hackles on my neck stood straight up.

"Yeah." His voice sounded disembodied.

"Out here? By yourself?" I asked.

"Yeah." Defensiveness crept into his voice.

I stood there, totally at a loss for what to do or say next. One man, alone on a wall, was controlling all the massive firepower of a national level asset with nothing but a radio and handset.

This is not the way you do business, especially in light of what had happened today.

He didn't even have a map. Hell, he was just staring into the dark of night.

What the fuck am I supposed to do now?

"HEY!" a gruff and booming voice called out from the 82nd Airborne's side of the wall. I looked to see PRO 6 rushing toward us. "Who is controlling that aircraft?" he demanded.

"I am," DOOM said.

"You have to be in our COC, you can't be out here alone. You've got to coordinate with us," PRO 6 ordered.

"We're tracking targets right now," DOOM said with not a little bit of *fuck you* in his voice.

As the AC-130 orbited, PRO 6 and DOOM got into an argument. DOOM didn't want to go into the COC. He didn't want to coordinate anything with the regular unit in the area. He told PRO 6 that they were tracking a Taliban fighter on a moped.

"Get down and get your ass over to my COC now," PRO 6 ordered.

DOOM split the difference. He gathered up his radio and moved over to the Hesco wall on the east side of the FOB. There he would at least be within earshot of the COC if someone needed to get ahold of him. PRO 6 apparently thought that was good enough, or at least as far as he was going to get with DOOM. He gave up and went back inside the COC.

I couldn't believe what I'd just seen.

I've got to talk to Danny about this.

I climbed off the wall and followed PRO 6. When I got to the door, I could hear a bedlam of voices coming from inside.

I opened the door. Total madhouse. PRO 6's staff was running back and forth, the place was packed, everyone was talking at once. Through the chaos, I saw Danny at his desk, headset on, focused on something.

I closed the door.

Nope. No way I'm going into that right now. I'll just add to the confusion.

BRRRRRRRRRRRRRRRRRRRRRRT!

The AC-130 tore off another burst.

I walked to the other side of the COC. DOOM was up on the wall, talking to SLASHER, the gunship's crew.

When there was a pause in the conversation, I asked, "Hey brother, are you doing all right?"

He looked at me, and said in a hollow-confident tone, "I'm good."

This guy is not okay.

He looked dazed. Like part of his consciousness had checked out. After the day his team had endured, it was no wonder.

Then it dawned on me. Did he call in the A-10s?

Was this vengeance for a mistake?

BRRRRRRRRRRRRRRRRRRRRRRRRRRRRRRRTTTTTTT!

A new series of crackles resounded through the valley.

"Did you want to use my VideoScout or MVR III so you can see what the gunship is looking at?" I asked.

"No . . . no," he said in that odd timbre.

"You sure?" I prodded.

"Don't need that."

How do I help this guy?

"You sure you're okay?" I asked, making it clear with my tone I was asking about his mental state to be controlling aircraft right now.

"Yeah. I'm fine."

He spoke into the radio again. The AC-130 shifted to another target.

This is like a bad Vietnam movie. Only it's 2009.

"Do you at least want a cigarette?" I asked.

He paused and looked back at me. His voice became more human. "I could really go for a smoke."

I handed him my pack. He took it and nodded. "Thanks."

Then he went back to work, killing Tangos with a giant weapon orbiting a few thousand feet overhead.

I cannot be a part of this. This whole operation is off the grid.

"You need anything else?" I asked.

"I'm good."

"Okay then," I said and walked away.

BRRRRRRRRRRRRRRRRT!

Distant crackles once again.

I climbed over the wall and headed back toward our team area, praying that this place wouldn't turn me into that guy.

13

★ Going Home ★

NOVEMBER II, 2009
FOB TODD

I sat at my workspace in the corner of our TOC next to Joe and stared at my monitor screen. I'd been reviewing everything posted in the BMG mIRC channel—the military's way of instant messaging through chat rooms. The 82nd COC had a dedicated channel just for the FOB. I was trying to keep up with what was going on around the valley. I never wanted to be out of the loop, just in case something suddenly came up again. I knew that if I missed a vital piece of information, I could make a mistake that cost lives. The A-10 blue-on-blue gave me an object lesson on that.

The TOC was quiet. Andy was head down in his computer, pecking away. Joe sat next to me, muttering under his breath while banging on his keyboard with his index fingers. Joe and computers did not mix together very well.

"Fucking piece of shit . . ."

"Hey Joe, can I help?" I asked.

"No. Just trying to write this damn e-mail."

"Oh, just hit control-alt-delete. You'll be good to go," Jack said from a nearby desk. Jack had a quiet voice and a soft-spoken manner about him that gave everything he said an understated sense of earnestness.

"Not falling for that."

"Again," added Andy.

"In all honesty, Joe, I don't even know how you can even read the screen with all of that dip-spit on it," I said as I started to crack up.

Joe shot me a grin. He was happy to be briefly distracted from the frustrating task of filling out and sending up reports to our MSOC. The moment faded as fast as it had come. I buried myself back in Task Force Professional's log of SIGACTs—significant events from the last twenty-four hours.

Things had been pretty quiet since November 6. A Black Hawk had taken fire later that night as it came in to land at FOB Todd. A few other firefights and minor dustups here and there followed the next day. But overall it looked like both sides had pulled in to lick their wounds. I could understand why, if the intel reports I'd seen were accurate. Supposedly, fifty Taliban had been killed that day, along with an undetermined number of wounded. Normally, such numbers seemed high to me. In Iraq, we took such reports with a grain of salt. But here, things were different. I'd tumbled across how we were getting our intel, and it seemed pretty solid.

Joe stood up and shuffled over to pour himself a cup of coffee. He looked over at Jack and asked, "Want some?"

"Got some."

"Ski?"

"Wait, is it the good coffee or the shitty stuff for the masses?" I asked. He brought me a cup. "Just drink the shit, you hippie."

"Thanks," I said as I took a sip. "Oh. For the masses. Gag."

It tasted like tar. Whatever. At least it had caffeine and it was hot.

Another sip, and I switched files on my computer and opened a recent intel report.

Yeah, the intel we were getting around here was pretty thorough. I'd never seen stuff this good before. Intel usually came from a variety of sources—human informants, communication intercepts, tips from locals, etc. But Task Force Professional had a secret weapon.

There was an Afghan who lived on FOB Todd, wore a white man dress and a badass leather jacket with a fur-lined collar. He looked like an Islamic version of a KGB agent. Cold, dark eyes, rugged jawline, wide frame—he gave off a vibe of somebody you didn't want to fuck with even though I'd never seen him carry a weapon, just a cell phone.

After seeing him on the base unescorted, it was clear he wasn't a local contractor brought inside the wire for a construction project, or to pump out the shitters. The guy was something else entirely, so I started asking around about him.

Nobody knew his name, but I did learn he worked for Afghanistan's version of the CIA, the NDS, the National Directorate of Security. He worked directly with Captain Perry and PRO 6 and fed them a steady stream of intel, all of which had proved to be amazingly accurate so far.

I'd heard that after the November 6 fighting, he whipped out his cell phone, sent a few text messages, made a few calls, and by the end of the night had the names of every Taliban fighter killed that day.

Impressive stuff, but I was having a very hard time focusing that morning. I caught my thoughts drifting more than once, and forced myself to get back on task by reminding myself of the stakes. I'd keep the focus, then gradually my mind would go elsewhere again. Boredom is sometimes just as dangerous as the enemy.

"Ski, you good?"

I glanced up to see Jack looking at me. Jack was one of our element leaders, a former Marine Recon instructor with two deployments in Iraq and one in Afghanistan under his belt. He was older than most of the other guys, which gave us something in common.

Since joining the team, I'd seen Jack more than once checking on the other guys. As one of the SNCOs, he made a point of trying to take care of his men.

"Hey Jack, can I ask you something?"

"Sure."

"You call home yet?"

The question caught him off guard.

"Not yet. You?"

I shook my head.

"You're married, right, Ski?"

"Yep. Seven years," I replied.

"Me, too. My wife's a teacher."

"Got kids?" I asked.

"Stepdaughter. She just became a teenager."

"God have mercy on you," I said.

"You've got no idea," he said with a smile.

I turned my flimsy folding chair away from the table so I could face Jack. "My girl is two. I've got some time before I have to deal with boyfriends and designer clothes."

"Enjoy it while you can, Ski." We both started to laugh. It felt nice to have somebody on the team who was a bit older and had a family, too. The team was composed largely of single guys. Being homesick was not any less of an issue for them. But for those of us with wives and kids, there was a different dimension to it. Marriage offered greater security in some ways, more to lose in other ways. Deployments wiped out countless families, and the divorce rate within the Special Operations community hovered around 90 percent. Every time we headed out the door, the bonds between husband and wife, father and children were tested and strained. The stress was cumulative, and once-solid marriages often fractured over the repeated burdens of our deployment pace.

"Don't wait too long to call," Jack said gently.

"Yeah. You, too."

We fell into silence for a moment, then returned to our work. I turned to face my computer, staring at the screen, and continued to study satellite imagery and read the intel reports from Task Force Professional.

I missed Sabrina; I missed our little girl, Devlyn. But I had been through all of this before, the different phases of loneliness while on deployment: this was my fifth one. I know there was nothing I could do to help the situation, and worrying would change nothing. You learn to put all of your emotions into a lightbulb, turning them off and on with the flick of a switch.

Managing that sense of longing was something every American fighting overseas had to face. I'd seen some just shut down, rather than contend with it. They abandoned thoughts of home, or gave up hope that they would ever return. Others were overwhelmed by the disconnect to their loved ones. Returning to them became their only priority. Mission, men, brothers—they were all subordinated to the desire to get back home to the perfectly fabricated life that they had built up inside their head.

Often, the way a warrior handled that separation defined how he fought in combat. A man who believes he has something to lose fights like it. He won't gamble or take uncertain risks. In extreme cases, his brothers brand him a coward.

On the flip side, what some would call courage turns out to be the actions of a man who simply has no hope for the future. He's given up any chance of home, and so he surrenders himself to the violence. He doesn't care if he dies. Death would be an achievement.

There are those whose home fronts destroy them. Combat becomes an out. Leon Uris wrote of this in *Battle Cry* when one of his Marines had his heart torn out by a Dear John letter. On Guadalcanal, he stayed behind to face a Japanese attack alone, ostensibly to save his platoon. Underlying his valor was the raw truth that he'd committed suicide by combat.

This struggle still goes on in war today. Weapon technology changes, warriors don't. It made me wonder how many times a man could risk his children's future before he finally asked if all this madness was worth it. And spoken or not, the thought of some other man raising your kids, screwing your wife was just something no man could stomach.

I may have turned the switch off, but I always felt my wife and daughter there with me. Their love was the constant presence in my life. When things were busy and stuff was going on, I could lose myself in the job. Even as a kid back home in Levittown, I could always slowly squeeze out life's white noise and fix my attention on one thing.

That was all great when there was stuff to do. But the last few days had been pretty quiet. The Iridium satellite phone sat on a shelf a few feet away from me in the TOC. I could grab it and be on the line with Sabrina in a matter of minutes.

What the hell am I going to tell her? I can't share what happened. I don't want to lie. Maybe someday I'll be able to tell her everything. Now is not that time.

I dreaded the call at the same time and needed the silence as part of my defense, to keep me focused. I could feel a war starting to rage inside me. Would I become overcautious, or would I give up hope altogether and stop caring if I lived or died? Either path could end up being fatal. The razor's edge in between was where the best warriors walked. Hope still burned within them, but their resolve held that fire in check. They never let home affect their decisions in battle, and they always did what needed to be done in the heat of the fight, even if it meant sacrificing themselves to save others around them. The best did that without question.

I'd seen very few men live for long on that razor's edge, especially men with families.

You got yourself into this. You didn't have to be here.

Sudden guilt stabbed me. I'd been proud of my journey to the team. Now I wondered if it would tear my family apart.

My eyes remaining locked on the flickering computer screen, I thought about the time when I told Sabrina about the opportunity to join MAR-SOC and finally get to Afghanistan.

I was in Iraq, at the tail end of my fourth deployment in 2008, when I called her from a phone trailer at Camp Al Qaim. She was living with her folks back in Goshen, New York, awaiting my return. I could hear our then one-year-old daughter, Devlyn, in the background as I explained what MARSOC was and what I'd get to do if I went that route.

"Isn't that dangerous?" she asked. I'd been turning and burning for six years. She knew about the brushes with death we'd had in Iraq, and she had suffered in silence year after year through sleepless nights, dread at the morning news, and jumping every time the phone rang.

This wasn't her life. Sabrina did it because she loved me. Before the Twin Towers, we'd have been more apt to join an Occupy Wall Street effort than an Occupy Afghanistan one.

Then I joined the Marines, and it was Sabrina who paid the price for my idealism. We gave up our life in Colorado. My private first class pay didn't come close to covering our bills, so we sold everything and Sabrina returned to live with her parents while I was overseas.

I'd made us give up everything but each other for a cause she was not completely sold on. Yet she had remained steadfastly loyal; her love and support never wavered.

Everyone had a breaking point, and I knew she was getting close to hers.

"Is it dangerous?" she asked again.

I wasn't going to lie. "Yes, it can be," I told her. I had this mental image of her curled up on the couch in her parents' basement, phone in one hand, a glass of Merlot in the other. She'd have been wearing sweatpants and a comfy T-shirt with Devlyn playing nearby. I heard her voice and could picture her soft chestnut eyes and straight brown hair. No matter where we were or what we were doing, she was home to me.

"What are you doing, Michael?" she asked. "We need to be a family."

"Sabrina, this is what I need. Let me go do this, then we can go back to our old life."

She sounded hopeful. "You will get out after this?"

"Yes." I meant it, too. I'd joined after 9/11 to serve in Afghanistan. I spent four deployments everywhere but there. This was a box I had to check, and MARSOC would get me there.

"Really?" she asked, a little more hope in her voice.

"Yes. I want to go back to being a normal person."

"We can have our old life back?"

"Yes. I just want to focus on our family. Be a father, be a husband."

I'd never had a dad. No way would I let Devlyn grow up without one—without me.

Those thoughts made the next thing I said even more difficult. "But I need to do this one thing first."

And now look where all that idealism took me. Five deployments—I'd done my share. What else did I have left to prove?

I pushed the memory out of my mind.

Such memories are like acid to a warrior's heart. They burn away resolve and risk acceptance. I couldn't afford that; too many people depended on me to do my job perfectly.

Still, I couldn't shake the mood off. Maybe it wasn't just the lack of activity that was affecting me. Earlier in the morning, the British divers had found the body of Ben Sherman, one of the two drowned men, not far from the original search site. He'd been swept under by the fifteen-knot current, weighted by his full combat gear, and thrown into a tangle of submerged debris. With great effort, the Brits had freed his body and brought him back to the surface. A Hero Flight was en route to the FOB from Herat to start his journey home.

Bullets, mortars, and bombs were dangerous enough. But out here, on the edge of the known world, there were so many hidden dangers, so many unseen traps residing in the terrain and circumstance, home seemed like a million miles away.

I didn't know Ben Sherman. He had died hours after I had arrived. But

I'd seen how the men in his platoon reacted to his loss. I'd heard stories about him. He was the kind of guy who elevated everyone around him. He made them better with his charisma and the example he set. He was one of those rare few who seemed to possess an innate nobleness. He had lived his life for others, and gave it trying to save a drowning comrade.

He'd been twenty-one years old, a paratrooper ever since he'd graduated from his Plymouth, Massachusetts, high school three years ago. At home his pregnant wife had been enduring the worst days of her life, not knowing if her husband would ever be found.

At least the Brits would give her and Ben's family closure. That wasn't much, but it was all anyone could do.

He'd been planning to take his mid-tour leave right in time to be back for the birth of his daughter. Perhaps he had been one of the few who walked the razor's edge and kept his balance in battle.

It didn't do him any good. In the end, the chaos and hostility of this godforsaken place ensured that whatever peace he'd found within himself was not enough to carry him through. Call it fate, call it whatever the fuck you want—it rose up and claimed him.

We can be prepared, do everything right, and shit will still go bad in some unforeseen way. The enemy strikes a blow. The wrong target is strafed. A river's power is underestimated. And lives will be lost every time. Historians and Monday-morning quarterbacks call it the chaos of war. Clausewitz called it the friction. The unforeseen happens. It just does. It is easy to see it with their perspective, but when the unforeseen has you in its crosshairs, how do you keep it together?

Some don't.

My laptop chimed; the soft sound broke my daydreaming. I refocused on the screen and saw a chat window had popped up. It was a private mIRC message from Barbarian Fires, Danny.

Bird inbound. Send-off for Sherman in twenty at the pad.

I told Andy and Joe the news. Joe ordered the team to drop whatever they were doing, put on cammies, and get over to the helo pad. It was time to say good-bye to one of the fallen. He was loved by his family, loved by his Airborne brothers, and we would honor that bond with our respects. He was about to make sergeant after only three years in the

Army, so he had to have been one hell of a soldier. Men like that deserved a hero's send off.

Closure for one family, but the divers were already back in the river looking for Brandon Islip, the other lost paratrooper.

This isn't over, not by a long shot. Hell, this is only the beginning.

14

★ PRO 6 AND THE ENTOURAGE ★

Sherman's remains lay within a flag-draped body bag atop a stretcher. Six of his brothers stood ready beside him. All the available personnel at FOB Todd had arranged themselves in two long lines that faced each other across a few feet of gravel on the edge of the helo pad. There were Navy divers in their retro tricolor desert camo, the Italians in their light green digital cammies, and the men of the 82nd wearing ACUs. Sprinkled among the Americans and Italians were Afghan police and soldiers. The ANA looked like shabby country cousins in their hand-me-down uniforms, oversized coats, and dingy boots. The ANP looked even worse. No standard uniform for them, they wore whatever could keep them warm. Most had thin gray-blue slacks that did very little to insulate from the cold. A few had camouflage parkas or grayish-colored jackets. One guy looked like he'd raided his grandfather's closest for a huge green overcoat left over from the Eisenhower years. Winter is not a season in Afghanistan, it is the time of year when many freeze to death or go crazy trying to fight it.

The ANA and ANP were mingled in with each other—unusual since they detested each other. For this one event, however, it looked like the stewing hatred between the two security forces had been stowed. The ANP stood, slope-shouldered and hunched against the cold in their ill-fitting castaway clothes next to the Afghan soldiers, their weapons a mishmash of stockless AK-47s, PKM light machine guns, and a few variants of the AK. For all the show of unity, it wouldn't have surprised us if a fight broke out between them. It had happened before on many Coalition FOBs.

I stood next to Jack and a soldier from the 82nd, waiting for the medevac bird to land. We could hear it in the distance, a Black Hawk by the sound of its rotors. The birds emerged out of the foothills to the west, the most direct way in without being shot at. They swung into a circuit around the FOB, passed over the ruins of the old factory, and sent pigeons fleeing from their rotor wash. One touched down and the pilots killed the engines. As its blades slowed, the crew chief jumped out and opened the side door facing the assembled causeway.

The six paratroopers bent down and lifted Sherman's litter to their shoulders. The two lines came to attention as the FOB's IDF warning speakers played a recording of "Taps." When it ended, Johnny Cash sang "Amazing Grace" as the paras slow-walked their brother to the helo.

They slid the litter onto the Black Hawk, then each pallbearer took a minute to say good-bye to Ben Sherman. They touched the flag on the body bag, then stepped away. As they did, PRO 6 and his Afghan Entourage stepped forward and lined up with their backs to us a few yards from the Black Hawk's door. There were four of them, and the only one I recognized was Chief Lewal, the commander of the BMG ANP who resided at the Castle. Short and pudgy, with a gray beard and ANP gray-blue pants, he was easy to pick out. I'd seen him rushing around looking busy but accomplishing nothing during the ODA/CMDO operation a few days earlier.

The lines broke up and the men clustered together at the edge of the pad to await their turn to say good-bye. Jack and I walked after everyone else, exchanging glances.

"Who are those guys?" I whispered.

He shrugged. "Well, Colonel Ali is up there. He's the really fat one."

They all looked fat to me. "The one with the green beret?"

"Yeah. He's the ANA Kandak commander."

"The dude's old as shit."

"Yeah, no kidding."

The Afghan to his right was clearly not military. He stood lazily, his arms crossed over his chest, looking around. I couldn't tell if he was uncomfortable or bored; either way, his demeanor at such a solemn event sent a spike of anger through me. Like this was some kind of fucking inconvenience for him to be here.

We bunched in with the rest of the men to await our turn to pay last respects. The Entourage was distracting. Clearly, they'd been invited by

PRO 6 as a symbol that we were all in this fight together. As dignitaries, they would pay respects before Sherman's friends and brothers, and that just didn't sit well with any of us.

The Afghan standing next to Colonel Ali was waved forward. He approached the helo, and I saw beneath his olive pants he wore purple socks and mud-encrusted Oxfords that looked like they might have been burgundy once. He stood at the litter for a brief moment, then turned and walked away from the Black Hawk. I saw his face in that moment—a cold one, with hawkish, heavy features and swarthy skin. He stopped beside PRO 6 and clasped his hands together across his stomach.

That guy looks like a fucking weasel.

Colonel Ali went next, followed by Police Chief Lewal. Last to go was the Afghan spook, leather jacket and big Saddam Hussein mustache. I could pick him out from a mile away. He was big and bushy and tall—so tall he towered over Chief Lewal, who couldn't have been more than five feet or so. He looked genuinely affected by the ceremony and said a small prayer. The others looked like they were simply punching the clock.

The paratroopers went next, approaching the Black Hawk in pairs to say their final salutes and good-byes. Most were stoic, but a few couldn't keep their emotions off their faces. The Italians and Afghan soldiers followed, along with the ANP and our team.

I paid my respects. With my helmet tucked under my left arm, I slowly rendered my salute. I had never met Ben but that did not matter; he represented every one of us. I took my right hand and softly touched our country's flag.

"Go on home, we will finish this."

The pilots restarted the Black Hawk's engines, and the blades began to turn as the assembled crowd looked on. A moment later, it lifted off, orbiting the base before turning west for Herat. Sherman had started his long, sad voyage home to Plymouth, Massachusetts, and his heartbroken family.

Jack watched the helicopter vanish into the hills. He'd been quiet, almost brooding, since we'd talked about our families. I wondered if he was thinking about his family back home again. Or maybe he was wondering how many of these ramp ceremonies we would endure before the end of this ordeal. I know I was.

"Ski?" he asked.

"Yeah?"

"What happened on the 6th? You got questioned by the investigators, right?"

I sighed. "Yeah. They didn't like what I told them."

"What do you mean?" he asked.

"I told them everything I'd seen. I said I'd offered the MARSOC JTAC a Rover and he refused it. Told them about the GRG. That stuff."

"What was the cause?"

"JTAC must not have known where the fuck he was and called in a gun run onto the wrong compound, seems like what they call GRG fixation."

"That ODA guy?"

"No. The MARSOC controller."

Jack shook his head and cursed quietly.

"What was it like inside the compound?" I asked.

"The worst thing I'd ever seen. I don't ever want to experience anything like that again."

I let it go at that. November 6 was a raw topic, and the investigation had not yet been completed. It looked grim for everyone involved, JTAC, team leader; even PRO 6 and his COC got pulled into it. If the war doesn't kill you, the politics and ramifications will. In situations like this, JTACs typically have their certifications pulled and get sent back to the schoolhouse to be retrained.

Soon after the Black Hawk left, the assembly dispersed. Men stood around in small groups talking quietly. Most eyes kept going back to PRO 6, though, and his Afghan Entourage. There was a bad taste in our mouths over their presence. This was an in-house moment, between the warfighters that called FOB Todd their home. Yes, we were fighting for a better Afghanistan, but turning final respects into a show for dignitaries whose allegiance was unknown felt like salt in an open wound.

"Did you see those fucking clowns?" George asked us indignantly as we linked up before we made our way back to the SOF compound.

"Yeah. Who the fuck are they?" I asked.

We told him what we knew, but the cat in the purple socks remained unidentified.

"We need to find out who they are and why the fuck they're always here."

"Always here?" I asked.

"Yeah, they follow PRO 6 around like they are fucking royalty."

King, our intel guy, had the answers for us. He joined the conversation and pointed over to Purple Socks. "That's the district governor."

"Governor of what?" I asked.

"BMG," King replied with a wry smile. He knew what I was getting at.

This seemed a little grandiose of a title to me, given that the Coalition's control of BMG extended about a hundred meters from FOB Todd's walls until about a week ago.

As we walked back to our tents, King explained the situation to us. Since PRO 6's arrival in the valley, he'd made a concerted effort to integrate all the various factions and nationalities into one fighting team. This was no easy task, as everyone had their own motivations or objectives, and some elements in the valley didn't get along. That was especially true with the ANA and the ANP. But to be successful in a counterinsurgency environment, PRO 6 was determined to work with the local authorities and make them feel like they were part of the team, having a say in everything. That was part of the reason for their presence at the ceremony. It was part of a broader effort to succeed in the valley with the help of the political establishment already in place.

Well, at least part of the political establishment. Purple Socks may have been Kabul's district governor of BMG, but the Taliban had constructed its own shadow government and military hierarchy. They were the real controllers of BMG beyond FOB Todd's wall, at least for now. Parallel power structures—it was an odd situation. Our job as American warriors was to invest Purple Socks with the authority and strength to actually be able to govern his region. Right now, with the valley in Taliban hands, the shadow government pulled all the strings.

Afghan politics was a minefield of intrigue and double-dealing, something that PRO 6 either didn't seem to realize, or ignored. Or perhaps he thought he could beat them at their own game. During the operation on November 6, PRO 6 kept the Entourage close to him, which was raising some concerns about operational security (OPSEC). Could Colonel Ali and the police chief be trusted? What about Purple Socks?

That night, after I'd seen him try to talk DOOM off the wall, PRO 6 took a small personal security detail, plus the Entourage, to meet with local leaders in an abandoned compound outside the wire. While meeting with them, the Afghan NDS agent began reading off the names of the dead Taliban his sources had sent him. He'd gone about halfway through the list when the BMG District Governor, Shawa Ali, broke out in tears. When he regained his composure, he admitted that his cousin was among the Taliban dead.

Not long after, a Black Hawk had passed over the southern village of Daneh Pasab en route to FOB Todd. A lone gunman carrying an AK-47 stepped onto a rooftop and opened fire at the helicopter. The news reached PRO 6 over the radio, who told the assembled Afghans that somebody was shooting at his bird.

Wakil, the elder from Daneh Pasab, pulled out a cell phone, spoke a few hushed words into it, and a moment later the man on the roof vanished. Was the village elder also a Taliban commander? King wasn't sure yet, but at the very least he knew whom to talk to on the other side. But all the evidence pointed to the fact that some of these characters had a foot in both camps. It made trusting them impossible as far as we were concerned. PRO 6 was getting into a very dirty aspect of the war, and the margin between working with the locals and inadvertently providing intel to the enemy seemed razor-thin.

We took a last look at Purple Socks, who was standing beside PRO 6 and the NDS agent. Colonel Ali was telling a story, which one of the 82nd's terps was translating. Counterinsurgency will always be a slippery slope. To make it work, good men have to get into bed with some seriously unsavory local characters. Ultimately, those same locals have to be able to defend and govern themselves and their people. The Entourage didn't look up to that task. Ali looked old, soft, and worn out. The chief was a pig. The district governor ruled a region the enemy controlled.

And what of Wakil, the village elder from Daneh Pasab? What was the real story behind him? SNAFU, this all seemed like such a bog of moral ambiguity.

As we walked back to our tents, I couldn't help but think PRO 6 had allowed the enemy inside the wire.

"I really hope he knows what he's doing," I muttered.

"I guess we'll see," King answered noncommittally. But his eyes told a different story.

15

★ DANEH PASAB, PART 1 ★

DECEMBER 4, 2009
SOUTH OF FOB TODD

The old man stared up at us from the side of the road, his face a warren of wrinkles. White beard, dirty white hair under his headdress, slightly stooped over, he looked as ancient as the foothills that flanked this valley. He was probably only about fifty, but life in Afghanistan ages everyone beyond their years.

Our GMVs rolled to a stop and settled in the mud beside him. We'd left the FOB only a few minutes before and had only gone about six hundred meters south before encountering the old man. Rob sat next to me in the trunk of our GMV, regarding the Afghan thoughtfully.

"Hey Andy, I'm going to jump out and talk to him."

"Roger," came Andy's reply from the backseat of our rig. Floyd was driving, and Jamie manned the .50 cal in our turret that day. The band was back together for this one, our first real combat and reconnaissance patrol (CRP) as a team. Brandon Islip had been found after a local villager had come forth saying he had seen a body near the shoreline a good distance downstream from the recovery site. Islip's body was recovered on November 30 by a team of Navy divers from his home state of Virginia. He'd been in the Army for only three years, but during that time he pulled a fifteen-month deployment to Afghanistan in 2007–08 straight out of Basic and Advanced Infantry Training. A short stint home gave him just enough time to get married before heading back out the door. His life reflected the frenetic pace we all faced to fight the War on Terror.

With his remains recovered, the Entourage returned to the FOB for a memorial service for both men. Once again, we'd been treated to the sight of these Afghans of questionable loyalty, sitting as honored guests during a deeply intimate and private service. Our dead were not honored by their presence; instead, it felt invasive. The district governor made it especially hard to endure. He sat through the ceremony, his arms crossed over his chest, and looked at times either disgusted or bored.

At least with both soldiers now found, Operation Hero Recovery had come to an end, and we were finally able to get on with the mission at hand: training the Afghan National Army and getting out into the valley.

Rob stepped down out of the GMV. His boots splashed into the mud and he sloshed through it to reach the old man. Our terp, Easy, dismounted and went over to facilitate the conversation.

The day was a cold one. When the trucks moved, the wind bit our faces and chilled us through our tricolored cammies. The clouds overhead were dark and gloomy, hinting of another rainstorm like the one that had lashed the valley the day before.

We were patrolling south on Highway 1 (Ring Road), the main road in Afghanistan. Calling it the main road was a joke. Glorified donkey trail was more like it. Since the Taliban controlled the area, this was the only stretch of Ring Road left in the country that had not been paved by the American taxpayers. The rains had turned it into a brown stripe through a landscape of farming fields and villages. We'd only been on it for a few minutes, and already our GMVs were coated with mud.

This sort of mission was an opportunity to gather atmospherics. Basically, what that meant was Paddy and Rob had put this patrol together to get out into the villages in the southern part of the valley to gauge reactions, talk to elders and locals to begin building the map of the human terrain. Who is friendly, who hides, who wants to share information—these are the things that really define the terrain, not mountains and rivers.

We intended to patrol down Ring Road for about seven kilometers, through the town of Daneh Pasab and to the very southern end of the valley. Two huge mountains came together to create a narrow pass that formed the exit from BMG that was referred to as Hell's Gates because it was unreachable to Coalition forces. The tiny village of Sini sat at the entrance to Hell's Gates. Rob and Paddy had decided we should check it out. Andy agreed. It would be a good first run through the southern half of BMG.

Officially, the SOTF classified our patrol as a Level Zero CONOPS, which meant a low possible threat of encountering the enemy. A Level Zero mission was the most basic, and considered most safe, operation we could conduct in theater. Because of that designation, my request for air support went unsourced in the hierarchy of availability. Aircraft were scarce; assigning them to a Level Zero operation was a waste of assets needed elsewhere. Just in case we ran into trouble and got something pushed to us, I had my VideoScout and Mover ready to go. In the meantime, I'd be functioning as another trigger puller for the duration of the patrol.

I stood up into the chill morning breeze and watched Easy make introductions. The old man seemed friendly enough. After a few back-and-forths, Rob got down to business.

"Easy, ask him if there are any Taliban around here," Rob said.

Easy translated. The old man nodded and replied matter-of-factly.

"He says he is Taliban," Easy said.

The answer threw Rob. He'd been looking at the old man instead of our terp, as we'd been trained to do during such conversations, but now he turned to Easy in surprise.

The old man amplified.

"He says, 'When Americans are around, I am not Taliban. But when they are not here, I am Taliban.'"

Kudos for the honesty. Rare in these parts.

I think Rob realized in that moment the old man's simple statement encapsulated the entire situation in Afghanistan. The people cared nothing of politics and nationhood. In this harsh and unforgiving place, survival was the only thing that mattered. Ideals and duty to something other than self, family, and livestock were useless luxuries. Loyalty got you killed around here. So the old man went with the flow and got by, just like the rest of the people in the valley.

This short pause at the edge of the BMG security bubble was making me anxious. *We are traveling into the unknown, let's get to it already.*

Rob retuned his attention to the old man. "Sir," he asked, "will we be safe in the village to the south?"

Rob pointed to the compounds in sight on the edge of Daneh Pasab. The old man looked that way and shrugged.

"Did you speak with the village elder to get permission to enter their village?"

Haji Wakil was the village elder of Daneh Pasab, the Afghan who had broken down and cried in front of PRO 6 when he had learned his cousin had been killed in the November 6 firefight. He'd also been the one who had made the phone call that stopped the attack on one of our helicopters that evening. What kind of reception would we get from that guy? We weren't laying any bets on a red carpet.

Rob answered, "No, we did not. We are going to the village to introduce ourselves to the elders and try to meet with them."

Easy finished translating. The old man was silent for a long moment. Finally, he said, "If you do not have permission to enter their village, I cannot say that you will be safe."

"Fair enough."

Rob and Easy bid farewell to the old man, then climbed back into our GMV. Rob squeezed into the trunk next to me.

"Let's go," Andy ordered. Floyd put the GMV in gear and we splashed forward through the mud, three GMVs and an ANA Toyota Hilux pickup strong. A moment later, we rolled past a few clusters of compounds and wide, empty fields on the north side of Daneh Pasab.

"We are the first Americans to travel this area. Ever," Rob noted. That wasn't reassuring.

Even less reassurance followed when I looked out toward the east and saw a small group of Afghan civilians hustling along the raised foot trails that divided the fields between owners.

"Check that out," I said, nodding in their direction.

Rob leaned forward and looked, shaking his head. "They're getting the fuck out of Dodge."

"Yeah."

Another group of farmers gathered up their hand tools and began hustling north out of their field. In Iraq, locals were always the combat equivalent of coal mine canaries. If they bugged out, you knew something bad was going to happen. No doubt, this was the same pattern here in Afghanistan.

"Not a good sign," I offered.

"Nope. Strike two on the shitty meter. The old man was the first one."

"Andy, you see those civilians?" I said.

"Yeah. Keep alert."

Right then, I really wished we had some type of air support overhead. I could have used the sensor to scan the road ahead to make sure we weren't driving into an ambush.

The road was a straight shot south through the farm fields, taking us into a series of compounds that marked the outskirts of Daneh Pasab. As we passed between them, Joe keyed his radio.

"Everyone on your toes. This place reeks of an ambush."

Rob and I turned and kneeled on the bench, looking forward over our M4s. As we searched for potential threats, the road narrowed even further. We bounced through long puddles and passed thick-walled compounds with padlocks on their metal doors. Between the compounds were more empty fields, some overgrown, some nothing but seas of mud. Nobody had tilled the land here in months, maybe longer.

The road skirted the west side of Daneh Pasab, disappearing into the hills as it led to the next village on the road to Hell's Gates. As we drew closer, I could see small and colorful burial flags on top of a lone hill about five hundred meters directly south.

"That hill must be Daneh Pasab's cemetery," Rob said.

"Not so different from home I guess."

"Okay, let's halt here," Andy said as we encountered a flooded irrigation trench that had turned the road into a quagmire. For the GMVs, this wasn't a problem, but there was no way the ANA rig could have made it across.

We dismounted into an empty village. I stood on the east side of the road, out of the mud, where I could see the cemetery hill and the small road that wrapped around it. To the east was a maze of mud walls and compounds.

Not one plume of smoke from a cooking fire in sight.

Short of climbing atop one of the compounds, there were no good fields of view. This place was a jigsaw puzzle of danger areas and was giving me a claustrophobic feel. Trapped.

"This is not good," Jack said as he came up the road toward me. He was in charge of our ANA detachment, and their squad leader kept pace beside him, radio in hand.

"Yeah, creepy, isn't it?"

"The place looks like it has been abandoned for years."

"Either abandoned or the people were forced out," I mused.

"Yeah. This doesn't make any sense. Why would they run the locals off like this?"

"No clue."

We took up positions on either side of a watering well made of mud bricks between two compounds. A metal bucket that looked like it came straight off the set of some medieval epic dangled from a length of rope. It made a quiet squeaking sound when hit by the wind.

Behind us, a GMV's engine revved. We looked over our shoulders to see the rig plow through the flooded irrigation ditch. Pat stood in the turret behind the 7.62mm minigun. Mark, Paddy, and Billy jumped out and began moving forward on either side of the road.

"Where they going?" I asked.

"Set up security on the hill there," Jack said.

Good plan. The hill rose up above the trees, and at least on the high ground they could see the rest of the village. Down here, the enemy could move right onto us and we'd never know it until they started uploading on us.

The GMV moved up the hill, even as the road narrowed even more. On either side of it, the villagers had built a berm perhaps three and a half feet high. Mikey, the GMV's driver, shoehorned the rig between the berms with only a few feet to spare on either fender. I watched them ease along, the dismounts in front scanning the heart of the village. A few of the ANA soldiers crossed the irrigation ditch on foot and followed after them.

The road bent to the east. By now the GMV was about eight or ten meters above us—just enough elevation to see across the leafless treetops and compound walls.

Pfoomp!

An RPG hissed overhead trailing a tongue of flame. It sailed over Pat's head and exploded against the hillside behind him.

Mark, Billy, and Paddy hit the berm, taking cover. The ANA guys looked confused. A moment later, a burst of machine gun fire sent them scurrying for cover as well.

"Contact east!"

Pat swung the turret out to his eleven o'clock and unleashed the minigun. Brass fell like rain across the GMV's roof as the weapon spewed lead.

Brrrrrrr! Brrrrrrrr! Brrrrrrrr!

Pat worked the gun like a virtuoso. Short burst, a split-second pause, another short burst. It gave the weapon a pulsing sound unlike anything else on the battlefield.

Another RPG sizzled past his GMV and exploded somewhere to the west, followed by a peppering of enemy small arms fire.

"Did you see the POO?" Mikey called up to Pat from the driver's seat. POO was short for point of origin.

The GMV was partially protected by the berm, but we couldn't support it from our positions inside the village. Andy realized they were out on a limb and called over the radio, "Vehicle 1, slowly push back. Maintain fire."

"Mikey, start backing up slowly," Pat yelled down through the turret.

There was no way to turn the vehicle around. As bullets cracked past, Mikey shifted into reverse and rolled backward, using the side mirrors to steer. Mark and Paddy tossed smoke grenades to conceal the withdrawal as the ANA soldiers moved back with the truck.

Pat laid down the hurt with the minigun. Whoever was shooting at us was quite a distance away near the river to the east. Every time somebody opened fire on them, Pat tracked their muzzle flashes and dealt payback.

Andy grabbed the SATCOM and contacted the SOTF. "Dagger 22 has troops in contact."

Now that we were in a fight, the SOTF air officer was working on getting us some air support. A moment later, Andy yelled over to me, "Hey, Ski, you've got two F-15s heading our way from the next valley over."

"On it," I said, already moving back to the vehicle.

I started keying my radio and made contact with the lead pilot, who was still three minutes out. It turned out, one was the outgoing squadron commander, the other was his replacement. Here I was, a staff sergeant, directing two lieutenant colonels in combat.

Only as a JTAC does this shit happen.

I gave them a quick brief on our situation and a center grid to the action as our lead GMV continued to back off the hill. I had no clear view of the enemy, or even any precise idea where they were. I couldn't engage them at the moment, but I needed to let them know we have air overhead. I called for an immediate show of force, altitude at pilot's discretion.

"Roger. DUDE 21, In from the north," the squadron commander radioed.

I had no visibility to the north. I could hear the F-15E in the distance, but I wouldn't be able to see him until he was at least halfway through his run.

A Taliban gunner lit up the GMV one last time. Pat flayed the area with his minigun right as the F-15E screamed over the battlefield so low I was afraid they'd take hits from 7.62 ricochets sparking off the rooftops. The ground shook; the air crackled as it torched the sky with its afterburners. The bird blazed southward beyond the engagement area, then arched up into a steep climb to the base of the cloud layer.

"Holy shit that was low!" I heard Jack say.

Joe and Andy were back by the road working on a fix to our situation. Neither liked the tactical spot we'd been caught in, and it didn't make any sense to stick around where we had no fields of fire. We couldn't continue the patrol to the south without running the risk of them cutting us off to the north. We had no idea of the size of the force opposing us, so assaulting east, through the heart of the village toward the river, would have just been reckless. That left only one option. They made the decision to pull out and head north, back to the FOB.

Mikey got the GMV off the hill, and we turned the vehicles around on the road, which was no easy task since it took triple X turns to pull off. With DUDE overhead, and our rigs out of sight, the firing ceased. We used the lull to get everyone repositioned for the move north.

I checked the little hand map I kept in the front pouch of my kit. We were less than two kilometers from the south wall of FOB Todd. The Coalition's control over this valley was a tiny footprint. Apparently, we'd just wandered outside that footprint and into the enemy's backyard.

"No wonder why the Spanish never left the fucking FOB," I muttered.

DUDE called in and told me they were starting to run low on fuel. There was a tanker orbiting about twenty minutes away, so I approved them to start conducting yo-yo ops, sending one aircraft at a time to the tanker. This would give us continuous coverage during our egress out of Daneh Pasab.

The lead aircraft peeled off and raced for the rendezvous with the KC-135 aerial tanker. The other throttled back and stayed low under the cloud layer to scan for the Taliban positions.

Andy asked, "Ski, you see anyone maneuvering on us?"

"Negative." The F-15 hasn't picked up any movement yet. I kept an eye on the video feed using the handheld Mover that I kept in my ammo drop pouch. So far, I hadn't seen a single person on it, empty like a ghost town.

I took another look at the map. Ring Road was arrow-straight from here to the FOB and ran through five open fields between clusters of compounds before leaving Daneh Pasab. Those compounds would give us little islands of cover between the open spaces. We would bound to them, consolidate behind the protection they offered, then bound through the next open stretch. Should the Taliban figure out what we were doing, they could turn those five open stretches into deadly kill zones. A few machine guns, that RPG gunner, and our exfil could get very dicey. We finished getting the rigs turned around. Andy radioed the team: "Everyone ready?"

Each vehicle commander and the dismounts checked in. Good to go.

"Joe, lead us out."

Time to make a break for it.

16

★ FIVE KILL ZONE GAUNTLET ★

DECEMBER 4, 2009
VILLAGE OF DANEH PASAB

Joe's GMV, now the lead rig, lurched northward. Aside from drivers and gunners, everyone else dismounted to clear the compounds on the edge of the first danger area. We had to make sure none of the enemy was waiting patiently behind us to hammer the patrol with point-blank gunfire.

Joe's vehicle entered the first clearing. Across the field to the east, Taliban eyes spotted his GMV and a few scattered shots rang out. Our guys laid down suppressive fire. The second vehicle rolled across as Joe's pulled up at the north edge of the gap, Jay snapping out bursts with his .50 cal from the turret. One by one, the rigs all made it north to defilade behind a large compound and its walls. The team's dismounts walked alongside the vehicle, using them as shields, or moved through the deep side ditch.

That first bound to the cover over these isolated compounds went pretty well. DUDE continued to scan. No sign of movement, and no sign of the enemy in any firing positions. They were out there all right, but maybe we'd caught them off guard with our reversal of direction, and the scattered incoming represented perhaps one or two surprised Tangos who took hasty advantage of the targets our vehicles presented.

I reached my GMV and jumped up into the trunk to study the video feed from DUDE on the VideoScout's bigger screen. A moment later, Danny called me on the air net.

"We've launched the QRF for you. They're staging near the New Bridge. Call if you need 'em," he said.

I passed the word to Andy. I was really impressed that the 82nd was already spinning up to help us. Another platoon with their vehicles and heavy weapons would be vital should the Taliban disable one of our GMVs, or we start taking casualties.

Mark, Billy, George, and Jack cleared the compounds that provided us momentary shelter from the incoming. No enemy inside them, and the places again showed signs of being abandoned for a long period of time. From the corners of the wall, some of the team established a base of fire. The men readied their weapons, searching for targets less than two hundred meters east across a field. There were compounds and dwellings and stands of leafless trees the enemy could use as hiding places. It was like playing Whac-A-Mole with machine guns.

The lead rig started across the second clearing of exposure. This one was bigger than the first, perhaps ninety meters long. The Taliban were waiting for us here. A sudden fury of incoming fire raked the mud walls. Muzzle flashes winked from the compounds and trees to the east, but only for a fleeting moment. These Taliban fighters knew the score: stay in place and their positions would be pinpointed in seconds. With aircraft overhead, that meant they risked a bomb if they were detected. So they'd fire a burst or two, then shift positions. Fire and move, fire and move. The muzzle flashes rarely came from the same place twice, and it soon looked like the entire northeast side of Daneh Pasab was crawling with Taliban.

Yet the F-15E's sensors couldn't see anyone. It was maddening. All this incoming, and not one Tango in sight. How were they moving undetected? These were cunning, disciplined fighters.

Joe's GMV slowed at the far end of the second clearing as Jay laid down some suppressive fire with the .50 cal. A moment later, our rig entered the kill zone. Some of the dismounts used it as cover, moving along with it on the unengaged side. The ANA soldiers still looked confused and scared, but they followed our lead. Jack had to keep telling them to scan for the enemy and not to bunch up. Green soldiers find comfort in their buddies. They tend to clump up, and these ANA troops were no different.

Jesus. We're supposed to be teaching these guys how to fight while not getting killed in the process.

I jumped out of the truck and added my M4 to the fight. Every time I saw a muzzle flash, I sent rounds back at it. I drained a mag, slapped a fresh one home, and dashed north to catch up to our GMV.

The ANA pickup sped through the kill zone, attracting bullets like flies on shit. The soldiers in back had a single magazine each for the AK-47s. A few fired as they drove, then huddled low, as if the thin-skinned pickup's metal hide would offer protection.

I made it across the second danger area and ran straight over to the nearest compound's gate. We needed to clear each one to make sure no one was lying in wait for us. These would be quick and dirty sweeps, no thorough searches. Just get in, get out, keep moving north.

Mark and Rob, Jack, Billy, and Ryan, our SARC (medic), continued to kick in doors along the roadsides. If it was locked from the outside, they kept moving. The few that didn't have padlocks, we entered and hastily secured. All of them had long been abandoned.

"Clear! Coming out!"

Other team members had swept through the other nearby compound. For the moment we were all hidden from the enemy. That didn't cause them to slacken their fire, though. Bullets grazed the treetops. We could hear them impacting against the compound walls and cracking past to the north.

The third open space awaited. Joe's vehicle pulled forward with Jay hunkered low in the turret behind his .50 cal as it rolled into sight. The Taliban unleashed a fusillade against it.

"Where are those fuckers?" Jack shouted in frustration. He'd taken a knee at the corner of a wall and was trying to find somebody to shoot.

I ran to our GMV and piled into the trunk to check DUDE's feed again. He was in orbit, low under the cloud layer, which limited the field of view the sensor offered. I stared at the monitor, frustrated. Not a single sign of enemy fighters.

The pilot toggled back and forth from narrow to wide view hoping to catch a heat signature. It's like trying to scan the battlefield looking through a straw.

George sprinted past the GMV out into the third clearing. I glanced up over the hull to see him fully exposed on the road. Half-bent at the waist, he drew his M4 up and scanned for targets. Something caught his eye, and he motioned to Jack.

"Right there! Left side, that closest compound!" he shouted and pointed.

Jack popped off an M203 grenade round he had loaded into his weapon, lobbing it into the area George had identified, just as our GMV moved into the kill zone. AK fire, light machine guns, beat the air around us. For all their cunning, the enemy couldn't seem to hit shit that day. Thank God.

As if to underscore the point, an RPG whizzed high above the road. The son of a bitch with the launcher was high again. He must have been too scared to stay exposed long enough to get a good bead on us. We reached the next cluster of walls and compounds, and I bailed out to cover the other guys as they kicked in doors.

The F-15E swept over us, still searching for any movement. The jet was loud and obvious, which usually was enough elsewhere in Afghanistan to convince the Taliban to break contact. Not here. These guys weren't going anywhere, and clearly knew how to mitigate our airpower advantage with stealthiness. I just wanted to stop this stupid game and start dropping bombs on likely enemy positions. But the rules of engagement and General McChrystal's tactical directive forbade us from doing that, so we'd just have to endure until the situation became just shy of hopeless.

Joe's rig started crossing the fourth open space. Floyd pulled forward to unmask Jamie's turret so he could cover them. As soon as Joe made it to the far side, his driver stopped at the edge of a compound so Jay could suppress for our vehicle.

We rolled through with Jamie snapping out bursts while I placed my hand over my ear and held the handset to the other, listening to the pilot's update. We had nothing positive we could drop on, and the biggest hurdle was just ahead. The last field was almost twice as wide as the others. As soon as we broke north of the cluster of compounds, we'd be exposed for several minutes. There was no other way back to the FOB; we'd just have to run the gauntlet.

We reached the next compound wall. Joe's rig eased behind it. We took his place at the edge so Jamie could cover the ANA truck and Pat's vehicle. Jack and George moved to the north corner and peered around it. Lots of open ground. If anyone was going to get hit in all this craziness, it would be on this last bound. Once we reached the far side, the final compounds on the northwestern edge of Daneh Pasab would shield us from further attacks.

The enemy sensed their moment had come. The volume of incoming swelled. The ANA guys looked panicky as they moved into cover. The ones who dismounted hadn't even shot their weapons through the entire ordeal. Our guys were standing up in open terrain, draining magazines without regard for their own safety, and the soldiers whose nation we were protecting hadn't even flipped their safeties off.

Just as well. Sometimes the ANA were more dangerous to us than the enemy when they started shooting. You had to have eyes on the back of your head or you might end up with a faceful of RPG blowback. Some had accidental discharges, which had proved fatal more than once to friendlies. Then there were the ANA who worked for the Taliban and would shoot an American if given the opportunity. Steadfast allies like the Brits? Not so much. More like mentally retarded cousins with guns.

Where do you even start to train soldiers like these when their hearts are so obviously not in the fight?

My radio crackled. "HALO 14, I got two guys moving around inside a compound. Hundred and fifty meters east of your position. I can identify at least one carrying a hot weapon."

I passed the word to Andy, who radioed it out to the whole team. Nobody saw any movement from that qalat, but the team laid down fire on it. DUDE kept his sensor on the two PAX. A weapon in clear sight, but they were not actively engaging us. Technically, they could have been villagers just trying to protect their property. As absurd as that sounded, the fact was if we dropped a bomb on them, and if they turned out to be civilians or just some lady carrying a hot pan out of the qalat, the shit would hit the fan so high in the chain of command that we would probably get kicked out of Afghanistan.

No direct attack. No imminent threat. Compounds had become safe havens for any Taliban wanting to take a tactical break from the action.

The pilot was pimping me to do a gun run, giving me every little gold nugget I needed to make it justified and legal. But one thing hung on my mind: I couldn't tell Andy that I was one hundred percent certain that they were not civilians. And therein lies the catch-22 of being a JTAC: unmatched firepower at our fingertips, but rules of engagement that hamstring our every move even in the thick of a firefight.

This shit is getting old fast.

I was dismounted, suppressing with my M4 as best I could between radio transmissions. The VideoScout was still in the back of the GMV.

Joe's rig had already started across the last danger area. Things were moving so fast, I decided to stay put and keep my rifle in the fight, at least for the moment.

"HALO 14, this is DUDE 21. In from the north for a dry gun run."

The call caught me off guard. I quickly radioed back.

"DUDE, confirm dry, acknowledge, over."

"Affirmative, dry, over," he responded.

The lead pilot on his own initiative had decided to make a simulated strafing pass to keep the enemy's heads down.

Floyd slow-rolled his vehicle into the kill zone. In seconds, it became the next exposed target for the enemy. Jack, Rob, and I kept firing, then I bolted for the rig as it drove by and jumped aboard. Once in the trunk, I took cover behind the bulkhead while Jack and Rob took shelter on the concealed side of the truck. I saw the aircraft as it came in.

The F-15E was coming straight toward that compound like a lawn dart. He made a beeline for the two PAX, who were now moving into shooting positions along the west side wall of their compound. They still posed no threat yet as defined by the ROEs, but it was only a matter of seconds before they opened up on us at close range.

The F-15E pulled up hard a mere thirty feet above their heads. With incredible timing, the pilot lit his afterburners, blasting the courtyard with deafening sound, heat, and flying debris. The ground shook. Anything not metal shattered. For the two Taliban, it must have felt like being on the pad at Cape Canaveral during a Shuttle launch.

The video feed showed them cowering on the ground, paralyzed by the overwhelming sensory input. Thanks to the ROEs, one of the most advanced jets on the planet had just been used as a hundred-million-dollar flash-bang. Priceless.

But it worked.

The team rolled through the last kill zone, taking fire and dishing it out. The Tangos buzzed by DUDE had fled to the back side of the building. Morale broken, they were done playing.

It was ridiculous that we'd been reduced to such measures. Those two guys would eventually get back into the fight. Unless we killed them, we were sure to come under their fire again. That was the only thing you could count on in Afghanistan.

We'd almost reached safety when the incoming seemed to slacken a bit. I kept my weapon up on the side armor, watching the compound DUDE had buzzed. Suddenly, a sharp crack rang out, and something impacted hard right between Jamie and me. Both of us ducked simultaneously—an instinctive reaction that made no sense since the round had already hit. When a second one did not follow, I yelled to Jamie, "You okay?"

"Yeah, I'm good," he responded.

I peered over and looked at the front of the chicken plate on the .50 cal and saw a big divot in the plate that was positioned between both of our heads.

"Whoa. That was a good fuckin' shot," Jamie said as he got back up on his sights.

I ducked back down so just my eyes and the top of my helmet were exposed over the trunk wall. "Yeah, that was pretty fucking close."

"Someone out there knows how to shoot," Jamie said.

That made me think about November 6 and the shooter who had caused such carnage on the rooftop. Was he out there now? Were Jamie and I in his sights? The thought of having a sniper with his scope on you will make anyone sit a few inches lower, I don't care how seasoned you are.

I kept my gun on the side of the GMV and sent the last rounds in the magazine downrange. I dropped it out, slid home a fresh one. I'd gone through about 150 5.56mm bullets as we ran the gauntlet.

We reached the edge of the clearing and plunged into a built-up area that offered significant cover as we moved out of enemy range. They wouldn't dare try looping to the north. If they did that, they'd run into the 82nd Airborne's QRF, and that would not end well for them.

As we reached the north end of Daneh Pasab, the Taliban RPG man looped around behind us. He stepped out into the road and aimed his launcher at Pat's GMV. When he pulled the trigger, the rocket expelled a long plume of smoke and flame as it shot forward. He'd been shooting high all day. This time, he was too far away. The rocket fell short and detonated against a compound wall.

"One last *fuck-you* from our lovely new neighbors," Pat said from the turret of Tail-end Charlie.

The RPG man vanished from sight. Fighting the Taliban cell in Daneh Pasab was like fighting ghosts. Ghosts and a well-trained shooter. I really don't enjoy going up against a sniper, but I knew we'd probably tangle with that son of a bitch again.

Mark always got on people that called an enemy fighter a sniper. "They are well-trained marksmen, not a sniper," he would say. "There is a lot more that goes into being a sniper than some shithead Taliban who takes a few well-aimed shots."

Who am I to argue?

We paused briefly in the same area where we had spoken to the white-bearded elder only two hours earlier. We linked up with the 82nd's QRF and made our way back to the FOB. As soon as we reached the SOF compound, I pulled my VideoScout from the truck and raced to the TOC. I still had DUDE on station for a few minutes before they got pulled from us, and I wanted to see if the enemy would show themselves now that we'd left the area.

Sure enough, we started picking up movement almost right away. Soon, we could see men slipping out of buildings and compounds, gathering at small intersections, all through the east side of Daneh Pasab along the river. I counted almost thirty fighters moving around in different areas, so the odds had been pretty even this time.

I got to work, getting grids to every gathering area, every building they walked into. There was one building along a road that had a large opening like a garage door.

Garage, got it. Next.

Connected to the garage was a large structure, a two-story building with roof access.

Two-story, got it. Next.

I recorded all of the grids and thanked DUDE for the great work, wishing them a safe flight back to base. I had no doubt that these places would come into play again at some point during our time here in BMG. Andy sat down at his desk and called the SOTF over the SATCOM. "Dagger 22 is game over at this time."

As he waited for our HQ to acknowledge, he turned to me. "Level Zero my ass."

17

★ Intel Dump ★

The firefight in Daneh Pasab changed everything for us, and the valley took on a different portrayal of danger afterward. The enemy had demonstrated he would fight us whenever we left the FOB and the tiny security bubble around it. This was their winter quarters, a place where the local Taliban's numbers swelled every fall as their brethren returned from the summer battles in other provinces to rest and refit for the next spring's offensive. For eight years, this had been their sanctuary, a haven from the violence and constant fear they lived with every day while being hunted by the Marines and the British Army around Kandahar and elsewhere.

Over the past fifty days, we had inadvertently destroyed their sense of security, driven into the heart of their refuge, and killed scores of their comrades in the process. Their response after the Daneh Pasab patrol turned into an intelligence orgy for us.

They lit up the airwaves with radio chatter, all of which our signals intelligence picked up and translated. They made cell phone calls and spoke openly of the developments in BMG. Our Afghan Man in Leather, the NDS chief, received dozens of tips and leads from human sources he had already developed around the valley. Even our own intel guys began getting reportings.

King, Rob, Paddy, James, and West formed our intel-fusion shop. King was part spook at heart. He spoke fluent Arabic, had access to technologies the Taliban could not even fathom, and worked twenty-hour days developing sources, tracing relationships, and identifying leaders. Rob and Paddy were his eyes and ears outside the FOB. They had been trained to cultivate human intelligence. This meant they knew how to meet locals who could help us, find their motivation, and turn them into assets. James handled everything that had to do with signal and communications interception, and West was our intel analyst and T-SCIF (Temporary Sensitive Compartmented Information Facility) hobbit, piecing everything together.

Their efforts paid off very quickly following Daneh Pasab. After a few patrols through the Bazaar and the neighborhoods around FOB Todd, the guys discovered that a few civilians left in the area hated the Taliban with almost religious zeal. Eighty percent of the families in BMG had lost somebody to Taliban terror raids designed to cow the locals into submission. Their ruthlessness and willingness to kill, torture, or kidnap wantonly had worked; the people of BMG either left or gave in to whatever demands the Taliban placed on them. And those demands were onerous to the extreme.

The enemy fed off the locals like parasites. They forced them to turn over food and to give them shelter, and they taxed them at the same time. The Taliban's shadow government ran the show and everyone knew it. There was no recourse, no appeals. The citizens of BMG either fled, died, or survived in servitude.

At the same time, the Taliban who stayed year-round to control the valley had entwined themselves with the drug trade. Opium flowed freely from the southern provinces through BMG and across the border into Turkmenistan. The Taliban controlled this smuggling pipeline and routes established during the reign of Alexander the Great and used some of the funds from it to tighten their grip on BMG. They bribed local officials and elders. Those who refused disappeared in night raids, their mutilated bodies found days later by villagers. These Taliban were not religious zealots, they were a mafia. The locals, whose traditional Islamic values made the opium trade anathema, hated the Taliban all the more for bringing narcotics into their communities.

Paddy and Rob discovered that the civilians despised the Taliban almost as much as they feared them. It was powerful motivation, and both men soon figured out ways to harness it. For the few people left in the area, basic survival was the only thing that mattered. The Taliban represented a threat to that, but so did supporting the Coalition. Taliban spies and

paid-off informants lurked everywhere, especially in the Bazaar area. To
be seen talking to Coalition forces was a death sentence.

Our guys figured out ways around that. They passed along cell phone
numbers where they could be reached and offered cash for information.
Rob was the smoothest at this. I once saw him pass his number to a village elder hidden inside a can of dip that he offered as a gift.

I looked at him later and just said, "Slick, brother, very slick."

He just grinned and winked. He knew the way to get business done
around here.

Along with the tip line, our team had set up a dedicated radio station
that played twenty-four hours a day to counteract the Taliban's propa-
ganda. Want the truth, just tune into 105.7 BMG, where freedom always
reigns, and local traffic reports at the top and bottom of every hour.

The tip line blew up that December. Our terps manned it twenty-four
hours a day, taking dozens of calls a week. Each one required a contact
report to be filled out, then passed along to the SOTF intel section. In the
days after the Daneh Pasab bullet exchange, King, Rob, and Paddy were
buried under hundreds of pages of paperwork. They read through everything, culling little details and discovering relationships between individuals that gave clues to the breadth of the enemy's networks throughout
the valley. At night, after patrols, Rob and King, West, Paddy, and James
would gather to brainstorm, connect dots, and draw logical conclusions
based on what they had gathered.

The best sources were those who wanted justice. They wanted the Taliban driven from the valley, or simply killed. Revenge for the loss of a loved
one usually formed the basis of their motivation. Others wanted money.
Those were the sort of sources that had to be taken with a grain of salt
and tested first, as they probably were selling information to the enemy as
well. In the *Lord of the Flies* world of Afghanistan, survival trumped ideology every time. If a man struggling to feed his family saw a way to make
a buck on the sly, he'd take it.

King, Rob, and Paddy set up drops and created a network of paid informants. Money transfers were tricky and had to be done very carefully
so the Taliban's spies would not notice and kill the informant. We established dead drops—hidden spots where we left cash on patrols that the informants could recover after we'd left the area. Sometimes we would have

in the windows of a nearby qalat caught his eye. Two enemy fighters brought their AK-47s to bear, but before they could open up on him, Eddie had his SAW on his shoulder. He pulled the trigger and held it. The weapon spewed 5.56 rounds. They impacted all across the adjacent building's wall, and he walked the fire into the first window. The Taliban gunman spun as Eddie's bullets cut into him. A second later, he fell to the floor, dead.

Laying on the trigger, draining the two-hundred-round box magazine slung under the SAW's receiver, he shifted targets and killed the second man. In a matter of seconds, he'd used almost all his ammo.

He reached Eugene and knelt beside him. Checking him over, he saw that he had been critically wounded by the sniper. If he couldn't get him off the roof immediately, he would bleed out and die.

He grabbed his brother and began to pull him toward the safety of the stairwell leading down into the compound. With Dagger 22 on the way, he had to get him into cover and try to stabilize his bleeding before he could be put into a vehicle for the ride back to the FOB.

He'd only gone a few feet when a single shot rang out over the cacophony of automatic weapons fire. The Taliban sniper lurking somewhere to the south had taken a snap shot at the corpsman. The bullet caught him in the neck. He kept going, dragging Eugene with all his strength.

The sniper fired again. Eddie staggered from another blow. The round hit him in the neck again, only a few inches from the first wound. Bleeding and weak, he tugged Eugene along, both men groaning with pain.

The Taliban shooter took careful aim and pulled his trigger. The 7.62mm Dragunov sniper rifle bucked. The bullet streaked across the battlefield at 2,700 feet per second. Unerringly, it found the shooter's mark. The round slammed into Eddie's shoulder, perhaps six inches from the other two wounds. He spun and fell beside Eugene. Both men now lay helpless on the roof, the two wounded Afghan Commandos motionless nearby.

Ignoring the threat posed by the shooter, two more Americans rushed into the house and ran upstairs for the roof. They saw the situation and dashed out to grab the wounded men. They were able to get Eugene and Eddie downstairs, along with the wounded Afghans.

With five men wounded, including their medic, the other ODA element pinned down nearby, and the volume of incoming increasing, the assault force found itself in dire straits. They needed help—and fast.

an informant come to a MEDCAP (Medical Civil Action Program) seeking medical treatment and then pull him into a side room.

What started as a quest for information on the enemy turned into a shadow war within a war. King became the architect of a network of sources that stretched throughout the valley, deep into enemy territory. He and his team even developed double agents and fed the Taliban false information. It was a dangerous, dark, and shady operation; we worked with some vile characters, but the effort paid off. When all the puzzle pieces were put together, the scope and nature of the enemy presence in the valley finally came into focus.

The southern end of the valley was a Taliban stronghold. Daneh Pasab was the center of that activity, the hub around which all the other cells in BMG revolved. The shadow governor operated somewhere outside the valley, perhaps around the city of Qal-e-naw. He was known as Ishmil. He was in overall command of Badghis Province, both the Taliban's political structure as well as the military arm. He also oversaw the smuggling and drug running as well as the financial operations.

Ishmil pulled all of the strings. His top military commander in the BMG Valley, the man who planned and executed all combat operations, was Haji Wakil Jailan, known as Mullah Jailan. His right-hand man was a midget by the name of Mullah Muslim.

Yes, a no-shit midget standing about three and a half feet tall. This is Afghanistan, you can't make this stuff up. This place is literally a fucking circus.

Mullah Muslim was a bomb maker extraordinaire. He'd become indispensable to the Taliban for his ability to manufacture devious IEDs using a variety of detonators and components. He had risen through the ranks based on those skills and had developed a genius for guerrilla warfare.

Mullah Jailan, as the Taliban military commander for BMG, possessed a core group of well-trained and disciplined fighters in his main operating cell. These guys were superb light infantry. The "shooter" was part of that cell, as were a die-hard core of loyalists who served as his palace guard. Unafraid to die, they protected him with fanatical devotion—to the point that some wore suicide vests full of explosives. Should an American Special Forces team raid his lair, they were committed to stopping us at any cost.

He was one of the key agents of terror in the valley. Should a village get out of line, Mullah Jailan would handle the problem. He would send his minions in to terrorize and murder. He was a dangerous individual, a ruthless leader who cared little for the suffering of the locals.

Mullah Jailan's cell was located in Daneh Pasab, where his father, Haji Wakil, was the village elder. But there were other ones spread through the valley that operated on his orders. Consisting primarily of locals who were paid from the drug and tax money the Taliban collected, these cells functioned sort of like militia units. Their job had been to keep order in their villages, maintain a Taliban presence, operate checkpoints, deal with any resistance from the civilians, and facilitate the smuggling operations. They often had loose associations or connections with the local police, and they formed the muscle that coerced the elders into collaborating with the Taliban shadow governor. The BMG district governor, Shawa Ali— Purple Socks—was just a puppet without real control and power. And he knew it.

There was no true chain of command as in a military organization. Instead, the cells operated semiautonomously within a framework established by Mullah Jailan and Mullah Muslim. It was a loose coalition of gangs, more a confederation than a unified force. At times, the cells feuded among themselves, and occasionally those disputes turned into gun battles. Still, when pressed, Mullah Jailan could get the local cells to fight the Americans and work within an overall strategy.

Every village had its own cell, or component, but some areas had become significant strongholds. Southeast of the Bowling Alley lay a largely abandoned village called Qibcaq, which had long since become a Taliban base of operations. The other villages in the area, including a tiny one called Taraz about seven hundred meters from the edge of the Bowling Alley, had large numbers of Taliban fighters quartered in them.

During the winter, the force in the southern part of the valley swelled as fighters returned from other battlefields. For eight years, they were quartered, fed, and trained during these rest cycles. They learned new skills, received fresh supplies of weapons and ammunition. These were hard-bitten fighters, men who had survived the bruising firefights around Kandahar and Helmand—veterans unafraid of facing the Americans toe-to-toe.

From the best we could gather, some of these fighters also wintered in the northern part of the valley with the cell that controlled the village of Burida. This cell remained mysterious to us. They didn't chatter like the ones to the south, and our human intel sources either knew little or chose not to share their knowledge. We did know a sizable force lurked up there between the 82nd Airborne's COP Corvette at Ludina and the Turkmenistan border. We'd skirmished with those guys during Operation Hero Recovery on the night I dropped a Hellfire on the east bank of the river.

We knew they were skilled and capable, and we knew they were a vital part of Mullah Jailan's organization. Beyond that, we had yet to identify the Burida cell's key leader or even how large a force they controlled.

Exactly how many fighters Mullah Jailan could throw at us was unclear. Some were part-time warriors, paid to plant bombs or spray us with AK fire. They'd carry out their assignment, get their paycheck, then go back to whatever their day job was if they had one. Above those hired guns were the Taliban's version of NCOs, men who formed the backbone of each cell; these guys were the cell leaders. They formed the core of the resistance we faced. Above them were the elites of the Taliban hierarchy, the loyalists who had received training in Pakistan or Iran and carried the best weapons and gear. Added into the mix were the veterans of Helmand and Mullah Jailan's personal security detail. Overall, the total Taliban strength in the valley had to have been upward of five or six hundred.

The Coalition troops at FOB Todd had two choices: live and let live, as had been the case for eight years prior to our arrival, or go after the Taliban and secure the valley. There was no room for half-measures or compromise solutions given the threat we faced and the number of troops we had on the FOB.

PRO 6 wanted to clear and hold. Dagger 22 just wanted to fight. But one reinforced infantillery company from the 82nd Airborne Division could not possibly destroy such a large enemy force, a dilemma that PRO 6 faced ever since Hero Recovery drew us into this fight. We could counter the numbers with the massive amount of firepower available to Coalition forces—namely airpower. But the rules of engagement had ceded that advantage except in dire circumstances, so that was a card that could only be of limited use.

To clear the valley and drive the Taliban out for good, PRO 6 had to rely on all the many nationalities and services represented at FOB Todd.

He took the broad view to counterinsurgency warfare—get the local leadership on board, bring in the ANA, ANP, the Italians, and even us Marines, and weld us into an integrated, mutually cooperating force. With all of us working together to defeat the Taliban and bring the valley under the Kabul government's control, the numbers opposing us would not be so daunting. Short-term reinforcements could be brought in via helicopter to support large operations. Smaller ones we could handle ourselves.

Coalition warfare came with dangers and one great trap. Each nation had its own agenda, its own rules of engagement, which made their participation more complicated and nuanced. The Italians, of course, could not fight back unless their soldiers were directly under fire. That alone ensured they would be a supporting role in any future offensive operations. The ANA and ANP would be of limited use. Both lacked training, equipment, motivation, and discipline. The conflict between the two organizations escalated in BMG to outright violence, thanks to the real power broker in the local police force. It was not Chief Lewal, who seemed inept and disconnected. We suspected he had a foot in both our camp and the Taliban's. For a local ANP, playing both sides was a matter of survival, just as it was for the civilian population.

The real power lay in an ANP sergeant, Shawali. The 82nd noticed him first during patrols through the Bazaar. He'd be kicked back in a chair, two minions washing his feet as people approached him to do business. How did he have such power? Nobody knew, and the chief refused to tell us.

The ANP sergeant had so much power that the locals feared him far more than any other police. They catered to him. They did business with him, though it was unclear at first what that business was. He was the man behind the curtain in the Bazaar.

One day, an ANA soldier was in the Bazaar trying to purchase some meat from a butcher when he was confronted by the ANP sergeant. A fight erupted, and the sergeant drew his weapon and killed the Afghan soldier. He escaped, at least initially, while the ANA vowed revenge. The 82nd located the sergeant's compound and raided it later that week, which was only a few hundred feet from the District Center building, where the district governor lived. They captured him and his brother, and when they searched his home they found it stuffed with humanitarian food-aid packages, ammunition, weapons, equipment, clothing, and explosives.

The ANP sergeant had been the godfather of smugglers in BMG. Even as he worked with the Coalition, he'd been supplying weapons and ammunition to the enemy. The sergeant was flown to Herat, where an Afghan court found him guilty of murder, and he was hanged a short time later.

As you can imagine, this did not go over too well back in BMG.

If the relationship between the Afghan security forces was bad, the situation with the local elders and political leaders proved to be even worse. Hardly a more craven, self-involved, and greedy bunch could have been cooked up by central casting. Purple Socks (the district governor) and many of his lieutenants were suspected of having deep ties to the Taliban. They were money-hungry, professed loyalty left and right, then as soon as the Americans turned their backs, they would sell or just give intel to the Taliban.

PRO 6's great challenge was to find Afghan partners he could trust while removing those too incompetent, corrupt, or who were Taliban operatives from positions of authority. To find out who could be trusted, PRO 6 first extended trust. Locals would not interact with the Americans unless they were shown respect. PRO 6 offered that and trusted them to be a part of the process. By involving them, he thought he could turn the fight into their own. At times, it even worked.

We later found out that when PRO 6 met with all the local elders in that abandoned compound, he offered a cease-fire with the Taliban. He told them the violence could stop. He only wanted to recover his men. In response, the elders offered twenty-five volunteers from their villages to swim the river and look for the bodies. Though we did not know for sure, rumors swirled around the FOB about the temporary cease-fire that had been worked out that night of November 6. That deal, brokered through the locals PRO 6 had trusted, had helped ensure the men were found and returned to their families.

In December, PRO 6 took these connections one step further. After Daneh Pasab, he and the Italian commander, Colonel Bruno (who was the true battlespace owner and had the final say for all major operations), began to plan a major offensive. Pro 6's goal in this offensive, dubbed Operation Buongiorno, or Good Morning, was to cut the valley in half by seizing key terrain features, building outposts, and throttling the Taliban's freedom of movement between Qibcaq and Burida. The FOB had already done this on the west side of the valley; now it was time for the east to fall.

Doing this would cut our enemies into two manageable elements that could be defeated in detail. It would also disrupt the smuggling and opium routes into Turkmenistan, which would cause havoc with the Taliban's funding.

The idea was solid. If we could pull it off, we'd put the Taliban in a very bad strategic position while at the same time crippling their financial networks. Yet, instead of bringing us all together into the planning process, PRO 6 dictated how it would be done, and who would have what part. That imperiousness went a long way to alienating much of Dagger 22, and when he received operational control over us from the SOTF commander for Buongiorno, the team was pissed to say the least. They didn't know PRO 6 like we did.

We have to answer to PRO 6 for this op? Are you fucking kidding me?

PRO 6's plan called for us to lead the way east into the fight. We would escort elements of the 82nd along with some ANA through the Bazaar, past the ANP checkpoint, and into the Bowling Alley. At the end of the Bowling Alley, part of the 82nd force was to peel off, Team Prius, and secure a couple of compounds that would be turned into a new combat outpost. COP Prius would dominate the main north–south road on the east side of the river and would cut traffic between Burida and Qibcaq. It would be one of the most important positions in BMG for that reason.

With the compounds seized, Dagger 22 would continue east the seven hundred meters through a section of compounds called Taraz. The village had been built at the base of a large hill that jutted out of the main dragon's spine of hills that defined the east side of BMG. That hill was one of the most significant terrain features anywhere in the valley. Whoever controlled it could see for miles in every direction. PRO 6 intended to first occupy it, then build a COP atop it that could support Prius and be a stronghold position. The two outposts would chop the Taliban forces in half and cut the Burida cell off completely. The hill was named Objective Pathfinder and would be seized by Team Pathfinder.

In mid-December, we were told our role in the operation. The 82nd and the ANA began to rehearse their roles. We worked internally on rehearsals of our own. The 82nd headquarters staff built a complete sand table of the battlefield in the motor pool's maintenance tent. It detailed each village, each objective and showed the roads in and out of the area. The sand table became a valuable planning aid for everyone as we all made sure this would not be another seat-of-the-pants operation.

As each group on the FOB practiced their role, PRO 6 briefed the Entourage. The district governor, Colonel Ali, and Chief Lewal were brought into the whole process from the outset. PRO 6 went out of his way to make them feel like integral members of the team.

King and the rest of our intel team watched with alarm as the details of each phase of this operation were passed to three Afghan leaders of dubious reliability. In their eyes, it became a threat to our operational security. The chief and the district governor were particular concerns, as King believed they were entwined with the Taliban. King talked this over with Andy, who agreed. Trusting these guys seemed to be a mistake. Chances were pretty good that our entire plan of attack had been fed from PRO 6 to the Taliban via these two characters.

There had been no set date for the operation. We waited for a few final pieces to fall into place; weather was a huge factor on when we could execute this operation due to the expectation that we were going to need a lot of air support, medevac, and resupply coverage. We took this extra time to prepare and rehearse our roles until we knew them backward and forward. In the meantime, Danny, who was without a JTAC, worked tirelessly, requesting as much air support as they could spare. King convinced me that the Taliban probably knew our plan, and CAS (Close Air Support) was my way to mitigate that. Should we run into an ambush, we would need firepower, and lots of it. And if the shit got heavy, fuck McChrystal's tactical guidance letter. My brothers were all that mattered to me.

I was assigned to this team for one purpose, to drop bombs, and that is what I intended to do.

At night, I lay in bed thinking about the last two months. I'd been overcautious after the A-10 incident. No more. If a compound needed to be dropped, I would do it. Let the chips fall where they may in the aftermath—I was not going to watch men I loved like family die because I felt constrained by the rules of engagement.

Christmas came with bad weather and the operation was rolled a day. The Italian chow hall cooked us a wonderful dinner but the mood was not very festive. A lot of men were wondering if this would be their last meal.

On the morning of December 26, 2009, the blanket of gray wintery clouds began to break up over the valley. The operation was a GO for that night. We would be stepping off from the FOB around 0200 in a mixed bag of vehicles and dismounts. I tried to get some rest before midnight but it was useless.

No one wants to spend the last hours of their life sleeping. Where's Pat? I need a cigarette and coffee.

18

★ **OPERATION BUONGIORNO** ★

In the last hour before kickoff for the operation was given, the SOTF managed to get us an AC-130 gunship. Scheduled to arrive just after we launched from FOB Todd, it would protect us only for a few hours—just long enough to get us to Pathfinder Hill. I considered us lucky to get the bird; there were only five AC-130s in Afghanistan, and the other three were supporting Special Operations units elsewhere in the country. Given the situation we faced, I had never been more grateful to have such destructive power at my fingertips.

As we had worked up for this operation, two things kept sticking out to me. First, the locals never went onto our objective, Pathfinder Hill. They would not even let their goats go up there, so the grass was green and undisturbed. Our intel guys scoured their networks to learn why they shunned the place and learned that the Soviets had occupied the crest during the 80s. After they abandoned it, the locals believed they'd left behind a minefield, and the villagers in BMG had lost plenty of loved ones over the decades to leftover Red Army explosives elsewhere. So they stayed away.

PRO 6 was sending us to occupy a twenty-year-old Russian minefield.

Ordinarily Licon, our EOD tech, would have led the way to the top of Pathfinder, sweeping for ancient Cold War explosives when we would likely be taking fire. But Licon was not at the FOB, as he had flown out a few days ago and still hadn't returned. George volunteered for the job.

This is what we are trained to do, we adjust to the situation.

The second aspect of PRO 6's plan that concerned all of us in Dagger 22 was the village at the base of Pathfinder Hill. Marked as Taraz on our maps, it began on the east side of the intersection at the end of the Bowling Alley, then stretched for a few hundred meters. It was really just a handful of family compounds built astride the road to Pathfinder, but the Taliban cell in that village had probably been in the thick of the November 6 firefight. They were hard-core veterans who stayed in the fight even as bombs fell on their comrades. To get to Pathfinder, we'd be moving straight through their lair in the dead of night. Thanks to PRO 6's Entourage, they'd no doubt know we were coming.

Dagger 22 prepared to lead out. Our MRAP would take point, followed by a pair of GMVs. Behind us would be the ANA, a reinforced squad of about fifteen who'd been attached to the 82nd Airborne for this mission. A platoon from the 1st Battalion, 508th Parachute Infantry, would cover our six on foot. We'd rehearsed the order of march on the FOB during the days before, unsure of when exactly PRO 6 and Colonel Bruno would give the order to execute. We walked through the mission with all the players, then continued to pre-gear, clean our weapons, and load ammunition aboard our vehicles. All of us expected a heavy fight as soon as we moved out.

We waited until 0145 to rally around Andy for our confirmation brief beside our vehicles. Practically the entire team was there, minus Rob and Paddy, who were back in Herat doing some intel paperwork with our MSOC. They should have been back by now but couldn't get on any flights heading to BMG. The team missed and needed them.

"All right guys, listen up," Andy said as he stood beside our MRAP. "We all know what's happened these past few weeks, and that there is a good chance that this operation has been leaked to the enemy. There is no timeline on this, we could be out for one day or it could be eight days. Be ready for anything; I need your best for this one."

Heads nodded. The team's mood was grim but resolved. Nobody liked going into a fight with the enemy waiting for us. On the other hand, we'd planned this out thoroughly. Rob had been instrumental in building our own piece of the operational pie. Danny had pored over the fire-support plan. We had a gunship until dawn, then a mix of fixed-wing, rotary-wing, and Predators to provide air cover for us through the daylight hours. The Italian 120mm mortar crews were ready; the 82nd had 81mm mortars at COP Corvette as well. In a moment's notice, we'd be able to smother any resistance with firepower—if PRO 6 would allow it.

That was a big if. He and his "Unified Command Team" would orchestrate the operation from the ANP Castle. As the situation unfolded, we would need permission from him to put any ordnance on the enemy. Given the ROEs and the fact that the district governor and Chief Lewal might be involved in that decision making, it could be a long day.

I noticed Joe standing close to Andy, listening to his final words. Joe's scowl was deeper than usual. He looked supremely pissed off. Since the mission came down, he'd been grousing about it, and as we began preparations, it became clear his heart wasn't in it. He went through the motions, but increasingly the team relied on Rob instead for things our team chief should have been doing. That had caused some internal grumbling, the first sign of any discord within the team. I watched this development with growing alarm. If we were going to make it through all this shit, we needed to operate as a team and be focused.

As I watched Joe, a conversation came back to me. We'd been working in the TOC together a few days ago, and I could see him slow-boiling at his desk. At first, I thought he was just fighting and losing the techno-battle with his computer again. But when I asked him how he was holding up, he launched into a diatribe about the mission.

"What the fuck are we doing?" he said.

"What do you mean?"

"We're going to go sit on a hill and get shot at. That is not a mission."

I was taken aback. I thought it was sort of an honor that PRO 6 had picked us to lead the way.

"Who knows how long we'll be stuck out there." Joe spat. He was really working himself up.

"Regardless, we've got no choice," I said, trying to be diplomatic.

He shook his head and bored his eyes into mine. "Ski, do you think there is a single piece of real estate in this entire fucking valley worth one American life? Worth the life of one of our guys?"

I had no response for that. We had a mission. We needed to execute. That's as far as my horizons went.

"Hey Joe, the enemy doesn't care if you wanna be there or not. But we need you."

"This is such bullshit."

The TOC had fallen quiet. In the silence, Joe had made me start to rethink the honor of our role in the assault. I was starting to feel expendable, like PRO 6 wanted to spare his own men from the danger ahead.

Andy finished his last-minute talk and then the men dispersed to their rigs. As we walked to our rides, I heard George grumble, "Fuck PRO 6, I don't work for him."

Pat was on him in a heartbeat. "Hey George. You think that's helpful right now?"

George just stared at him.

"Come on man, we need your head in this game."

"Screw this, Pat! PRO 6 and his Entourage of butt buddies calling the shots? What a crock, man. Colonel Ali's probably beating off to his stash of white-chick porn as his men are about to go into battle. That's how much he cares. Talk to Jack, he'll tell you how that fat old bastard keeps pestering him for porn; it's all he talks about. And now? That shit puppet didn't even bother to see his men off. And I'm supposed to be okay with him being part of this dis-fucking-functional committee that's telling us what to do?"

Pat put a hand on his shoulder. "George. Relax."

George's eyes flashed with defiance, but Pat's even gaze wore him down. "Okay. Sorry, but I am still not happy with this," he said reluctantly.

This was not a time to be petulant. Pat was right. George needed to learn to hold his tongue.

Just then, my radio crackled.

"HALO 14, this is SLASHER, over."

The AC-130 had arrived. It was time to go to work.

Nine thousand feet above us, four turboprop engines purred smoothly as the Spectre Gunship entered an orbit that would cover our movement. BMG's first Level 2 offensive after eight years of war had begun.

I saddled up in the back of the MRAP, my gear piled in heaps around me. The rumble of the big diesel engine drowned out the comfort of the AC-130's turboprops. But I knew that our fearsome beast was overhead, its crew ready to rain death on any son of a bitch willing to oppose us. Pending PRO 6's approval, of course. In an extreme circumstance, Andy could trump his authority as the ground force commander (GFC). Still, that would not be pretty, and it could cause us a lot of problems down the road if it came to that. And Andy would be hanging out there, exposed to investigation or even prosecution if anything went wrong.

Floyd slipped into the MRAP's driver's seat. Jay crawled past me and pushed into the remote gun seat. Andy was already settled into the passenger's seat, studying his computer screen. Mark climbed in back with me, carrying his .50 caliber sniper rifle.

"You guys set?"

Rogers all around. Game time.

Andy gave the word, and the column rolled for the gate. Outside, I could see men lined up on either side of the road through the FOB. All the support troops had turned out to see us off. A few saluted. Most stood and watched silently, their breath fogging in front of them in the subfreezing temperature of the night.

The gates opened and Dagger 22 stepped off. Five hundred meters behind us, Team Prius followed. Aside from two ANA Toyota pickups, they had no vehicles. We would be the muscle for them should things get rough. At least until they reached the end of the Bowling Alley, where they'd secure a few compounds on the southwest side of the fourway intersection and establish the new COP.

Across that intersection stood another high-walled compound that intel told us the Taraz Taliban cell had turned into a pillbox. Reports had flowed in through December that they'd knocked a loophole in the wall that gave them a clear shot down the Bowling Alley. They'd also built overhead cover behind it to defeat our aerial sensors. A couple of their men, armed with AKs and an PKM light machine gun, supposedly kept watch from that vantage point twenty-four hours a day.

If this had been World War II, we'd have just pounded the area with artillery until the compound in question was nothing but rubble. Then we would have rearranged the rubble with air strikes. To ensure the complete destruction of anyone left alive, we'd have sent in Marine engineers armed with satchel charges and flamethrowers to make absolutely certain the pillbox would inflict no casualties.

McChrystal's ROEs forbade us from doing anything close to that, even though we knew that the area had been abandoned by civilians. Instead, we had to test the Taliban's resolve by walking right into their line of fire.

If they opened fire, then maybe we could bring our firepower to bear. Maybe not. It depended on what PRO 6—safe from bullets and roadside bombs at the Castle—decided was the best course of action for us.

Has there ever been a war where American lives were so wantonly risked when there were so many ways to limit losses and remove threats? History is full of examples of troops misused in battle—Cold Harbor being one that cost eight thousand lives in a few minutes. The assault on the stone wall at Fredericksburg was another. But in those Civil War cases, as well as most others, it was tactical ineptitude that caused the carnage, not official strategic policy. Where else but in Afghanistan have we ever faced an enemy who played without a rulebook at the same time as our own ceded almost every advantage to the foe?

We crossed the river via the old bridge and passed the District Center building at the edge of the Bazaar as I dwelled on this. Risking our lives for the sake of protecting civilians—we all understood that concept. To win an insurgency requires the local population to side with its government, not the guerrillas. Killing them accidentally only pushes them to the wrong side.

Here, there were no civilians. We were risking our lives for a principle, not for people. To lose one of our team members that way would be a blow I doubted the team could recover from, no matter how successful the mission.

This all played out in the back of my head as I continued to monitor my handset for any transmission from SLASHER. The gunship loitered just below the overcast layer, scanning the Bowling Alley's environs with its thermal sensors. So far, they'd seen no signs of life.

It was only a partial reassurance for me. After the patrol into Daneh Pasab, we'd seen how the enemy could maneuver on the battlefield in the face of our technology and air support. They could be hunkered down behind that PKM right now, just waiting for us. We'd never know until the first bullets cut the air around us.

Our MRAP reached the ANP checkpoint. The Afghan police looked sleepy and totally disinterested. No doubt Chief Lewal had briefed them of our approach and mission. I couldn't help wondering who they'd sold that information to as soon as they learned it.

We paused at the checkpoint to kick out dismounts. Behind us, Team

Prius moved quietly in the darkness. The ANA carried no night vision, so they were already nervous and jumpy despite still being within the security bubble.

The Bowling Alley served as a canal straight down to the pillbox. The walls on both sides ensured we'd have no escape should the PKM open fire. We'd just have to neutralize it as quickly as possible. Jay, controlling the remote .50 cal on top of the MRAP, would be the key. He possessed the heaviest weapon we could bring to bear on the enemy at a moment's notice. But even the feared Ma Deuce would not be able to penetrate the walls of these compounds. He'd need a miracle to put a burst into a loophole only a foot or so high and wide. It's a machine gun after all, not a sniper rifle.

We could have kept everyone in our rigs and just relied on our armor to defeat any machine gun fire. I'm sure Andy considered that. Yet another threat lurked out there. Mullah Muslim and his bomb-making ability ensured we had to deal with potential IEDs. If one of those things went off beside a GMV, we could have a mass casualty event on our hands.

Combat requires hard choices; we risked the machine gun fire instead of the IED threat. Billy, Jack, George, Mark, and the rest of our assaulters climbed out of the trucks, formed up behind the vehicles, and snapped their night vision goggles in front of their eyes. As we moved through the Bowling Alley, they'd be able to get eyes onto any potential IED, but that would always be a crapshoot depending on how well Mullah Muslim concealed his devices. Everyone would be vulnerable until we reached the intersection at the end of the Bowling Alley.

"Okay, Floyd, let's go," Andy said.

Floyd threw the MRAP into gear. We crossed the threshold beyond the ANP checkpoint and entered the Bowling Alley at about three miles an hour. Our dismounts loped along behind us.

"Eyes up, Jay," Andy reminded our gunner.

Jay grunted an acknowledgment. He had the .50 trained straight ahead, ready to open up on the pillbox should we come under fire. A thought hit me just then. Here I was inside one of the most modern vehicles ever built by the United States being protected by a weapon our great-grandfathers relied on at Guadalcanal. Tarawa. The Bulge. The M2 had seen us through five wars across three generations. Rolling blind into a potential ambush dependent on 1930s technology to kill our enemy, while our ride was something our grandparents would have thought came straight out of a Buck Rogers comic book—I didn't know if that was irony or not, but it certainly lent a sense of the surreal to an otherwise tense moment.

Our dismounts crunched along over frozen ground frosted with ice. As cold as the night was, I had already started to sweat inside my flak vest. Anxious, I guess. It seemed like an hour, but we'd only gone about a hundred meters down the Bowling Alley.

I had popped the MRAP overhead hatch and stood up in the frigid air. I needed to have eyes on, in case I needed to get SLASHER into action. Besides, the team needed all eyes for this one. Goggles down and my M4 up, I had attached my IZLID (IR pointer) to the rail of my rifle to quickly designate targets. The SMP-1000 radar beacon that was Velcroed to the back of my helmet pulsed my location to the gunship's radar.

Through my NVGs I could see the compounds around us to the north and south. I could see the intersection in the distance ahead, and the faint outline of the walls on the far side. That was the edge of Taraz, where the PKM pillbox had been built. Nothing moved around us. No signs of life anywhere, not even smoke from fires meant to keep the chill out of hearth and home. This whole area, like so much of BMG, had been long abandoned. It was like driving through a Third World version of a post-apocalypse movie.

SLASHER checked in and reported the way ahead to be clear. The fear and tension didn't diminish with the news. In fact, it heightened in me. I couldn't believe they weren't out there waiting for us. That cell from Taraz had fought us fiercely on November 6. How could they just let us occupy their neighborhood?

Scan left. Scan right. Check the twelve o'clock. The shades of green in my NVGs revealed nothing but structures, bare trees, and walls. Any moment, bullets might come. I had to remain alert. The threats fucked with your head. Bombs on the road, perhaps hidden under some of the debris and trash littering the sides of the Bowling Alley. Gunmen anywhere, lurking in the shadows of dark and empty rooms, concealed from the gunship overhead. The shooter—he was out there somewhere. Was he boring his reticle into my skull even as I thought about him?

In such moments, we entered a trancelike state of hyperawareness. Every sensation, every organic sensor a man possesses kicks into full gear and opens wide for input. The slightest things are noticed and instantly assessed as a threat or not a threat. We were suspicious of everything. Nothing in this country was as it seemed. To stay alive, we expected the worst; our default assumption was that even an innocent pile of trash could kill us, for it could conceal a Mullah Muslim special. The mind played tricks on us, and in the darkness I was mesmerized by all the dangers my brain could conjure.

Those back home wonder about their returning warriors and the hypervigilance we cannot shed. Families watch our paranoia, our constant and unconscious search for threats, and feel cut off from the person they once knew us to be. Nights like these change a man forever. In the years ahead, we'll jump at unusual sounds, fear threats in what others see as harmless, and find it impossible to let our guard down. To do so out here could mean the death of a brother. One slip, one moment of inattention, and the Taliban might deliver a blow. We feared that, not for ourselves and our own lives, but for the lives of the men we'd grown to love. To let them down was a fate worse than death. We all knew what the cost of such a mistake would be: a lifetime of living but not living, as the burden of our error crushed the soul and the memories of the mistake we made played out across every day remaining to us. We'd be little more than breathing husks. Nobody wanted that burden; a bullet would have been mercy compared to that.

We slow-rolled to the intersection without encountering a soul. As the MRAP stopped beside the first compound that Team Prius was to take, Jay and I put eyes on the pillbox's loophole across the road to the east.

Nothing. No movement, no heat signatures. No gunfire.

Instead of relief, the stillness offered only more tension and heightened fear.

"Nothing Andy?" Jay muttered.

The assault force remained quiet and ready.

We idled at the edge of the intersection, our dismounts covering the area with their rifles as we kept an eye on the pillbox. Minutes passed like hours, all of us expecting a rocket or a sniper round from some unexpected quadrant. It was hard not to be spooked.

Team Prius pulled up. They stacked up on the compound gate to our south and stormed inside. This was the same area where the November 6 firefight took place. This time, we'd come to stay.

The 82nd found the first compound empty. The second was just as deserted. They fanned out to cover the area and prepare for the arrival of the Italians, who would bring out the construction supplies needed to turn the compounds into a Combat Outpost.

Andy got on the radio to tell higher our first objective was secured. The radio chattered to life. A voice cleared us to continue the mission. I closed my eyes and drew a long breath of cold air. Taraz loomed in the darkness across a narrow, rickety bridge.

"Okay, Floyd," Andy said, turning to our driver. "Let's go."

Floyd goosed the accelerator. The MRAP crossed the intersection and led the way forward into another village no American had ever entered.

19

★ OBJECTIVE PATHFINDER, DAY 1 ★

0330, DECEMBER 27, 2009
VILLAGE OF TARAZ

The MRAP waddled across the dilapidated bridge that separated the intersection with the edge of Taraz. The structure groaned under the weight of our heavy vehicle, but it held. The Afghans might not have much, but they make the most with what they have. Behind us, the GMVs made it across as well. We were seven hundred meters from the hill and our objective.

It seemed unreal that we hadn't taken any fire, not even a stray shot or two. It made things even more stressful and eerie as we tried to figure out what the enemy was doing. Around us, the compounds of Taraz looked desolate in the greens of our NVGs. As we drew closer to the heart of the hamlet, the road narrowed so dramatically that it didn't look like the MRAP would fit between the ten-foot compound walls that lined either side.

We rolled forward slowly, shielding the dismounts with the lead MRAP. A squad of 82nd Airborne troops, along with six or seven ANA guys, trailed behind our small convoy of vehicles. They would occupy Pathfinder Hill with us and hold it until reinforcements arrived to begin construction of the COP. Together, we formed about a platoon-sized, polyglot element composed of two services and nationalities.

We inched along, the sides of the MRAP almost scraping the walls. I stayed in the hatch, using the perch to peer down into the compounds and study the windows and doorways of the dwellings within them. Nothing moved. Not a sound rose above our engine and the reassuring drone of the AC-130's big turboprops.

Jay kept his .50 trained forward on the road as he acted as the tip of our spear. I heard him mutter, "I got nothing."

Anticipating the first enemy shot is the worst part of combat.

SLASHER called in to tell me they would have to pull off station in twenty minutes. I checked my watch, 0330. The beginning of nautical twilight, the very first light of sunrise, was in about two hours. The AC-130s never operated past dawn. They were far too valuable, expensive, and vulnerable to be risked in daylight. I had them continue to scan the area around us and to give Pathfinder Hill a good once-over for anything suspicious.

If the enemy did attack us, I hoped it'd be in the next few minutes, when we had that gigantic sword of Damocles hanging overhead just waiting for the chance to carve up our foe. An AC-130 was the only platform I was comfortable having light up targets within thirty meters of the team.

It took only a few minutes to get through Taraz. The place was deserted, not even an animal had been left in the courtyards. Now the dark silhouette of Pathfinder Hill loomed before us, a massive pile of earth resembling a small volcano.

The slopes were too steep for our vehicles. We'd only be able to get them a little ways up the base, so we planned to use them as support for the 82nd and ANA as they took the crest. First, we had to determine if the local rumors were true. Did the Russian army leave behind a minefield? Certainly, the few people left in the valley never tread upon it.

The MRAP approached a lone qalat that sat at the base of the hill. Jay rotated the crow's-nest turret slightly to put the .50 on it as our dismounts approached it. A boot in the gate flung it open, and the men swiftly went through the entryway to confirm that the mud hut in the center of the courtyard was as empty as the rest of the area.

We came to a stop here as the 82nd squad prepared to mount the hill. The ANA looked dreadfully unhappy; no doubt they'd heard plenty of stories about Pathfinder from the locals at the Bazaar. Now they were being asked to walk to the top and dig in. For the risk-averse, this seemed like a bad idea. The only feasible way to the top was to walk up a gradual spine that ran along the east side of the hill.

George would be on point with Jack in tow. We needed his expertise badly, but George was game to blaze the trail ahead. I watched him climb out of one of the GMVs and pull out a small metal detector like the type beachcombers use stateside. That was the sum total of our anti-mine-warfare equipment. He strapped on his assault pack, held the detector in his right hand, and strutted over to the 82nd Airborne squad with Jack.

"Those guys have brass balls," I said to myself.

What a shitty moment. Two-days after Christmas, he and Jack would soon be mucking around in an old Communist minefield.

He took point. Jack and the 82nd formed up behind him, their ANA counterparts staggered between the Americans. George looked back at them, nodded, and stepped off. With each step, he swept the metal detector from side to side. The 82nd followed exactly in his footsteps. I watched him follow the goat trail around toward the north side of the hill, a figure silhouetted against the gray-blue light of the early morning sky.

George stopped suddenly, which made the 82nd paratroopers instantly freeze. He regarded something on the ground by his feet for a long moment. "Nothing," he whispered.

George continued forward, sweeping as he went. He followed the trail up the slope of the hill, and we lost sight of him as he crested the top.

I dismounted and took a position by the qalat's wall to help reinforce our perimeter. Mark appeared, holding his SR-25 7.62mm rifle with its free-floating barrel. Inside our rig, he'd also brought his M4, which was still stowed in the MRAP. Elvis, his Barrett .50 caliber M107 SASR, had been left behind at the FOB. Two guns were more than enough to lug around, and the Barrett weighed as much as an M240 machine gun.

"Well that was pretty fucking spooky," Pat said as he nodded to Mark.

Mark grunted. "Not what we expected."

"No," Andy said as he walked toward us. "Look, I figure one of two things is going on here."

He paused as the radio crackled. George had reached the top of the hill and was starting to sweep its plateau.

After acknowledging the message, Andy looked back at us. "Either the Taliban's holding back because they can't see shit at night and the size of our element intimidated them—"

"Not likely," Pat interrupted. All of us were thinking of November 6. These guys didn't seem like the type to get intimidated.

"Maybe they didn't want to fight us in the dark," Mark offered.

"What's the other alternative?" I asked

Andy answered quietly. "They want us to be here."

Mark said, "Well, that would make sense if word leaked out from PRO 6's gang."

"Yeah. No shit," Pat said.

I glanced back up at Pathfinder's crest. I could just see the top of George's silhouette working to clear the hilltop, his metal detector moving back and forth. We'd heard about some of Mullah Muslim's insidious bombs. They'd plant homemade explosives (HME) in the ground, then run wires to a pressure-plate detonator ten or twenty feet away. The pressure plates were usually Styrofoam, or wood with just two wires taped to the top and bottom. Minimal metal. Almost impossible to detect with the sweeper George had. Step on it, and the bomb goes off to your left, or right, or in front of you. It was a low-tech solution to counter our detection devices, and it had been grimly successful elsewhere in Afghanistan.

If the enemy knew we'd occupy the hill, it made sense that they'd plant something up there to welcome us.

As if reading my thoughts, Pat said, "Ground's pretty frozen. Be hard for that midget fucker to emplace something."

"Maybe that's why we haven't seen any IEDs yet," Mark added.

"Yeah. But it works both ways. We're gonna have a hard time digging in up there," Andy said.

Joe, who had been talking to the vehicle drivers, passed by us and stopped to throw in his two cents. "There ain't no fucking way the Taliban's gonna let us walk into their backyard without firing a shot. I'm going to put the trucks up around the north side of the hill. Give the guys on top some flank protection."

Andy nodded. "Good idea. Go for it."

We saddled back up and inched up the base of the hill. The trail wound around the east side to the north, then grew too steep for the trucks to go any farther. Joe set up a half-moon perimeter with the MRAP in the middle. Each gunner could cover a sector from north to east. The guys atop Pathfinder would be responsible for covering the south, and Prius would anchor our western flank.

North of Pathfinder, the slope flattened out into a small gully, concealing our vehicles from observation. It was really the only place we could put the vehicles; the terrain forced them to defilade and drastically degraded their effectiveness.

The eastern flank concerned all of us. Pathfinder was the last hill in a series of them that stretched toward the rising sun for several kilometers. The rolling slopes were bare, but there were plenty of folds between them that the Taliban could use to conceal movement toward us. The crests and ridges would serve as excellent firing positions, too.

At the MRAP, SLASHER called in to let me know that they were checking off station and heading for home. We'd have air support later that morning, but for now we'd have no orbiting eye in the sky protecting us. A thick blanket of gray clouds stretched over the valley, making things trickier.

"Hey Andy, the gunship's off station," I reported. "Just us now."

Pat heard this and grinned. "Alone and unafraid."

Over the radio, the AC-130's pilot said, "Stay safe guys."

"Roger that, and thanks," I said, keying my mic.

We heard the aircraft break out of its orbit and exit the area to the south. The reassuring sound of its engines disappeared in the early morning, and silence fell across Pathfinder Hill as our drivers shut down their rigs. Now I could hear the faint sound of hand tools attempting to dig in up above.

"Alone and unafraid?" Mark said. "Brave words, Pat, from a guy who can't grow a fucking beard."

"You're rocking that Doc Holiday–looking soul patch and stash," I said as I helped unload gear.

"Soul patch? I thought it was a caterpillar fucking your face," Pat responded.

We shared a laugh, and the tension eased

Pat continued to rib him. "Mark, brother, I love ya man, but have you looked in the mirror? You look like fucking Davy Crockett at the Alamo."

Mark's eyes moved to the hilltop. "Given the situation, I'd be careful with Alamo references, Pat."

Mark was usually all business and rarely made jokes. At first, I'd wondered if he even had a sense of humor. But over the last few weeks, I'd seen it emerge. He was a careful man who played things close to his chest.

But around a few close friends, he would sometimes loosen up. Pat was the only one of us who seemed to always draw Mark out.

I was looking at the hilltop when George and Jack appeared over the crest. George walked down the slope toward us still hefting his detector.

"Hey, where's Joe?" he asked.

Pat said, "In the GMV over there."

George went over and reported that he'd found no mines, nothing suspicious.

"Good job," Joe said

Jack added, "Looks like there was a Russian position on the hilltop at some point. Shallow trenches—remains of them here and there."

Jack added, "I guess the local rumors were bullshit."

Joe nodded. "Well, they believed 'em. That's for sure." Then he added, "Good work, guys."

"Thanks, I'm going to put this gear up," said George.

He walked away from us. The sun was just starting to break the horizon to the east, revealing a dense white wall of heavy fog surrounding us.

"Eerie," Pat said in a whisper.

"Sure is."

Above the whistle of the thermal wind caused by the rising sun, we could hear the clang of entrenching tools still coming from the hilltop. The paratroopers were trying to dig into the frozen ground. Beyond that, not a sound. The place seemed deadly still.

"Well, Tom Petty said it best," I muttered.

"What's that?" Pat asked.

"The waiting's the hardest part."

"Well, if they didn't know where we were going, they sure will know where we are when the sun's up," Pat said, again his voice barely audible over the morning breeze.

"Maybe. But we've done our part. We got the 82nd to the objective."

"You wait, Ski. As soon as the Taliban figures out we've cut the valley in two, all hell's gonna break loose."

"We'll be ready if it does." Inside, my gut told me Pat was right.

At the back of the MRAP, Mark reached for his SR-25 and grabbed a couple of magazines for it. I'd been watching him for months now, and I'd never seen anyone so meticulous with his gear. He never played around, never goofed off. Whenever we had downtime, he was cleaning his weapons or buffing the glass of his scopes—optics he'd purchased himself. He used only match-grade 7.62mm ammunition, which was hard to come by, but he had his own private stash.

"Hey Joe," Mark called to our team chief. "You wanna go up to the crest with me?"

"Yeah," Joe replied, climbing out of his GMV to join us.

Turning to me, he asked, "Wanna come, too, Ski? See if we can get a good view of the area?"

"Sure." I'd taken a knee beside the MRAP to lighten the burden of my gear. Now I straightened up and felt the weight of all my extra JTAC shit on my shoulders. I adjusted my pack and tightened the straps.

"Let's go."

We started up Pathfinder Hill. There was only one way up—that narrow path on the east-side ridgeline. We climbed it at a steady pace, saying little along the way. The sky now glowed pink as the first rays of sunlight reflected off the overcast layer above us. Below us, the fog encircled the base of the hill. We were sandwiched between weather formations.

We reached the crest and found the 82nd squad furiously digging fighting positions. They knew they'd be exposed to the whole valley up here. Anyone looking would see them silhouetted against the sky. The only solution was to burrow into the earth.

They'd made scant progress. The ground proved so hard that each swing with their entrenching tools only chipped away at the frozen soil. Sweating through all their layers of clothing, they hammered away at the ground, sensing that they were running out of time.

The ANA troops claimed the east flank of the hill, taking turns with a broken shovel to try and carve out a fighting position. Mark and I briefly watched them work, then walked over to the southwest corner of the crest. We figured there'd be a good view of Prius, the ANP Castle, and the Bowling Alley from that side. But the fog had socked in the entire valley. A few trees here and there poked through it, a few rooftops of compounds were visible. Pathfinder looked like an island jutting from a white sea.

The sun had fully vanished into the overcast layer. What little color was left drained from the landscape, leaving us in a dark and gray winter morning. It felt depressing and alone.

As we took in the view, the fog began to lift and thin. Not much at first, but gradually the tops of buildings appeared, and in the distance we could see the ANP Castle, standing like another island in this ethereal ocean.

Mark turned his attention to the south. Two hundred meters away stood a small village called Kapeh Baba. It was a large hamlet—about forty compounds scattered along a few alleys that flowed off the main road that ran straight south. Beyond the hamlet, the road passed a large lone compound on a hilltop similar to Pathfinder. We'd named that Objective Fiesta. Further south, the road dumped into Qibcaq. South of Objective Prius, the sub-village of Khasadar began to materialize from the mist. Three villages, perhaps a hundred compounds. From where we stood, once the fog dissipated, we'd be able to see almost all of them. And anyone inside them would surely see us.

Mark, Joe, and I stood shoulder to shoulder and scanned them for any signs of life.

Nothing. Each town looked as abandoned as Daneh Pasab, or the area around the Bowling Alley. No civilians, no sign of the enemy. Once again, I got that post-apocalyptic vibe.

We were waging war amid ghost towns. Towns that the Russians waged war against twenty years before.

"You think the Russians had the same idea we had?" I asked Mark.

"Cut the valley in half?"

"Yeah."

"Probably. Why else dig trenches up here?" Joe replied.

"I wonder if it worked," I said.

"They lost the war, didn't they?" Joe answered. "So did it really matter?"

It felt odd, following in the footsteps of our former Cold War adversaries. But terrain and basic strategy are timeless. This chunk of real estate had value in any war, no matter the weapons or tactics.

I checked my watch: 0730.

"Mark—" I said, turning to say that thought aloud. But before I could, my words were cut short by a hail of gunfire.

20

DAWN, DAY ONE
PATHFINDER HILL

Red-orange muzzle flashes glowed through the fog in the village. The sound of furious hornets tugged at my ears as bullets pierced the air around us. A dull explosion, the ground trembled as an RPG struck the side of the hill. Dark figures ducked around walls or appeared in windows like wraiths. The moment seemed to have no end. Mark dove for cover, flattening himself within a shallow fold in the ground. Joe did the same.

I paused for a brief moment before hitting the ground, stricken by the sensory overload that comes with being on the wrong end of a surprise attack. Not far away, I saw a young paratrooper, his face chiseled by fear. Between us was a small dip and berm in the ground. It was probably too shallow to once have been part of the old Red Army trench system, but enough to offer us some protection. We lunged for it and rolled atop each other.

The enemy shooters lowered their aim, and a row of bullets chipped out chunks of the berm. More stitched their way across the crest, miraculously missing Mark, who was already on his SR-25 and scanning for targets.

"Contact south!" I heard him say into his radio's handset. "PKM in the village below us!"

AK-47s barked. More bullets whistled past. The kid from the 82nd and I molded ourselves to the ground. Even so, the tops of our helmets remained exposed above the berm.

The ground felt as cold as an open grave, with crystals of ice striping the nearby weeds and blades of grass. I hugged it, my cheek to the frozen soil as my mind caught up with the moment. There are times in combat where things happen so fast, the brain just can't follow. With the brain disengaged from the moment, people do odd things. They run into the line of fire. They freeze. They react impulsively. Mistakes are made that way. People die, or they get other people killed in those disconnected moments.

Slow and deep breaths. Focus.

Another series of bullets stitched across the berm and into the dirt. The gunner walked his aim toward Mark's prone figure a few meters away. He didn't even flinch.

I felt a warm calm settle over me. My mind went from feeling as if it were encased in concrete to a sensation of complete liberation. It dawned on me that my body was getting used to these kinds of situations. Another breath, and I had assembled a mental list of everything I needed to do. I would stay focused and execute. For the team and everyone on this hill.

I lifted my head from the icy soil and peered over the berm at Kapeh Baba, the village two hundred meters to the south. The enemy was there, using the abandoned compounds for cover and concealment.

I brought my M4 to my shoulder. Right now, more than anything, we needed to establish fire superiority. They'd pinned us down with their surprise attack. We needed to break that stranglehold on us and force their heads down. Everything else could wait.

Off to the right, Mark found a target and pulled his SR-25's trigger. The rifle bucked against him. I wondered if he'd dropped his quarry. He looked utterly unflappable behind his scope, cool and steady, his breathing no different than if he'd been reading a paper at a Starbucks. Seeing him so steady in the middle of this maelstrom inspired everyone who witnessed him.

Billy came charging up the hill, bullets cutting the air around him. Others smacked into the hard ground by his feet. He sprinted from man to man, dumping off extra ammunition to the machine gunners, and extra mags to those with rifles. He was the most exposed man on the hill, but he looked almost as if he were enjoying the moment.

He dashed back over the crest, disappearing from view as he returned to the vehicles to get more ammo for the guys. He came back, M4 across his chest, hands full of boxes of belted 7.62mm ammo. He never ducked, never took cover as he picked his way around ANA troops cowering against the ground and paratroopers giving back all they had. He looked invincible, larger than life, as he ran among us ignoring the messages of death the enemy tried to send his way. He'd been manning a turret in one of the RGs and wasn't even supposed to be up here. But where there was a fight, Billy was the kind of warrior who always found a way to get in it.

What would his dad say if he could see him?

Billy's dad had done three tours in Vietnam. He wore two Purple Hearts by the time Billy's Uncle Bud joined the Corps and was wounded in action outside of Khe San. His dad was ready to get out, but the news of his brother being wounded enraged him. He reenlisted and volunteered to go back over and ended up in the siege of Khe San as well.

That's the sort of Florida farm-boy mettle from which Billy had been forged. His dad came home with shrapnel in his head, knee, and legs. But what bullets could never do, smoking did. When Billy was a junior in high school, his father lost an agonizing fight to lung cancer.

He dumped off the last box of ammo, spun, and raced back down the hill. We were good to go for the moment, but if this shit lasted we'd need a resupply run from FOB Todd to stay in the fight.

And Billy's recruiter wanted him to be a Humvee mechanic. This is no man to be left on an FOB.

Bullets raked across the hilltop. The guys around me either fought or tried to dig in deeper. A few ANA started to poke their heads up and join the battle. One, an impossibly skinny NCO with a yellow, Hulk Hoganesque bandanna and no body armor, seemed almost as unflappable as Mark. Hefting his AK, he crawled to a good vantage point and began to blaze away at something below us in the village.

We dueled for fire superiority. The enemy had it first, but now the balance was shifting. The more guns we got into the fray, the faster we'd master the moment and drive the bastards off.

I scanned for targets with my ELCAN optic. About 250 meters away, I thought I saw something move in a window of a squat mud dwelling. I focused on it until I saw a muzzle flash. I triggered off a couple of quick shots, then really laid down the return fire. I drained the thirty-round magazine in a matter of seconds.

As I dropped it out and slapped home a fresh one, Danny called me on the JTAC net.

"Ski, we've got a B-1 inbound right now."

I put my helmet to the ground again and keyed my radio's handset. "Roger, I'm standing by for them to check in. Thanks, brother."

"You got it, Ski."

A Rockwell B-1—Uncle Sam's sledgehammer. The Lancer was one of the last of the Cold War strategic bombers, a swing-wing aircraft whose bomb bays were designed to carry twenty-four B83 nuclear warheads—enough power to destroy every Russian city with a population of 500,000. When not carrying nukes, its ordnance crew could load aboard almost 125,000 pounds of bombs in three bays and six external hard points. That's more firepower than an entire thirty-four-plane bomber group of World War II. This aircraft possessed more destructive power than any other weapon in human history. And the United States Air Force owned a hundred of them.

In Afghanistan, the B-1 took on a precision-delivery role armed with five two-thousand-pound and fifteen five-hundred-pound JDAMs. These surgical weapons possessed accuracy down to five meters.

Keep fighting down there, fuckers. Give me something to drop on.

The bullets flew. The guys reloaded. Pat showed up with an M240 machine gun and started snapping out bursts, still panting from the steep climb. The paratroopers emptied their magazines and rammed new ones home. We ate through our ammo supply at an alarming rate.

But it started to work. We could feel the momentum shifting in our favor. Just as we tipped the balance with sheer volume of lead sent downrange, the enemy went silent and a lull fell over the battlefield. The Taliban either went to ground in the face of our return fire or had crawled off to resupply and grab fresh ammo. Firefights were often like that—a sudden, violent spasm lasting ten or fifteen minutes at most before things quieted down. But the lulls never lasted long, and what followed tended to be a steady, sustained exchange of fire as everyone settled into a rhythm. If things were really heated, though, a second furious spasm might follow the lull if one side was trying to break contact, or the fighting took place at close range.

"Mark, you okay, brother?" I called over to him.

His eye never left the scope. In his slow Texas manner, he said, "Yep. Think I got a few."

I poked my head up over the berm again with my Vector 21 binos, determined to figure out where the enemy was hiding so I could pound them with the B-1 bomber. The fog was thinning fast now, just a few pockets lingering here and there. No shadows moved. No figures darted from wall to wall. The village seemed deserted again.

No way they are done.

I dropped back down behind the berm and pulled out the GRG for this operation. Unlike the one used on November 6, this GRG had been meticulously put together so that every single dwelling, compound, building, and terrain feature had a number. In a tight spot like this one, that attention to detail was a huge help. SSgt. Miller with our MSOC intel section built this one and it was huge—twenty pages stapled together. I'd folded the corners of the pages detailing my sector for quick reference.

Before leaving FOB Todd, I'd stuffed the GRG into an upper utility pouch on my kit so it would be easily accessible in a pinch. Unfolding it, I studied the numbered buildings and compounds in Kapeh Baba, looking for the one I'd been shooting into. I found it, poked my head over the berm, and began orienting my view to what was printed on the GRG. When the B-1 arrived, I wanted to make sure I could put a bomb quickly on any location the enemy decided to use against us.

This is where you make all of your money as a JTAC: target locator. The bomb is only as good as the information you program into it.

A shot rang out. A single AK-47.

"Anyone see where that came from?" somebody called.

Another AK cracked off a second round, which slapped into the crest with a sharp *thwack!*

These single bullets often preceded another full-on onslaught, letting us know halftime was over and the Taliban was game for another half.

If things were about to get crazy again, I needed a smoke first. I kept my pack of cigarettes in the same utility pouch as the GRG, so I reached in and plucked one out. As I stuck it between my lips, I realized I'd put my lighter in a cargo pocket. Since my legs were pinned under the 82nd Airborne soldier with me behind the berm, I could not get to it.

"Hey, do me a favor," I said. "Reach into my cargo pocket and grab that lighter and light this cigarette for me?"

We were slightly tangled together, which also made it hard to get my other arm free.

The solider looked over at me, eyes like saucers. He couldn't have been more than nineteen years old.

"Yeah. Hang on." He dug into my cargo pocket and found the lighter, then sat up slightly to reach me.

Another AK report echoed across the valley. The paratrooper's hands were shaking. I regarded them as he struggled to spark the lighter.

"Hey," I asked softly. "Are you okay?"

He brought his trembling hands to the tip of my London, holding the lighter with one and shielding the small flame with the other. As the tobacco ignited, I saw that his face was waxen and drained of color. I started to worry about him.

"You okay?" I asked again.

He glanced up from the cigarette and whispered, "How are you so calm?"

"Being scared will change nothing," I said. "We're all in this together."

He nodded quickly, but he looked unconvinced.

"We've been in this situation before. And we're not going anywhere."

That seemed to register, until a short burst of automatic gunfire drummed from the village. The Tangos were starting to find their groove.

I stuffed the lighter in my open utility pouch. I took a long drag on the London and exhaled. God, that first lungful felt almost transcendental, especially in this moment.

"You're gonna feel fear. You just will. But you can't let it control you. You've got to accept it and focus on your job. That's what I do, anyway."

"Thanks," he mumbled.

More gunfire rattled from the village. The angry hornets returned. We ducked slightly lower.

"Look, brother, we won't let anything happen to you."

"Over here," I heard Mark yell.

I looked to see Andy, Billy, and George sprinting through the Taliban fusillade. They'd come up over the crest in a three-man wedge, Billy with his M249 PARA-SAW light machine gun with its collapsible stock held across his chest. George and Andy hefted their M4s, leaping over obstacles and darting around fighting positions.

George dove down next to Mark. Lying prone, he unslung a spotter's scope, stuck his eyeball to it, and began searching for targets for our sniper. Andy flopped down a few feet away from them, somehow shooting and talking on the radio at the same time. The king of multitasking.

Billy, six feet tall and all muscle, stood atop the crest long enough to unfold the SAW's bipod. Then he, too, dropped prone. In seconds, he was laying on the trigger, his 249 roaring.

"I'm telling you, dude, if you gotta be pinned down, these are the guys you want with you," I said to my berm-mate.

"No joke," the paratrooper replied. I saw relief wash over his face.

Mark's SR-25 bucked against his shoulder. If he had a target, I had a target for the B-1. I grabbed my binos, slithered up to the top of the berm, and focused on where George was directing Mark.

I could see movement in the compound he'd targeted. The shadows darted from windows, lurked around corners. I counted four or five before I heard Danny on the JTAC net checking in with the B-1 and sending its crew a situation update.

Gotta figure out which compound this is.

The bird would be overhead any minute. I pulled the GRG out again and looked it over. I thought I found the right compound on the map, but I wanted to be sure, so I brought my binos up again and studied the area. Memorizing the terrain features, the other nearby dwellings, and their relationship to the road, I got a good fix on the enemy's location. Head back down, eyes on the GRG, I knew I'd found the right compound: Number 26. The page on the back of my tactical pamphlet had a ten-digit grid associated to each number. This is too easy.

I double-checked, putting the grid into my small handheld GoBook MR-1 computer, thinking of November 6. The chance of hitting our own people in this situation was low, but I didn't want to waste a bomb and hit an empty compound because I'd made some stupid mistake in the heat of battle.

Number 26. That was the one.

From a few potshots that signaled the end of that initial lull, the firefight reignited in full fury. The enemy poured fire at us. No RPGs, thank God, but lots of automatic weapons fire swept the hilltop. Rounds skipped and whined around us. The rest of the team, along with the two paratroopers on our side of the hill, blazed away with everything we had. The enemy wasn't foolish enough to assault us—this hilltop, though terribly exposed, would have been suicide to mount in the face of our gun power. Instead, they focused on driving us off with sheer volume of fire. It had worked in the past; they figured it would work now.

"They're backfilling from those other villages to the south," Mark reported.

Andy asked, "Can you get on 'em?"

"No. They're too far out. Fifteen hundred meters. I need the SASR."

"Roger," Andy said. He got on the radio and asked the 82nd to bring out Mark's massive M107A Barrett with the first resupply run. Zappala was leading the resupply effort and would ensure the weapon made it to us as soon as possible.

The din of battle grew into a full-scale assault on the senses. Our ears rang. The smell of gunpowder filled the air. Men shouted. Weapons boomed and cracked. The enemy refused to break contact, doing everything they could to take advantage of our vulnerable situation. With little cover, we could be seen for miles to anyone in the valley to the south. A pair of binos, a radio, and a mortar crew somewhere down there would be devastating to us.

All we could do was hang on and dish it out. But a sense of dread kept trying to break through my focused calm. If this continued, I knew we'd start taking casualties. There was just too much incoming for any other outcome.

"HALO 14, this is BONE 11. Radio check, over."

"BONE's on station," I yelled to Andy, who was now with us on the hill.

Our own arsenal in the sky, a super-bomber that represented a pinnacle of American combat technology, had come to tip the scale. The sense of dread evaporated. Now was my chance to make a difference and end this shit.

I couldn't help but grin. The Taliban in that compound were about to get their shit pushed in by this bomber.

I keyed my handset. "Roger, BONE, this is HALO. I got you loud and clear. Say when ready for a grid."

"BONE 11, ready, send it."

Over the sound of the gunfight, I heard the Lancer's four massive General Electric F101 turbofan engines thundering in an orbit above us.

BONE was at twenty thousand feet, well above the solid overcast that darkened the morning in our valley. This meant they would have no sensors on the target area. Instead, they would be entirely reliant on Danny and me to get them on target.

"Danny, this is Ski," I called. He reconfirmed the grid and building number I'd passed to BONE. He would relay this to PRO 6 at the Castle and get final approval for the drop from him.

"On it. Give me one sec," Danny radioed back.

As I waited, the firing intensified. In combat, there are two speeds: too fast and too slow. Which mode you were in depended entirely on what you were doing in that moment, and what the enemy was trying to do to you. As I looked around the hill, watching my brothers fighting as bullets tore chunks of ground out of the crest around them, I realized their moment was too fast. Mine seemed to last forever. Strange how combat splits reality for men who are fighting side by side. It is probably one of the reasons why everyone has different memories and sequences of events in the wake of a large battle.

"HALO 14." Danny's voice rose from my radio.

"Go ahead, Danny," I replied.

"Okay, PRO 6 talked it over with Colonel Bruno and the leadership element."

A stab of panic hit me. What was Danny telling me? Was PRO 6 looking for input from the Entourage on whether we should drop a bomb?

"What's going on, Danny?" I asked, forcing calm into my voice.

"They want you to do a warning shot first before they will approve dropping on a compound," Danny said with embarrassment in his voice.

"What the fuck is a warning shot with a goddamned B-1?" I asked.

"Find an uninhabited area nearby, give me the grid, and we'll drop a GBU-38 on delay."

I stared up at the overcast.

Our dicks are hanging in the breeze up here, and PRO 6 wants us to put a bomb in an empty field?

"Danny, we are under heavy fire."

"I know, Ski." I could hear the frustration in his voice. PRO 6 was gambling with our lives. For what? To send a "message" to the enemy that we had the resolve to use force if they didn't back off?

What the fuck are we doing? It's like Vietnam all over again.

Gradual escalation on the battlefield, in the middle of a dangerous situation with my brothers in the direct line of fire? I couldn't believe it. The enemy had already proved they'd stay in the fight even when A-10s strafed them or we dropped bombs on them. These Tangos didn't run. Obviously, PRO 6 hadn't gotten that memo.

"Andy?" I called out through the cacophony of battle. "Are you tracking this?"

"Just do it, Ski," he said.

"What the hell is going on, Ski?" George shouted.

"PRO 6 won't let us drop the compound. He wants a warning shot."

"What the fuck is a warning shot?" George raged. "Why are we even out here if we aren't allowed to kill the people shooting at us?"

The word quickly spread, and the level of anger it caused was reflected in the sudden escalation of fire into the village. The guys took out their indignation at PRO 6 on the Taliban. At least we were allowed to use the weapons in our hands.

"Okay, Danny, give me a minute to work up a grid."

I stuck my head above the berm and brought the binos to my eyes, searching for a suitable place to blow up that would cause no damage, but maybe inspire shock and awe in the enemy.

Yeah. That worked well in Iraq.

I found a patch of open ground on a slope on the east edge of the village with no compounds within a five-hundred-pound bomb's radius of destruction.

"Danny, got it," I said. I read off the grid, and Danny went silent for a moment as he sought permission for this location from PRO 6.

"Good to go, Ski," he radioed a moment later.

We worked up a 9-line and called it up to the bomber's crew.

"Execute immediately," I said. I wanted that emphasized, so I repeated it.

The bomber called in a moment later. "Roger, will call when inbound."

High above us, the B-1 completed an orbit, then turned onto a new heading to get on its bomb run. I knew we were only minutes away now, and my throat went dry. My body tensed. First drop of the day—even if it was onto an empty hillside—was one of those gut-check moments.

Had I made all the right calculations? Was the 9-line accurate?

A million thoughts ran through my head as the men around me fired and reloaded in the thick of the fray. I knew the bomber was on approach when it turned back around and its engines went silent. The enemy had to know what was coming.

And they were still shooting at us.

"BONE 11, In from the east," the bomber crew reported.

"BONE 11, from HALO 14, Cleared Hot," I replied.

"One away, thirty seconds," the pilot reported.

The five-hundred-pound bomb plunged through the overcast, sounding like a runaway train. Anyone within earshot would know something was about to be smothered by American firepower.

I wondered if the Taliban thought it would be them.

The bomb struck the hillside. It punched through the crust of frozen ground and embedded itself deep in the earth. No explosion followed. Either the bomb was a dud, or it was never armed by the crew.

The Taliban's fire never slackened.

21

★ First Wave ★

I stared out at the hillside impact point, radio in hand. Nearby, Billy blasted away with his SAW. Mark took shots with his SR-25. Beside me, the paratrooper had joined the fight, banging away at targets with his M4 rifle. Between the drumming of automatic weapons, I could hear Andy talking on his radio. As always, his voice was that of the consummately cool professional even in the middle of all this chaos.

This amazing combat ballet played out as my brothers fired, reloaded, shouted, cursed, and cheered. The Afghans dug. The paratroopers dished out everything they had, firing from shallow holes they'd scooped out just before the battle began. The moment seemed unworldly, so disconnected from the life I'd known in Colorado.

What the fuck is going on here, this is madness. I'm dropping warning bombs on empty hillsides as the men around me fight for their lives.

"BONE 11, HALO 14. Negative detonation," I heard myself say.

I didn't want to give PRO 6 a chance to chime in on this. I already had a clearance to detonate a bomb on that grid, and that is what I intended to do.

"You are approved for immediate reattack," I said in the same breath.

The B-1 crew responded right away and turned out for another run.

"BONE 11, In from the east."

I keyed my handset to talk, just as Billy went cyclic with his SAW. The din of that machine gun spewing 5.56mm rounds downrange drowned out my words. I cupped the mic with one hand.

"BONE 11, from HALO 14. Cleared Hot!" I yelled into it.

Billy triggered another long burst as Pat swapped out barrels on his

240 machine gun. The bomber was silent again as it approach the ballistic release point of the bomb, the sky as gray as our situation.

"One away."

"Andy," I shouted. "One away!"

The bomb fell through the overcast layer and plunged straight into the hillside almost exactly in the same spot as the first one. It exploded and sent a shock wave rumbling through the valley. On Pathfinder, the hill shook as if some tectonic plate had shifted miles below us.

It rattled not only our bodies, but our sense of permanence as well. We go through our daily lives believing that the one unchanging constant is the ground beneath our feet. In battle, when a bomb goes off, you feel it in your gut. You feel the bomb's power telegraphed through earth, through concrete buildings, and through the air when the shock wave reaches you. It destroys any sense of safety or hope that the earth can offer succor if only you dig into it far enough. But the truth is, no matter how deep you burrow, there are always bigger bombs.

I looked at the smoking crater on the hillside. Chunks of sod and rocks rained down around the impact point. They stippled Pathfinder's southern slope and drummed onto the rooftops in Kapeh Baba. Tendrils of smoke coiled up over some of the larger pieces.

The enemy stopped firing. Mark and Billy lost sight of their targets as the Taliban went to ground and tried to figure out what had just happened. Within a minute after the bomb's detonation, the scene had gone quiet.

The warning shot had worked? I couldn't believe it. Maybe PRO 6 was on to something after all.

But it didn't work for long. Before most of the guys had a chance to even reload, the enemy began taking potshots at us again. Instead of pouring the rounds at us, they became more cunning and cautious. Inside buildings throughout Kapeh Baba, they fashioned mouse holes to aim through so they would not have to risk detection by appearing in a window. In some buildings, they just pulled out old pipes that ran through the walls, creating instant fighting positions. In others, they carefully bored firing ports in the walls with whatever implements they had at hand. On their bellies, barrels poking through these tiny openings, they would let fly with a few rounds at

a time, then would go quiet. The bomb hadn't persuaded them to stop trying to kill us. It only made them harder to locate.

Way to go, PRO 6. Thanks for this.

As they harassed us, First Sergeant Z arrived with the resupply convoy. They'd run the gauntlet from Prius through Taraz, taking fire along
the way, but they got to us intact to deliver ammunition, food, and water—
plus Elvis, Mark's M107A semiautomatic .50 caliber sniper rifle. We used
the moment to regroup, reload, and run supplies to the hilltop.

Mark made a dash down to the convoy, where he uncased Elvis and
brought it up into the fight. All morning long, he'd seen the enemy send
small groups of reinforcements into Kapeh Baba from the south. They'd
been too far away to hit with the SR-25, but the range was right in Elvis's
performance envelope.

As the occasional shot smacked into the hillside, we started digging
with renewed fury. None of us had any doubt that we would be hit hard
again at some point. So we dug, and filled sandbags that Zappala had
brought us. We piled them around our fighting positions, but the digging
was slow and tiring. Periodically, we took enough fire to force us to drop
our entrenching tools and get back into the fight. Those flare-ups didn't
last long, and I had no chance to try and get another bomb onto the enemy in Kapeh Baba.

We settled into a routine: *Dig–fight–dodge incoming.* Repeat as needed.

Mark finished digging for the moment. He'd moved enough dirt to
have a decently protected hide site, complete with a crown of sandbags.
He tore off a chunk of an MRE box and settled down behind Elvis with a
map pen in hand.

"Range card?" I said to him.

"Yep."

He began using the Vector 21, recording the range and direction to
multiple points on the battlefield. In a fight, such information would help
him get on a target faster. He also made note of the temperature and hu-
midity throughout the day. The man was meticulous about his craft.

"Hey Andy, we've got movement," he reported from behind his scope.

Andy, who'd dug in only a few feet from George and Mark, grabbed
his rifle and asked, "Where?"

"South of Kapeh Baba. Moving north toward us and northwest across an open field toward Khasadar and Prius."

Andy peered over his sandbag-lined hole to see where Mark was looking. I did the same. To the south, I could see the triangle of villages— Kapeh Baba below us and Khasadar over to our right, the village of Qibcaq was in the far distance with its lone compound fortress on the hill named by the 82nd as Objective Fiesta. The enemy was using a deep wadi as a ratline to run reinforcements from Qibcaq up to the other villages. There was plenty of cover and concealment almost all the way to the back side of Kapeh Baba. From there you only had two options, go into Kapeh Baba proper or make a mad dash to the west for Khasadar. That route was perilous, as they would be exposed for most of the last three hundred meters to reach the outskirts. It was a perfect kill zone for Elvis.

Mark covered the area. The range varied from fifteen hundred meters to over two thousand, but he began to take shots. Trying to hit a running man at that distance with a Barrett is nothing like the way it is portrayed in the movies. In the real world, there are few one-shot, one-kill moments. But Mark's fire harassed them and slowed down their reinforcement process.

While we took sporadic fire from Kapeh Baba, Elvis's thunderous report boomed across the valley. The damn thing sounded like a cannon, and each time Mark pulled the trigger, the weapon made the hilltop tremble. The Barrett was so powerful that its concussion could be felt in our guts. Back in the States, snipers were limited to a certain number of shots with the M107 every time they went to a range or participated in a field exercise. Because of its concussion wave and recoil, too many shots can cause internal damage to the weapon's users. Out here, there was no such concern.

Mark targeted one enemy fighter, who dove behind a low-lying mud-brick wall just as our sniper pulled his trigger. The high-explosive round struck the wall and blew a chunk out of it. The man hugged the wall and didn't move.

Mark checked the range. Eight hundred meters. Patiently, he stayed behind the scope and watched the wall. The insurgent was patient, too. Knowing he was under the eyes of an American sniper, he didn't move for several minutes. When he did, Mark put another HE round into the wall and the man went to ground again.

The waiting game continued. Mark kept him pinned behind that wall while we started digging shallow connecting trenches between fighting positions. He'd give us updates every few minutes between shots. Every time the Taliban fighter exposed any part of himself, Mark made sure to let him know the American sniper was still watching him.

Even though they were hundreds of meters apart, there was something intensely personal about such moments in combat. All too often the enemy has no face, he is just a black blur moving in the shadows of a building, or hunkered down in a stand of trees. He's the human shape exposed by the muzzle flashes of his PKM. But here, with Mark's eye in his scope, he saw the man, his features and his face. It became a contest between two men on a battlefield where hundreds lurked. One-on-one, hunter and prey maneuvered for advantage. The Taliban wanted only to elude Mark's crosshairs and get his AK into the fight. Mark was determined to protect us on the hill from that outcome. And so he watched and waited like a raptor, looking for the moment where he could deliver the fatal strike.

The duel went on for almost two hours. The insurgent finally lost patience. Staying low, he tried to crawl away from the wall. Mark was ready, having already glassed all potential escape routes the insurgent could use. He'd mapped out the entire area around the wall, picking the best spots to take a shot. The Taliban fighter crawled right into one of those, and Mark put a round right into him. A .50 caliber HE round travels at 850 meters a second. That's enough kinetic energy to punch through a lightly armored vehicle. When such power impacts human flesh, the results are gruesome.

The man exploded.

Mark pulled his eye out of the scope only long enough to jot some notes down on his range card and drink a little water. Then without saying a word he shouldered Elvis again and looked for a new target.

I hadn't seen his shot. At length, I finally asked, "You get him?"

"Yep."

★ ★ ★

Just after noon, the enemy struck again. This time, they hit the 82nd platoon at Prius from Khasadar. The shooting started with a sudden outburst of AK-47s and PKMs as they laid down a base of fire to support a sudden rush from the south and southeast. Squad-sized elements broke cover, sprinting forward across open ground to get closer to Prius. The enemy was bounding and gaining a foothold around the COP.

"Andy, do you see what they're trying to do?" Mark asked.

"Yeah. They're attacking Prius. If they can push those guys out, they'll cut us off."

They couldn't knock us off the hill with small arms fire alone. They knew assaulting up Pathfinder would be suicidal. So they switched gears and sought to isolate us. Whoever was directing the enemy had a good tactical mind.

The enemy flowed up through Khasadar and pressed the attack. While the hill was not under heavy fire, the situation at Prius soon grew desperate. Knots of enemy kept bounding forward, closer and closer to the nascent COP despite the constant chatter of the 82nd and Italian machine guns, which had been positioned on rooftops.

Captain Perry, commander of Bravo Company, 1st of the 508th, 82nd Airborne Division, stood inside one of the Prius compounds and realized that if his men didn't get support, the enemy would soon be on top of them. He called Danny for help.

I was the only JTAC in the field. Fortunately, from my vantage point, I had a million-dollar view of the enemy attack. I could see exactly which compounds the enemy had already infested.

We picked one, got the grid, and prepared the 9-line. Danny called over to PRO 6 to get approval to drop.

The clock ticked. More Taliban broke cover and charged forward. They hopscotched from one compound to the next, getting closer to Prius.

"Danny?" I asked impatiently.

"Still working it," he said. I could imagine him sitting in the 82nd's operation center, a radio handset in each ear, trying to give us what we needed while talking to PRO 6, who no doubt was second-guessing us.

Mark fired Elvis as a large group surged forward toward Prius. Shooting this close to a friendly position required extremely precise accuracy.

"Come on, goddamnit! Come on," I whispered under my breath.

"Danny, they're pushing hard here," I said.

"Still waiting for approval," came the terse reply. I could hear the strain in Danny's voice. He only wanted to help us, but the circumstances left him trapped in the middle.

Another minute passed. I was ready to scream. Finally, Danny had an answer for me.

"Ski, they want another warning shot. Find someplace unoccupied that will work."

"You have got to be shitting me," was all I could manage. One of PRO 6's platoons was under direct assault by an enemy unafraid to maneuver in the open with a B-1 orbiting overhead, and he wanted to send them another message?

"How about between the two compounds southeast of Prius?" Danny offered.

"Roger."

We worked up the solution and fed the 9-line to the bomber crew. The B-1 broke out of its orbit for another run. The seconds passed—more time for the enemy to push forward. Soon they'd be too close to Prius to hit with a bomb. Maybe that was the whole point. They knew us and our tactics. They knew that they could negate our firepower advantage if they assaulted to point-blank range. In such a situation, we'd be unable to use aircraft or artillery to break up their attack.

"Cleared Hot!"

"One away," the bomber's crew finally called over the radio.

I let everyone on the hill know we had another bomb inbound. It freight-trained right into an empty field between two enemy-held compounds and exploded.

The enemy paused. Most stopped firing. Nobody broke cover. The momentum of the attack evaporated, as the Taliban tried to figure out what had just happened.

They must have decided we had missed, because within a minute or two, the fight was back on. They hammered Prius with RPGs, machine guns, and AK fire as their buddies bounded ever closer. The situation hadn't changed, and the enemy quickly regained their momentum.

"Danny," I said, trying to control my emotions. "This is not working. You have to tell PRO 6 these warning shots are not working."

"I already did," Danny said, his voice weary and frustrated.

"Listen to me, brother, this is getting out of control."

"I know."

"We have to stop this attack."

Captain Perry reported in and said the enemy had taken over two compounds about ninety meters from his men. They were fighting at point-blank range now. He gave the building numbers, and I took a hard look at them on my own GRG.

"If we wait any longer, we won't be able to do anything, Danny. They'll be right on top of Perry's men. They're 'danger close' as it is now with GBU-38s. We need to take out those compounds."

As long as the guys at Prius kept their heads down, and we put a 5 millisecond delay on the bomb, we could do this. The walls of the compound would contain the blast and the shrapnel, killing anyone inside but leaving the surrounding area unharmed.

This was what we were trained to do as fire-support guys. And we'd already worked up solid ten-digit grids to the compounds.

"Hold on," Danny replied. I hoped he had the juice to convince PRO 6; otherwise, it was about to get really ugly down there.

Rocket-propelled grenades exploded against Prius's outer walls. Machine gun fire laced the rooftop fighting positions where the Americans and Italians were sprawled on their stomachs. AK reports echoed through the valley. The Italians and 82nd paratroopers chewed through their ammunition at a furious pace as they tried to keep the enemy at bay.

"Okay, we are cleared to hit those compounds."

The gloves are coming off now. About fucking time.

We worked up the solution for the first compound and sent the 9-line to BONE. Once again, the pilots abandoned their orbit to execute another bomb run.

I warned everyone on the hillside that we had a GBU-38 coming in. Andy, George, Billy, Mikey, and I kept our eyes on the target, waiting with tense anticipation for the moment those inside firing at our comrades at Prius would finally get pummeled into the ground.

The bomb punched through the bottom of the cloud cover and speared

straight into the small building in the middle of the compound. The delay
on the bomb caused it to puncture the roof before detonating, sending a
huge ring of dirt, debris, and brown-gray smoke boiling laterally from
the impact point. Simultaneously, a thick black spout of smoke rocketed
hundreds of feet skyward.

Warheads on their foreheads. Direct hit.

We stared at the scene in awe of the bomb's power. A few cheers rose
among the men on the hilltop. Then George casually announced, "Well,
that compound is fucking gone."

Over the radio, Captain Perry called to Danny, "Holy shit! I felt the
heat of that one on my face!"

The Taliban inside the second closest compound fell silent after their
compatriots were obliterated by the JDAM. But that did not save them
from the same fate. Danny and I worked together to get the B-1 onto it, and
another five-hundred-pound bomb soon plunged down into the valley to
flatten that second Taliban position.

After that, the assault slowed, then stalled altogether. The paratroopers and Italians drove off the Taliban's final attack. By the time afternoon
prayer rolled around, the fighting had died down completely. We dug in
deeper while the enemy bowed to Mecca. Here and there, a scattered shot
rang out across the valley, but nothing like what we'd been facing throughout the day.

After prayers, the enemy began to move around again. A few groups of
reinforcements bubbled up from the ratline to run the gauntlet over to
Khasadar. Mark calmly thinned out their ranks. The ones who made it
joined the shattered remains of the Prius assault force. At the same time,
more fighters flowed north straight into Kapeh Baba. Mark interdicted
their movement, but we couldn't stop them all.

Within an hour, we were taking heavy small arms fire again and their
aim was getting better. Operating in two- or three-man teams, the enemy
slipped from building to building, shooting and scooting. They coun-
tered our airpower advantage with constant movement. With plenty of
ammo and rockets now, thanks to Zappala, we hammered back at them
every time we spotted their muzzle flashes.

Shortly before dusk, our B-1 departed to refuel and then head back to
Al Udeid Air Base in Qatar. The one that replaced it was flown by a female

pilot. When she checked in, her voice proved a surprising comfort in the midst of all the tension, frustration, and anger I had felt through the day. Her sweet voice was soothing, even over the flat tone of the headset radio.

I gave her a thorough brief on our situation, and it wasn't long before we had a target for her. We'd spotted a PKM crew inside a building due south of Pathfinder Hill in the heart of Kapeh Baba. I called Danny to start working clearance to drop a five-hundred-pounder on delay.

As we waited for PRO 6's answer, the team poured fire at the PKM crew. Small arms did little good, however. The thick-walled mud dwelling was as impervious to bullets as a World War II pillbox. The PKM kept chattering, and the gunner's long bursts chewed up the ground around our fighting positions.

Goddamnit, somebody's gonna get hurt while we're sitting here waiting for daddy to give us permission to fucking kill those bastards.

I checked my watch. Five minutes had passed since I sent the request to Danny. What the hell was PRO 6 doing?

The PKM went silent. The gunner was probably swapping out magazines. Our guys laid on their triggers and even popped a few M203 40mm grenades down their way. It did no good. The PKM blazed to life again from a different mouse hole. Another one opened fire from another compound. Our guys ducked as the 7.62mm rounds raked the hillside.

At last, Danny's voice crackled over the radio, "Ski, we are good. No civilians are in that compound."

I wanted to slam my head into the side of the berm.

No shit there aren't any civilians. Except for the fuckers shooting at us, the place is deserted.

Wait. A thought struck me. Was Danny sending me a message by telling me that? Is this what PRO 6 has been worried about? If so, how'd he know if someone was there or not? What the hell was going on?

We dropped another five-hundred-pounder, and the building collapsed onto itself in a cloud of smoke, flame, and dust.

Did we kill them? The PKM had gone silent a few minutes before the impact. Did they escape to another building?

The sun hung low over western mountains by this time. The enemy knew they had only about ninety minutes' worth of fighting left before darkness made continuing the battle impossible for them. They stepped up their rate of fire. Bullets swept across the hill again, snapping and whining past us.

The PKM gunner spewed short bursts at us, and nothing we did could suppress him. The mouse hole was no larger than a cantaloupe. All we could see was the muzzle flash of his weapon. The windows were shuttered and dark, no movement.

We needed to take that gun out. I radioed the situation to Danny. I gave him the compound's number on the GRG, and he told me he'd pass the request to PRO 6 for approval.

We had dropped five bombs so far. Two warning shots, three dead-on that produced casualties. I wanted to end the day on a high note, take out that stubborn son of a bitch on the trigger of that PKM and keep our guys safe.

The PKM went silent. I checked my watch. Three minutes since my request. No word yet from Danny.

Elvis boomed. Mark had found another target making a run from Kapeh Baba back toward the ratline. He must have been looking to escape the ass-whupping his pals had taken. At the same time, George was firing at something inside the village. Billy reloaded his SAW, sliding home another box magazine with 250 5.56 rounds. Mikey, Pat, and the other 82nd guys were on their weapons as well, as they had been all day. I saw weariness on everyone's face. We were all burnt out, exhausted, and tense as violin strings. Most of the ANA with us had punched out by this point. They'd get tired and simply stop fighting, no matter what the situation. Now, aside from the soldier with the Hulk Hogan do-rag, the whole lot of them had taken refuge in their holes. Hunkered down, out of the fight, they sat and smoked while the rest of us protected them.

The PKM opened fire again, causing heads to duck as the gunner traversed across our tiny hilltop. Bullets impacted on sandbags, cracked overhead, and slapped into the slope before us.

Eight minutes since my request. The B-1 was burning a hole in the sky, just waiting for the word to help.

"Danny, things are getting a little desperate here. Are we good to go?"

No response.

Ten minutes passed. The PKM crew reloaded again. As the gun peppered our positions, Danny finally answered.

"Ski, PRO 6 cannot positively confirm there are no civilians in the compound. We can drop one in the clearing next to it, but not on it."

"What?" I thought I was beyond being surprised by anything, but apparently I wasn't.

Danny repeated the directive.

"Andy?" I shouted over to him.

"Yeah, Ski?"

I explained what Danny just said.

"That's what PRO 6 wants you to do?" he asked, his voice devoid of emotion. Andy was supremely good at that. Always matter-of-fact and unflappable, he never conveyed any emotions that the team could pick up on or be affected by in the heat of the moment. To me, that was the hallmark of an incredible leader.

"Yes."

"Go ahead and do it."

"Roger that."

I called Danny. If we were going to do this silly bullshit, I wanted to push the boundaries to help the team as much as possible. We picked a spot about ten meters from the compound's outer wall. It wouldn't kill anyone in the building on the other side, but it would rattle the hell out of their nerves and hopefully rupture their eardrums.

The PKM gunner paused as I sent the 9-line to the bomber. I settled in for another interminable wait as the huge aircraft lined up on the target.

The PKM stayed quiet. I kept expecting the gunner to open back up, but they appeared to have either run out of ammunition or moved positions.

The female Lancer pilot announced the bomb was away. It was like sweet poetry to a ground pounder's ear.

Seconds passed. The PKM never opened back up. The bomb landed right beside the compound. Its blast scorched and blackened the outer wall but left everything inside intact.

As smoke snaked skyward from the impact point, I wondered how the hell PRO 6 was making his decisions. It took over twenty minutes to get that bomb dropped between the wait for his approval, recalculating the aim point, and the actual run on the target. For most of those twenty minutes, we were taking fire from that compound. I wondered how he would feel if one of our guys was hit or killed during that huge lag time in execution?

Something else nagged at me. These guys seemed to keep going quiet just before we got the bombs onto their location. Were they splitting out of the compounds, displacing to another part of the village and going to ground?

We took no further automatic weapons fire before sunset, but I knew we hadn't killed that machine gun crew. It seemed their timing could not have been better. As we struggled with our own chain of command, they had slipped away.

As darkness engulfed the battlefield, another thought nagged at me. How was PRO 6 confirming that there were no civilians in the compounds we bombed today? Was the NDS spook playing a part here? What about the rest of the Entourage? If that was the case, how the hell did they know? As far as I knew, they'd been at the Castle with PRO 6 all day.

This is all out of my hands, I have to work with what I've got. I can't get worked up about things I have no control over. But sooner or later whatever luck we have had is going to run out, and we are going to take casualties.

With night came a sharp drop in the temperature. By midnight, the thermometer had plunged into the single digits. The fighting may have ended, but there would be no rest for us. We dug in deeper, filled more sandbags, and took turns standing watch with our NVGs just to make sure the enemy didn't try and sneak up on us.

Danny, who hadn't been to sleep in two days, stayed up with us. All that night, he worked up new grids and TOTs (Time on Target) to the 81mm mortar section now based at COP Corvette to our northwest. He was determined to make sure the enemy would not sleep either, and so he pulled an old World War I trick out of his hat.

The mortar teams loaded their tubes with illumination rounds—star shells that are so bright, they turn night into day. We heard that distinctive hollow *thunk* as the crew fired their weapon. The round sailed over Kapeh Baba and detonated hundreds of feet in the air. For several minutes at a time, the battlefield was bathed in eerie, white artificial light. Anyone underneath surely must have felt a sudden sense of panic that they'd been detected and HE rounds were going to land next.

Wear the enemy down mentally; make him fatigued, not knowing if there is an assault force creeping just on the other side of the wall. Brilliant, Danny, brilliant.

Twenty-five minutes later another star shell appeared over Khasadar, followed by one farther south over the ratline.

Between the star shells, Mark stayed on the SASR, using night optics to search for targets in the valley. He saw not a single fire in any of the three villages. The Taliban could not risk giving up their location just to keep warm, so they suffered and froze in silence just like us.

If we weren't going to get any sleep, neither were they. Misery loves company.

22

★ MISERY LOVES COMPANY ★

Dawn found us shivering in our shallow graves, eyes scratchy from the ever present Afghan dust. Like talcum powder, it coated our faces, clung to our beards, and got into everything, including our weapons. Without sleep, the dust irritated our eyes to the point where we blinked and squinted constantly.

We had established a rest cycle, but I don't think anyone actually got any. Now, as a new day's worth of fighting appeared to be in our future, we waited for the enemy and cursed the bitter winter weather.

I left my position, leaving my MBITR (radio), and made my way through one of our connecting trenches past Mark and Andy and George. My radio needed a fresh set of batteries, so I figured with first light I'd go down to the RG and swap them out. On the east side of our position, Pat had dug in his M240 machine gun. He had a great view of the sun's rays just now spearing over the hilltops. I saw him sitting next to his weapon and staring out at the birth of the new day.

He must have sensed me watching him. He turned from the spectacular view and said, "Ski. How ya doing?"

I walked over next to him, and he handed me an energy drink.

"Rip It, the breakfast of champions," he said as he took a long pull from his own can.

I popped the lid and leaned back against the dirt wall of his emplacement.

"Smoke?" he asked, offering me one of his.

"Sure, thanks." I took the cigarette and lit up.

"We're the picture of fucking health this morning, aren't we?"

"Could go for some bacon and eggs right now," I admitted.

"No joke."

We smoked and watched the sun chase the morning shadows away as we chatted. I polished off the energy drink and finished my cigarette.

"You think Rob and Paddy will get out here in time for this shit today?" Pat asked as he tossed back the last of his Rip It. The two had been recalled to Herat for some intelligence work. Last we'd heard, they'd been trying like hell to get a seat on a helicopter to get back up to BMG. That was hit-or-miss, though.

"I think they are coming out on the resupply convoy this morning with Zappala. Sure hope they make it," I answered.

"Yeah. They were born for fights like this one. Like Billy and Mark and George."

"And you," I added. Pat was most certainly one of the meat eaters.

"Well, it sure beats the hell out of stocking shelves at Home Depot."

"Yeah, I bet face paint wasn't part of the dress code."

He laughed at that as he tossed his cigarette butt out onto the slope. "Yeah, that sucked. But you know, at least we know that there's something here, no matter how shitty it gets."

"Like?"

"Purpose, I guess."

Truth was, my sense of purpose had been rattled yesterday by all the weirdness with PRO 6.

"Well, I'd like to be left alone to carry out our purpose," I said with more than a little bitterness.

Pat nodded. "That stuff with PRO 6 is fucking retarded. He needs to get his boots on the ground and get a grasp of what's really going on here."

"I see no point in risking our lives like that. Can you imagine if somebody had been hit while we were waiting for permission to drop? And not drop on a real target, but drop on a fucking field?"

"Would've been ugly, that's for sure," Pat agreed. Then he undid his chin strap and pulled his helmet off. He ran one hand through his hair, which caused a plume of Afghan dust to billow from his head. We all were filthy—that's when you know you're having fun.

"Hey, Ski," Pat said, his voice softer and lower now. "Where's Joe been?"

I thought about that for a minute. "Well, he was up on the hill yester-day morning with Mark and me when we first got engaged. Not sure where he is now. Down at the trucks I suppose."

Pat shook his head. "His heart isn't in this," he said in frustration. "That's gonna cause us problems."

"Hard to be gung ho if your heart's not there, I guess."

"That's not it. There's something else."

"What?" I asked.

"I don't know. But when this is all done and we're back at the FOB, I'm going to find out what."

"How?"

"Joe and I need to clear some air."

With Andy on the hilltop, it made sense for Joe to be with our rigs. But Pat was right, our team chief, our Marine gunnery sergeant, should have been more present during the past twenty-four hours. His absence on the hill was noticed by everyone, and it was eroding his moral authority to lead us.

I changed the subject. "We need to find out what the fuck has been go-ing on with PRO 6. You know it took almost fifteen minutes for Danny to get an answer on the last drop yesterday?"

"I know. All the while, we're taking it in the ass."

"And then after all that wait, we're told to drop it next to the com-pound. That is fucking stupid, Pat. But there is something else that is not sitting well with me," I said.

"What?"

"That last bomb we dropped—the Taliban we were trying to kill . . ."

"Got away?"

"Last bomb for sure. Number six. They stopped firing and vanished just before we dropped the bomb."

"They sure as hell didn't hear it coming. Inbound aircraft are almost silent because the thrust is going away from you," Pat said.

"Exactly."

"So how did they know when to split?" I left Pat and I puzzled over it.

The sun now loomed above the eastern hilltops. The sky turned gold beneath the clouds. In the valley, the morning fog began to burn off. If things developed as they did yesterday, we'd be hit as soon as it lifted.

We were socked in again with thick clouds, no aircraft sensors. Fuck I hate this.

We waited in silence for the enemy to attack. The fog cleared. The sun rose above the clouds and vanished. The valley below remained still and quiet.

The morning dragged on. "Maybe they had enough yesterday," I offered.

"Don't bet on it," Pat replied, lighting another cigarette.

"MBTR's almost dead. Gotta go swap the batteries out," I said, turning back to Pat. "Thanks for the Rip It and smoke."

"Ski, be careful."

"You too, brother."

I pulled myself out of Pat's machine gun nest and walked down the east spine to the vehicles. First Sergeant Z's resupply convoy had made it out, and the men were unloading boxes of food, water, and ammo. Sure enough, Rob and Paddy had made it out to us. They'd already climbed a hill to the north to set up an observation post and protect that flank.

As I got closer to the rigs, I could see Jay standing watch in the turret of the GMV on the east end of our perimeter. Joe was sitting in the passenger seat of the RG-33 MRAP with the door open. I saw him and felt a sudden conflict within me.

Somebody had to be in charge of the vehicles, relay communications if need be, and do the myriad of things to support Andy as he directed the fight from the front. I guess.

There was something else going on here. Joe's words clung to my mind. The mission, this country, this fight—he didn't see it had any value. It certainly wasn't worth the life of any of his men, or his own. He'd grown bitter and had given up on our role in Afghanistan. Others had, too, but Joe's position within the team was so central that it couldn't help but affect us.

It wasn't about the mission or the war to me. At times, the way we were fighting bordered on the ridiculous. Thinking about that, investing everything in it, would only cause anguish. In that respect, I understood Joe completely. I couldn't hang myself out there for this war alone either.

Joe saw me come off the hilltop and nodded at me.

"Good morning Ski balls," he said.

God, I fucking hate that nickname.

I greeted him as I climbed into the MRAP through the back door. I'd stashed the MBITR's chargers inside. The fresh batteries were ready to go. I sat down, my feet on the back step, putting two charged batteries into my cargo pockets. A moment later, I placed the used one onto the charger.

First Sergeant Z's boys finished unloading. They saddled back up and rolled back to COP Prius.

Mission first, men always. Isn't that what the Army says?

This thing with Joe could get ugly. It was the first sign of division within the team. Anything that affected unity would impact each one of us. If it got bad enough, it could compromise our ability to function. It had happened before. Dysfunctional teams operating in combat never fared well. Not in MARSOC, not in Naval Special Warfare, and not with the Green Berets.

That ODA team we saw in action on November 6 was a prime example.

Boooom!

A ball of dirt and smoke erupted right next to the rear wheel of an unoccupied GMV about thirty meters from where I sat. I stared at it, wondering what had just happened. Did a tire on the GMV blow out?

A few seconds passed with my mind still processing the sight. Suddenly, a Taliban machine gun opened up to the east. Assault rifles joined in.

"Contact east . . . !"

More gunfire erupted to the south and southwest. Within seconds of the blast, Pathfinder Hill was engulfed in a latticework of crisscrossing streams of bullets.

Joe tried to radio Andy, but the hill had fallen silent. He tried again. Andy was off the net. So was everyone else. That was a terrifying development.

This is the main assault. I can feel it in my gut. And I'm stuck down here without a radio.

I grabbed my M4 and slid off the back of the RG. The last group of hills to the east formed a ridgeline running north–south only about 400 meters from Pathfinder. They were higher, too. That meant if the enemy was on that ridge, they'd be able to fire *down* at the hill and into the trenches.

The guys are in a bad spot.

I started to run, then held up. The RG was safe. I could ride out this entire attack if I stayed inside it. The path up to the crest and the rest of the team was totally exposed to anyone on that ridgeline to the east. I'd be running through the line of fire if I went up there.

Joe's right. The mission, this war, isn't worth the blood it is costing us.

I took a step. Pat's 240 roared to life. He fired a short burst, paused, and adjusted. Then he laid on the trigger. The frantic burst he tore off echoed the desperation of the moment. Defensive, furious, it was a back-to-the-wall, *pour-all-the-lead-you-have* sort of gesture. Holding the trigger down like that would melt the barrel for sure. Pat didn't care. It was his only gambit to force the enemy to take cover.

It wasn't working.

The mission may not be worth dying for, but living without doing everything for these men would not be living.

Your brothers. Your brothers are worth it.

I started to run. The weight of my gear was crushing, but I kept moving, the thought of my brothers filling me with resolve. I reached the trail and began picking my way up the spine toward Pat's machine gun. I could see the tongue of flame spouting from the 240's barrel. I could hear the mini–sonic booms of AK and PKM bullets passing overhead. I sprinted into the full fury of the firefight, my back to the enemy as I struggled to reach the summit. I could see rounds impacting against the slope up ahead, could see them smacking into the sandbags crowning Pat's machine gun nest. Each burst from that PKM made me hunch my shoulders, the sense of exposure so intense that all my instincts screamed. I kept moving, sucking air from exhaustion.

"Marine coming in! Marine coming in!" I shouted.

"Ski! What the fuck are you doing?" Pat yelled.

Ryan, our team's SARC, was next to Pat, his rifle leveled and blazing. I reached the crest as bullets raked across the hillside.

"Ski! Get in here!" Ryan bellowed.

Panting now, I dove into the trench that ran into Pat's emplacement.

"Where are they?" I shouted.

An RPG sizzled past and exploded behind us. I glanced back and saw that it had detonated in midair. A second one followed and did the same, spraying the hilltop with shrapnel. Something else impacted into the ground and blew up. RPG? Mortar? Didn't know, didn't care.

"Where are they?" I asked again. Ryan pointed to the east ridgeline.

I flung myself against the east-side wall and brought my M4 up over the sandbags. There, on the nearest ridge to the east, I saw them. Muzzle flashes—lots of them—winked and flared along that crest. And then I saw two figures in the distance. One was wearing a black head wrap and brown man dress.

I put my sights on him and pulled the M4's trigger. *Pop!*

I turned the weapon on its left side and saw the 5.56 round stuck between the bolt and the ejection port's opening.

You've got to be fucking kidding me.

"Jam!" I told Pat and Ryan as I took a knee and tried to clear it. I pulled the charging handle back as hard as I could, but it did no good. I dropped the mag out and tried again. No luck.

Pat tore through his ready ammo. Another rocket exploded overhead. I heard men shouting all around the hill.

I couldn't get the weapon clear. In frustration, I looked around and saw Pat's M4 resting against the berm. I reached over, snatched it up, and got back up on the wall.

"I'm out," Pat reported as his gun went silent. Automatically, Ryan and I popped back over the parapet and covered him as he reloaded the machine gun. Pat's M4 had an ELCAN 3 power scope, and as soon as I put my eye into it, I saw Black Headdress again. He stood up, the top two-thirds of his body exposed over the ridge as he shouldered his AK. As I pulled my trigger, I saw the muzzle flashing.

The man disappeared behind the ridge. Had we hit him? There was no way to know, and no time to wonder. His nearest pal was blazing away at us with his weapon. Ryan was silent and focused as he unloaded the rest of his magazine on him.

I ducked down to reload just as Pat finished laying a new belt in the 240's feed tray. A heartbeat later, the weapon roared again. One of his tracers hit an insurgent center mass. The enemy dropped like a stone behind the crest. It was an incredible shot.

I could hear rifle and machine gun fire coming from Kapeh Baba. More gunfire echoed in the distance, too far away for me to get a fix on it. Were they hitting Prius, too? I couldn't tell. I needed to get eyes on what we were facing, then get bombs on these assholes. But I couldn't do that without my radio, my GRGs, and the rest of my gear.

I looked down the trench line. My stuff was over on the southwest side, where most of the rest of the team had dug in. Pathfinder's crest was tiny, only a few dozen meters long, but crossing it in the middle of this storm looked anything but appealing.

I can't just stay here and not do everything I can. Me shooting a rifle doesn't help the team.

"Fuck this! This shit ends now," I said aloud to myself.

Another explosion rocked the hilltop. The pissed-off hornets swarmed just above our heads. The battle's intensity seemed to surge. The enemy sensed they'd seized the upper hand, and they threw everything they had at us to exploit it. There was no way to wrest fire superiority from them. They had us outnumbered and outflanked.

I put Pat's M4 beside him and turned to run down the trench, staying as low as I could. I moved down the trench to the crest; the main team position lay just on the other side. When I ran up over it, I stopped suddenly, surprised by the sight that greeted me. George, Mark, and Andy were all tucked down in their fighting positions, hugging the ground. The nearby ANA and paratroopers were doing the same thing—all except for one soldier named Cory Ballinger, who sat almost completely exposed behind an M2 .50 caliber machine gun, hammering away at Kapeh Baba without any regard to the incoming fire tearing up our position.

"SKI! GET DOWN!" somebody screamed at me. The sense of urgency in his voice kicked my heart rate up. I dove for the nearest hole and landed atop somebody already at the bottom.

"Mikey! Mikey!" Heath, our other medic, yelled over the .50 cal.

A rash of machine gun fire clawed the ground. Bullet spouts erupted seemingly everywhere at once. The enemy on the east ridge had a grandstand view of this side of the hill. The trench I was in crossed Pathfinder east to west. They could see down into it and walk their fire through it without any obstructions.

This is bad, real bad.

"Mikey! You okay?" Mark cried out. I'd never heard his voice like that before.

"What's going on?" I asked.

The man below me shifted. I looked down and realized I was lying on Mikey.

Heath was in the next hole over. I heard him, his voice shaky, wailing, "Mikey, stay with me man. Stay with me."

Mikey looked at me with saucer eyes.

An RPG sizzled over the hill, blowing up over the west-side slope.

"You okay?"

His head tilted forward. Blood poured from under his helmet and flowed down the side of his head into the dirt wall of the hole.

"Mikey, what happened?"

Dazed and unfocused, with effort he looked back up at me. "Hit," he said woozily, "in the head."

"What?"

"It's okay, though. I'm all right."

23

★ This Ends Now ★

DAY TWO

FIGHTING POSITION, SOUTHWEST CORNER, PATHFINDER HILL

"Mikey, did you just say you got shot in the head?"

"Yeah. I'm fine."

"You're shitting me," I said, dumbfounded.

Billy, who was only a few feet away in his own hole, exclaimed, "No fucking way."

I shifted around so I could get a better look at Mikey. "Hey, let me check you out."

Billy's voice rose over the sounds of the battle. "No fucking way. I don't believe it."

He was behind an M240 instead of his SAW at the moment, and I glanced up over the lip of the berm to see what was going on. Billy was staring southward, binos to his eyes.

"They're massing at the treeline behind Kapeh Baba. Can you see this shit, Mark?"

Mark was crawling back down the trench toward his position as the enemy to the east kept a steady fire on us. As he moved, he cradled his M4 with his elbows.

"No man. They hit Elvis. Gimme a minute."

Mark had been shooting at an RPG gunner 550 meters away on the south side of Kapeh Baba when the burst that hit Mikey swept across his position, too. A brass-sheathed bullet struck Elvis and knocked Mark back into his hole. A bit of metal cut Mark under the chin at the same time another rash of automatic weapons fire flayed the space between him and Jamie's hole. The two men ducked down as Elvis caught fire. The weapon had been hit in the magazine well, and the enemy bullet had touched off one of the .50 cal rounds just beneath the chamber. A fire flared in the magazine, which could have caused all the HE rounds inside to detonate. But as it burned, Andy had jumped out of his fighting position, grabbed the rifle, and pulled the magazine out.

Mark reached his position and brought his M4 up into the little firing loop he'd created with sandbags.

"Can't see," he told Billy.

"Six to eight dudes. Six hundred meters in front of the treeline now. Comin' straight for us," Billy reported. He had a note of eagerness in his voice that seemed out of place in the desperation of the moment.

"Get some now," I heard him add.

Heath cried out, "Mikey! Mikey, are you okay?"

"Heath, shut the fuck up. I'm checking him now," I said.

I put my fingers around the back of Mikey's head and gingerly slid them under his helmet. I felt skin. Then hair. Then bone and blood.

I probed around further. The bullet had hit Mikey's helmet, which deflected it enough to keep it from penetrating his skull. Instead, it rode around the side of Mikey's head, leaving an ugly red halolike wound that was bleeding badly, but was not life-threatening.

Heath cried out again. He and Mikey were close friends, and the shock of him getting hit had clearly shaken Heath.

"Heath," I said sternly. "Stop yelling! The bullet didn't penetrate. He's bleeding, but he's gonna live."

I grabbed some gauze from my medical pouch and held it to the back of Mikey's head.

"Jack, throw me my GoBook," I called.

A moment later, he slid it over the side of the berm, and I opened it up.

"Andy, I'll get whatever I can onto the east ridge."

"Go for it," he said.

"Here they come!" Billy shouted. The enemy squad broke cover and sprinted for the south side of Kapeh Baba. Billy rode the 240's trigger eagerly, strafing back and forth as they ran. Next to me, the 82nd Airborne paratrooper, Cory Ballinger, spotted them too. His .50 cal roared. I was so close to its barrel that the sound nearly deafened me.

"Whoa! Did you see that?" somebody yelled. "Cory just nailed that bastard carrying an RPG!"

Mark reported, "Can't do shit with this M4."

He reached for Elvis. "Heath, get over here and help me."

The bullet hole in the mag well made it impossible to load a fresh magazine into the weapon. That wasn't going to stop Mark from using it. Quickly, he cleaned it out. The fire had left all sorts of crud and carbon inside the weapon, which he expertly removed in a matter of seconds.

Heath crawled over to Mark's position.

"You load. I'll shoot," Mark told him.

"Okay."

Mark racked Elvis's bolt. Heath slammed home a .50 cal round.

"Ready," he reported.

Mark shouldered the weapon and looked for a target. An RPG exploded overhead. Another one hit the south slope and shook the hillside. The machine gun to the east traversed back and forth across our positions, driving everyone to ground again.

Except the ANA soldier with the yellow do-rag. He popped up onto the berm and blazed away to the south with a PKM machine gun on his hip.

"That fuckin' guy is an animal!" one of the 82nd guys said.

My GoBook finished booting up and I tried to move the cursor using the touchpad with my right hand. Nothing happened. Frustrated, I tried again. The cursor wouldn't move. I glanced down. I'd smeared Mikey's blood all over the touchpad and the computer's outer casing.

I wiped my fingers clean while still holding the gauze to Mikey's head. At the same time, I needed to get my GRG. I clearly didn't have enough hands for this.

"HALO 14, this is Barbarian Fires," Danny called over the radio.

I seized the handset and replied, "Barbarian Fires, HALO 14. Go."

"BONE inbound, fifteen minutes out."

Shit. We have no air in the middle of this crap.

"Andy," I shouted. "Got a bomber en route, fifteen minutes out. Will work something else."

"Roger."

"Barbarian Fires, this is HALO 14. Fire mission, over!"

"Fire mission, out."

We had access to the 81mm mortars at COP Corvette. Though they wouldn't be nearly as effective as a bomb, at this point we needed anything and everything we could dump on the east ridge.

Together, Danny and I worked up the fire mission and plotted the grid. The 81mm crew fired a single aiming round. It landed long.

"Shot, over!"

I called in the adjustment, and a second one struck a minute or two later. It didn't have any effect on the incoming fire, so obviously we weren't on target yet.

We'd dropped two more rounds as BONE did a hasty check-in with Danny.

"Now we can do some damage," I said to myself. Then I glanced at Mikey. "How ya holdin' up?"

"I'm fuckin' fine," he said, still dazed. The bullet had concussed him badly.

"Andy, I want to drop a two-thousand-pounder on the east ridge."

"I trust ya, Ski."

This time, we weren't going to ask PRO 6 for permission and go through that agonizing bullshit again. With Mikey wounded and the men under accurate fire, Andy was well within his rights as ground force commander to make this call. We'd let the chips fall where they may once Danny relayed what we were doing to PRO 6.

From the ridge came the distinctive sound of an RPG launch. The guy must have taken his time to aim because this one flew straight and true— right at Mark. For a split second, our sniper thought it would actually hit him. Instead, it passed just above his position and exploded somewhere above the west-side slope.

I had to block out all the craziness unfolding around me to focus on the task at hand. I was able to get the GoBook to work and dropped the cursor on the east side of the ridge. That allowed me to pull a ten-digit grid coordinate. Okay, we had our target point.

"BONE, from HALO 14, prepare to copy 9-line, over."

"BONE 21, send it."

"This is a type-2 control, lines one, two, and three from the overhead . . ."

I wanted that two-thousand-pounder to land right in the middle of those assholes on the ridge. But if we did that, we'd run the risk of friendly casualties if the bomb missed and fell on our side of the ridge. The vehicles would be "danger close", and so would the rest of us on the hilltop. So I plotted a target point farther down on the back side of the ridge. It put the rigs a hundred meters from the impact point, but the terrain would angle the blast up and over them. And us, too.

"BONE—" I started to say into the radio, but Ballinger chose that moment to go absolutely crazy on the Ma Deuce. The weapon's din drowned out my words and made thinking almost impossible. The man was a spectacle of courage.

This is why I love the 82nd. They have heart and balls.

He eased off the trigger and I used the short break to confirm the 9-line with the B-1 crew. There'd be no second-guessing. PRO 6 was out of the equation.

"BONE 21, In from the east," the pilot called.

The morning was overcast and ugly gray, just like the others since we got here. I watched the bottom of the scud layer, waiting for a glimpse of the massive GBU-31 certain to come plummeting down at any second.

If you screwed up this one, Ski, you could get a lot of the team killed.

I pushed the thought from my head. Too late to second-guess myself. I had to trust in my abilities.

"One away," the pilot reported. I relayed it to the team.

The loud, thundering sound of the B-1 passing overhead forced the enemy to ground. The firing had stopped as the JDAM plunged through the air. I pictured the Taliban racing down the back side of the east ridge, hoping to get clear before we hit it.

You can't run. Destiny is always on the side of the bomb.

There! The GBU-31 punched through the cloud layer and dropped dead on target. It struck the slope and 5 milliseconds later detonated.

There is no possible way to describe the magnitude of force unleashed by such a weapon. To see it up close, to feel its effects cause the earth beneath you to shudder violently as a gray-black mushroom cloud shoots hundreds of feet skyward—is beyond the senses to process. All who witnessed that explosion went silent for a moment. Then on the hilltop, cheers rang out along with a few "holy shits."

"That's the end of those guys," Andy said matter-of-factly.

The southern force arrayed against us inside Kapeh Baba suddenly went nuts. They must have known what the blast meant, and they unloaded everything they had on us in a hailstorm of bullets and rocket-propelled grenades.

"I am targeting the village now," I yelled over to Andy. The smoke from the GBU-31 continued to rise, merging with the cloud layer overhead. It was almost an apocalyptic sight.

"Mikey, you're going to have to hold the gauze," I said.

"Yeah, okay," he replied and reached up under his helmet to free up my hand.

"We'll get Ryan over here to bandage you up in a minute. Just keep pressure on it."

"I got it. I'm fine."

"You sure?"

"Yeah, Ski. Just a motherfucker of a headache."

With Mikey taken care of, I turned my attention to Kapeh Baba. Poking my head up over the berm, I tried to figure out where the enemy was hiding, where the best place was to put one. I was going to need Mark's help for this one. Until I could get a fix on them, we were at the mercy of all their incoming.

I brought my binos up as I asked our sniper, "Mark, which compound? Let's end this shit."

"They've been moving around all along the south side," he reported between shots. Heath reloaded each time for him.

I watched carefully and soon saw muzzle flashes winking from mouse holes in the walls. These guys were good. They kept us guessing, and they stayed fluid. Rushing from one compound to another, they made it difficult for me to get a bomb on them. By the time I had a grid and 9-line ready to go, they'd shift positions and make the drop pointless. I didn't want to waste a single bomb today. The taxpayers had been shafted the day before, so this was the reckoning.

Without warning, an ANA soldier suddenly rose from his hole. It was the guy with the yellow do-rag. Tall and lanky, he hefted a rocket-propelled grenade launcher. He looked as skinny as the tube. Screaming, he climbed out of his position and ran through the maelstrom of lead straight down the slope toward Kapeh Baba with his shaggy surfer's hair streaming behind him.

"Where the fuck does he think he's going?" George asked Mark.

"Who the hell knows. But that's the ballsiest thing I've ever seen one of those guys do."

He ran another twenty or thirty feet, then dropped to one knee. Oblivious to the bullets chewing the ground around him, he shouldered the launcher and took aim at one of the enemy-held compounds. Flames vented from the RPG's rear as he triggered the weapon. The warhead blazed down into the village, exploding right on target. He stood back up and ran up the hill and gave us a thumbs-up as he passed.

Perfect shot. If every Afghan solider was like this guy, we'd be out of a job here.

"Did that really just happen?" George asked.

"Yes. Yes it did," Mark said.

"Don't mess with the Zohan!" somebody shouted. Billy let out a long, bellowing laugh. Then we all started laughing. The tension of the moment broke. The ANA had a hero, and now he had a nickname.

"Zohan!"

He jumped back into his hole, smiling as he picked up his machine gun, and let fly from the hip again.

The fight continued, and gradually it became apparent that the enemy was relying on three compounds in close proximity to each other. This triangle must have been where they'd stashed extra ammo, food, or water, because they kept returning to them. They must have grown tired of moving around, as the majority of the enemy seemed to drift back there. Soon, the incoming largely originated from those three structures.

It was time to take them out. But what would be the best way? I thought about this as I studied the compounds. Muzzle flashes winked from mouse holes in their walls. The compounds were in such close proximity, I thought I could destroy all three with a single two-thousand-pounder. If it worked, we could break their back with one blow. The other option would be to drop three five-hundred-pounders, each targeted to a compound. But that would take a lot of time to work up and to drop. By then, the enemy might have moved, or PRO 6 might try to interfere.

Fuck it. I bet we can get all three if I drop a GBU-31 on the road between them.

I radioed Danny. This would be a tricky one, as we wouldn't be dropping on a building already numbered and preprogrammed on the GRG.

"Danny, this is HALO, over."

"HALO, this is PRANKSTER 42, send it."

Who the fuck is PRANKSTER 42?

Matt was his name and he had just jumped off a helo from Herat. He had rushed to the COC and linked up with Danny. Turned out, he was the 82nd's JTAC that was supposed to be here for the beginning of Good Morning/Buongiorno. Due to bad weather, he'd been delayed along with Paddy and Rob. Now he was in the hot seat with little time for a friendly introduction. We needed to put a bomb on the ground.

Matt started talking to the B-1 crew, and they made a radar pass over Kapeh Baba using the SAR (Synthetic Aperture Radar) to generate the coordinates we would need. The SAR paints a radar image of the surface of the earth for the bombardier to study, creating a ghostly silhouette of anything car-sized or larger. Matt did a beautiful job working with the bomber, and after that one run we had our target point dialed in.

The B-1 banked into a 180 degree turn and came back on the bomb run.

"Cleared Hot," I heard PRANKSTER say over the radio.

Matt had literally just shownd up to BMG a few minutes ago and he was already dropping a bomb. This place is awesome.

"One away!" I yelled to the hill.

This time, we'd set the bomb to detonate on impact. No delays. It would strike the ground and explode, causing maximum damage to everything in its blast radius.

The bomb fell four miles, its fins navigating based on feedback from its GPS guidance system. A long wait later, we saw it fall out of the cloud layer sounding like a freight train passing by. Everyone in the valley could hear it coming, but it was too late to react.

It struck Matt's target point with incredible accuracy. One second, the southern half of Kapeh Baba looked like any other abandoned Afghan village. The next, it was smothered in dirt, dust, smoke, and flame. A cyclone of debris spewed outward. Rocks, chunks of walls, plaster, glass, metal, tree limbs, and tree trunks spun through the air in a huge arc. The village disappeared, utterly consumed by the bomb's power. The roiling mass of smoke and dust gushed upward, looking again like a mushroom cloud. To the uninitiated, it would have seemed as if a small tactical nuke had been touched off.

It felt that way, too. When the pressure wave struck Pathfinder, you could feel it pushing the air around us as the ground quaked violently. When the explosion's rumble finished echoing through the valley, cheers arose from all over the hill. We even heard a few from Prius.

The firing stopped. If there was anyone still alive in the village, they'd be choking on dust and smoke for a while, their eardrums surely blown out. That was great for us, though I would not be able to get another bomb on Kapeh Baba until we had decent visibility again.

What next?

We need to cut off the village. Make sure those left can't escape, and those in the ratline heading north can't reach it.

Just north of Objective Fiesta ran the treeline where Billy had seen the enemy massing earlier in the fight. The foliage ran along an irrigation ditch that eventually dumped into the wadi system they'd been using to conceal their movements. At the edge of the ditch stood a small mud hut on a little hill. With our optics, we'd seen an enemy fighter passing stuff, most likely extra magazines of ammunition and RPGs, to the insurgents pushing up into Kapeh Baba. Danny relayed intel to us that the hut was their last jump-off point before they went into the fight. They'd stationed some of their leaders at the hut, and according to what we'd been picking up through our various networks, the fighters were getting last-minute briefs from them.

This seemed like a logical thing to blow up next.

"Hey, Andy?"

"Yeah, Ski?"

"Can we take out that ratline?"

"What are you thinking?" he asked.

I sketched my idea. Andy approved. Danny, Matt, and I went to work, plotting the grid. The B-1 loitered overhead, ready to deliver on target when we provided the 9-line.

We dropped two GBU-38 five-hundred-pound bombs simultaneously. One hit the hut with such force that all that remained when the smoke cleared was a blackened crater. The other we had set to air-burst over the treeline. Anyone inside the irrigation ditch would have been shredded by shrapnel as the explosion blasted the trees to matchsticks. If they tried to use that route again, we'd now be able to see them in the ratline through the new clearing the bomb created. Seeing the ratline consumed in flames and smoke possessed its own terrible beauty, a sight only an infantryman could love.

We'd just finished those two drops when the remaining enemy in Khasadar hit Prius again. The attack was pressed with fanatical intensity driven by fear, as the Taliban recognized they were now trapped. They couldn't fall back without running the risk of a JDAM landing on them, or Mark and Elvis hunting them down. They couldn't stay in place for much longer without running out of food and water. So they tried to execute their original mission.

Mark talked me onto a compound where he was seeing activity. Through our optics, we could see them running around the courtyard, climbing makeshift ladders, popping up over the wall, and firing into Prius. It was only a few dozen meters south of the compound the A-10 hit during the November 6 blue-on-blue incident. Working as the eyes and ears for Danny and Matt in the COC, I located the compound on the GRG and relayed the building number.

"One away!"

It was so close to Prius we had everyone on the rooftops hunker down and wait for the blast to pass.

The two-thousand-pounder on delay dropped right on the enemy's heads. The bomb blew the compound to dust and rubble but amazingly left the massive perimeter walls standing even as another massive mushroom cloud shot skyward. As I watched the scene, something caught my eye. At first, it didn't register. There was a piece of debris sailing upward above the top of the mushroom cloud.

No. Not a piece of debris.

"Is that a person?"

Billy spotted the man also, cartwheeling, arms out hundreds of feet above the impact point. "I've seen some shit in my time, but this . . ."

The Taliban's momentum slowed. One more cartwheel and he seemed to hover midair for just a second, like a scene from an old Warner Brothers cartoon. Then he fell into the mushroom cloud and disappeared.

24

★ ENEMY INSIDE THE WIRE ★

PREDAWN, DAY THREE, DECEMBER 29, 2009
PATHFINDER HILL

"Hey, Mark?"

I glanced over to see George looking at our sniper. The morning was bitingly cold, and I was still in my bag trying to hold on to what little warmth my body produced.

"Yeah?" Mark answered.

"Could you smell any worse right now?"

Mark sniffed an armpit. "Have you been over by the ANA guys recently?"

"Those guys always smell like shit," Billy said as he lay at the bottom of his hole, eating an MRE, a can of Rip It next to him. He was a brawler and looked almost larger than life—Hollywood's version of an action star. A big old gator-wrestling fellow with an intensity about him that intimidated the crap out of people who didn't know him. Billy's default setting always seemed to be *Front Toward Enemy*. But this morning, it was clear the last seventy-two hours had taken its toll even on him. He looked less badass and more bedraggled warrior with his raccoon eyes and layers of grime on his face and hands.

"Hey, Billy, got any crackers?" Andy asked. Billy flicked him one of the pouches from his MRE. Andy tore it open with his teeth and began to eat.

George pressed the stench issue. "No, seriously, Mark. You've got a funk that's burning my lungs. What's the matter with you?"

"This from the fucker who's afraid to get sweat on his Gucci gear," Mark fired back. George had bought his own very expensive flak vest and helmet, and the guys constantly ribbed him over it.

"No man, I'm telling you, you've got a glandular problem or something."

"You're probably smelling yourself, George," Andy added.

"You need to get that checked out."

"George, you need a tampon. For your mouth," Mark fired back.

I put my head down and started laughing.

"Verbal diarrhea," Billy agreed.

Ryan weaved down the trench line toward us. "Hey, guess what the 82nd dug up?"

"More fucking Afghan dirt?" somebody quipped.

"No."

Ryan moved between us, still in the trench, which was now so deep we didn't need to crawl through it, just bend over slightly to stay below the enemy's line of fire.

"They found a body."

"What the fuck?"

"Well, bones anyway," Ryan added.

"We're sitting in a graveyard?" Billy asked incredulously.

"No," Ryan answered. "Probably a Russian soldier."

Everyone fell silent. It wasn't a villager or Taliban fighter, as their graves would be marked with the flags we'd seen on the hill outside Daneh Pasab. No, he had to be a Russian, a warrior from a long-forgotten conflict, missing for maybe three decades. And here in the midst of our own battle atop this hill, the paratroopers had uncovered a soldier's grave.

"They found a femur. Some other stuff."

"Someone's fucking leg bone. Awesome," said George.

Ryan made his way over to Mikey to begin checking over his bandages and wound. During a lull in the fighting yesterday, Ryan had taken good care of our wounded man. Now he fussed over him like an attentive parent.

"I'm okay," Mikey protested. He'd said it so much, it'd become his mantra. He'd refused to be evacuated off the hill, despite the pain the bullet caused him. He was still concussed and dizzy, but his eyes had regained focus. He wasn't going to let being shot in the head keep him from fighting alongside his brothers. Whether he liked it or not, though, Andy was going to send him back to the FOB as soon as First Sergeant Z showed up with the next convoy.

"Shut up. Let me do my job," Ryan ordered.

"What are we going to do with the remains?" Mark asked.

Nobody answered for a long moment, perhaps thinking about this Russian soldier's fate. None of us would want to spend eternity here. The American military goes to extraordinary lengths to make sure we come home: living, broken, or dead. There are forensic teams still scouring World War II battlefields in search of our MIAs.

Not so with the Russians. Abandoned by his brothers, his body left atop this anonymous hill as the Red Army scurried back across the Turkmenistan border in 1989 as his family waited for news of his fate. It seemed a terribly lonely end for somebody so far from home.

"Maybe just bury them back in the ground," I suggested.

It was the least we could do given our situation. No one would ever claim the bones. His family would never know his final resting place. So perhaps it was best to just leave him where he died.

"Hey Mark?"

"Fuck you, George."

"Still wanna tell us how rough the Dallas PD was?"

"Fuck you twice, George."

Billy looked out over the valley and said, "Fog's burned off. Seems weird not to be killing people right now. We haven't fired a shot since yesterday evening."

"Nice not to be shot at for once, though," Jack replied. He'd been sitting in his hole by Mikey's position, listening to the banter but not contributing much.

"Well, maybe they really are done," I said.

"Maybe," Billy answered as he finished another MRE.

We waited for the enemy's next move, but not with the same level of tension we had yesterday, thanks to our intel section. They'd been listening to the enemy's communications and deduced why their attack on day two had started so late in the morning.

Each evening, the cell tower in the valley shut off, killing phone service throughout BMG until after dawn. This was done partly to conserve fuel for the generator that powered it, but also as a result of pressure from the Taliban on the tower's operator, who lived on site. The Taliban wanted to ensure we couldn't track their cell signals and pinpoint where they slept at night. They knew we'd come and get them as soon as we figured out where they bedded down. Cutting cell service for the entire valley was a way to ensure nobody got careless and violated their own operational security rules.

While the first day had seen the enemy launch a local counterattack as soon as the fog had lifted, their assault on day two had required thorough planning and close coordination. To hit us simultaneously from three sides meant they needed to communicate, something they couldn't do without their cell phones. So they waited for the tower to come back on, then jumped off.

We figured they'd try something similar today. The morning had been quiet, marred only by a few distant shots somewhere farther down the valley. We enjoyed the momentary respite, eating and bullshitting and digging in even deeper.

Ryan finished up with Mikey and started back for his own hole. As he passed me, he said, "Your wife would've been pretty fucking unhappy with you yesterday, Ski."

"Fucking fighting hippie. Peace, love, boom," George added.

"Dropping bombs on shitheads is very Zen."

"Doesn't that sort of thing mess with your tree-hugging karma?"

"Karma's a bitch, Billy. And sometimes it comes in the form of a GBU-31."

"Those guys on the east ridge discovered that yesterday," Mark said.

"Dan said it killed at least fifteen," Andy agreed

"What's he think their strength is now?" Jack asked.

"From the sound of it, they're pretty beat down. Not sure how many they've got left," Andy replied as he dug into another MRE pouch.

"Seems like they've always got more to backfill the fuckers we kill."

Billy had a point. It seemed like the Taliban had an endless supply of willing bodies to throw at us. Whether money or religion or ideology motivated them, they'd keep coming at us no matter how we raked their ranks with our firepower. We may have inflicted a lot of casualties on them these past two days, but I don't think any of us really believed they were done yet. So we stayed alert, bantering back and forth as we kept watch over the east ridge, Kapeh Baba, and Khasadar.

Around noon, a helicopter appeared over the western mountains. It was an old Soviet-era Mi-8 Hip transport bird, flown by contract Russian pilots who, rumor had it, were usually drunk off their asses when in the air. They terrorized other helicopter crews, as they flew without regard to airspace rules or procedures and could barely speak English. At times, they would land simultaneously as another bird tried to take off from the opposite direction. As crazy as they were, they'd been bringing most of the supplies into FOB Todd since Good Morning began three days before.

The helo dropped directly down onto the landing pad to minimize exposure to enemy gunfire. Whenever a resupply bird arrived, everyone available on the FOB would turn out to help unload so it could get out of Dodge as fast as possible. If they weren't working on wounded men, the surgical support team would always be the first to come out to offer a hand.

The sound of a second Mi-8 filled the valley. These were the same helicopters that supported the Soviet occupation in the 80s. Their engines were heard by an entire generation of soldiers and mujahideen. I wondered if some of the senior leaders we were facing right now carried memories from their youth of that noise. Those who held this hill all those decades ago had seen those Mi-8s as a lifeline as surely as the enemy saw them as juicy targets for their American Stinger antiaircraft missiles.

The first bird rose above the FOB and buzzed off for Herat. The second came in and touched down. The crew of this one shut down their twin Klimov TV3 turboshaft engines. Apparently, they were going to stay for lunch, risk to their bird be damned. The Italians had good food, and everyone tried to take advantage of it when they could, even drunk Russian pilots who ought to have known better.

The valley grew quiet again. We chatted and smoked and used our optics to keep eyes on the playing field.

In the distance, shots rang out. Heavy, thick-sounding, the signature of an AK-47.

"That sounded like it came from the FOB," Billy said, alarmed.

A second or two passed and we heard a single crack of an M4.

The radio erupted in chatter. Andy tried to make sense of it. So did I, but it seemed like everyone was talking at once.

Andy finally picked up enough to figure out what was happening. "There's been a shooting on the FOB, I think it was a green-on-blue," he told us. "One American wounded."

"How bad?" Jack asked.

"They didn't say."

Heads came up above every position on Pathfinder Hill. We looked around at each other in stunned silence. Green-on-blue meant one of the Afghans on the FOB had attacked an American. These incidents had increased over the past few years as the Taliban penetrated the ANA and ANP. They were close to becoming the leading cause of NATO casualties.

"Who's down?" Mark asked. At such times, names are never mentioned over the radio, but each man has a number attached to him and those sometimes are shared over the net. Andy didn't recognize the number, so it was not one of the few guys from the team left back at FOB Todd with our intel section.

Unconsciously, our eyes shifted to the ANA with us. Would they do something like this to us?

Zohan was sitting behind his machine gun, his yellow do-rag now so filthy it looked almost brown. His face was set. He looked grim, even angry. Khybar, our terp that was with us had passed along the news. The other Afghans smoked and said nothing. Whatever trust we'd extended to our allies had taken a big hit this morning. Aside from Zohan, the rest of the lot we'd have to watch closely from now on.

This is Afghanistan, the enemy is everywhere. Sometimes right next to you.

Andy's radio lit up again. He listened to a report and shook his head.

"What's the word?" George asked him.

Andy didn't say anything at first. We waited in silence, eyes casting glances at the ANA in our midst. Finally, he told us, "An Afghan soldier from the ANA headquarters element walked onto the helicopter pad as the guys unloaded supplies from it. He shot one of the medics from the surgical support team. It doesn't look good."

Andy paused to let the news sink in. We couldn't help but think of the surgical team working frantically to save the life of one of their own. The scene over at the FOB would be indescribably awful right now. Part of me was glad I didn't have to see it.

"The ANA soldier shot up the helicopter, then he was tackled by his supervisor and a couple of soldiers from the 82nd."

"You mean the fucker is still alive?" George asked harshly.

"Apparently."

"Why?"

I knew what George was thinking. We were all thinking it. If this had happened to us, no way would that Afghan get taken alive.

"Don't know. He was shot in the leg as they subdued him. They're going to fly him to Herat."

"Unfuckinglievable," Billy spat.

"They're interrogating him now. Maybe they can get something useful from him."

"Yeah, like why the hell would he kill a medic," Jack said bitterly.

Khybar, one of our two terps with us, answered that. "When the Taliban can identify an ANA soldier, they seek out his family. They tell him that if he doesn't do what they say, his family will be tortured or killed."

"So even if they're loyal, they can be compromised," I said. "That means we can never really trust any of them."

"No. We can't," Khybar agreed. "The best we can do is try to make sure our ANA cannot be identified and singled out."

"He was high when he did it," Andy told us. "Heroin probably. Makes sense if he was being coerced. Just wonder why now. Why activate that guy after two days of ass kicking?"

"Hey, Andy," Mark said from his sniper position. He was on his scope, watching something intently to the west toward Prius.

"Andy, I have one civilian pickup truck moving slowly east through the Bowling Alley. The ANP let it go through their checkpoint without stopping it."

Through my binos, I spotted the truck. It was white, with two men in the cab. The bed had been covered with a dark canvas tarp. It was traveling a very nonthreatening ten to fifteen miles an hour. In Iraq, we'd learned that vehicular suicide bombers tended to drive fast and recklessly into their target. This was not the case here, which made the truck's presence on our battlefield even more puzzling.

"The guys at Prius'll check it out," Andy said.

We waited for that to happen. The truck drove sedately past Prius. To our astonishment, nobody came out to stop it or talk to the driver.

Andy keyed his radio and reported this to the COC. But in all the chaos after the green-on-blue, he received no guidance and no explanation.

The truck rolled right past the base of our hill and into Kapeh Baba and vanished among the tightly packed compounds toward the middle of the village.

"Mark," Andy said.

"On it."

Over the past three days, Mark had assembled a veritable arsenal with him in his sniper nest. Besides Elvis and his M4, he'd brought up his M40 bolt-action 7.62mm rifle and his SR-25. He'd stacked his gun cases nearby, along with extra magazines, ammunition, and his cleaning kits.

He grabbed his M40 and pulled Elvis from the loophole in his hide and started to glass the village for signs of the truck.

Andy called the FOB again to report that the truck had gone into Kapeh Baba, but again he received no response, aside from an acknowledgment of his transmission.

Ten minutes passed without any sight or sound of the vehicle. We were starting to wonder if it had just parked somewhere and the occupants had dismounted to get into the fight against us.

"There it is!" Jamie called out. He was dug in on the other side of Andy's position. Sure enough, the truck had reappeared coming out of Kapeh Baba, moving along at about ten miles an hour.

A single civilian truck coming from our section of the battlefield traveling into and out of an enemy-held village?

"Billy, George," Andy said.

"On it," George said, rising from his fighting position. Billy waved to a few of the other guys. Jack, Jamie, and Khybar immediately stood up. Together, they all climbed over the berm and rushed down the steep south slope to the road.

The truck cleared the village and started to head back toward Taraz and Prius.

Mark adjusted and got the M40 on the truck. "Andy, what do you want me to do? Our guys aren't going to make it in time."

Andy was hung up in thought and not responding.

"Andy?" Mark said again.

"Hit it," I said softly, standing right next to Mark.

The truck was about two hundred meters away, but moving a bit faster now. It would be a high-angle shot since the vehicle was coming toward the base of Pathfinder Hill. Mark carefully lined up on it and said, "Taking the shot."

The M40 barked once. The truck's front passenger tire exploded, and the vehicle slowed to a stop.

"Holy shit, dude. That was a perfect shot," I said to him.

It came to a halt with the front grille pointed toward the hill. This meant we could clearly see the two men in the truck's cab. Both sat motionless, the driver with hands still on the steering wheel. For a tense moment, both sides waited to see what the other would do next.

I watched from the hilltop, binos to my eyes as Billy approached the driver's side. The two men inside the cab stepped out cautiously. They were Afghans, dressed neatly in civilian clothes. They looked ridiculously clean juxtaposed to Billy and George. Our guys searched them both thoroughly. Finding no weapons, they went around to the back of the truck.

Four young men, all in their twenties or early thirties, slid out of the covered bed under orders from the Marines. All four looked beat to hell—shaggy and filthy, their clothes stained and impregnated with dirt. Even from this distance, we could see through our optics they had the thousand-yard stare of men who'd seen too much battle. They gazed out from sunken eyes at Billy and George, Jamie and Jack, but didn't really see them.

"What the fuck is this?" I asked aloud. "Are those some of the fuckers we've been fighting?"

"No idea, but it sure looks like it," Andy replied.

"Then why the hell are they in a truck leaving the village through our lines?"

"Andy, why didn't the 82nd stop them at Prius?" Mark asked.

The questions had no answers.

Billy and George searched the four men as Jack and Jamie covered them. Again, they found nothing.

Our guys separated the driver and passenger from the other four Afghans and put them to one side of the vehicle, where they sat on their haunches. A conversation took place, and for a long moment I watched as Khybar translated whatever had just been said. Billy and George looked stricken by whatever the terp had passed along. Khybar was an incredible Afghan and he had long since proved his loyalty. He'd fought alongside us, carried a weapon into every battle. He shared the same hardships without complaint. And he'd told us a little bit about himself during quiet moments, where boredom was our biggest enemy.

He'd gone to college before the war had come, and ever since he'd been trying to get out of Afghanistan. All he wanted to do was escape his devastated country and live his life out in Stockton, California. Why Stockton, we could never figure out, but nobody had the heart to tell him his dream city was the armpit of the Golden State.

Though easy to smile and quick with a joke, Khybar had seen a lot of nastiness in his years as a terp. He'd worked with many Special Operations teams all over Afghanistan in some of the worst battles of the war. Now, as we watched him from the hilltop, we could see that even he looked affected by whatever those Afghans had said to him.

Two of the dirtiest Afghans suddenly stood back up. Billy nodded to them, and they walked slowly over to the truck's back gate. They lowered it, then leaned forward to reach inside for something.

No, not something. Someone.

They pulled out a little girl. Her arms hung limp, her head lolled. The two men lowered her to the ground. She was covered in dust, eyes closed, hair matted and filthy.

My hands started to shake. The scene grew blurry through the binos. *She can't be more than Devlyn's age.*

I saw my little girl's face down there, and it wrecked me. My heart stopped. My body was wracked with shuddering spasms. I had no doubt how she had died.

Three compounds at once. A single two-thousand-pounder that had wrought such devastation on the southern part of Kapeh Baba. And now, we knew for sure. There had been civilians in there after all.

My bomb did this. Oh my God. My bomb did this.

George and Billy stared at the motionless figure on the ground.

You were killing enemy fighters. You didn't know.

I couldn't rationalize this. I couldn't marginalize my role, no matter how logical and necessary the bomb had been. I had killed somebody's child.

The two men returned to the pickup.

Oh God, not more. Please, no more.

I shuddered again. My hands trembled. I had to force myself to breathe.

The two Afghans extracted another body. This one was an older woman, perhaps middle-aged. She was as dirty as the little girl.

A mother and her child.

They laid her corpse next to the girl's. Billy, George, and Khybar seemed rooted where they stood.

This isn't happening. This isn't happening.

"Easy, Ski," Andy said gently.

I couldn't stop shaking. The binos fell from my eyes. My head dropped. Dizzy and uncomprehending, I felt myself losing control.

I will never live this down. Ever.

I couldn't look.

I had to.

"Hey, Andy, something's seriously wrong here," Billy called over the radio.

Do it. Own it. Own this mistake. It is the least you can do for them.

I forced the binoculars back to my eyes.

25

★ The Truth Hurts ★

DAY THREE
AT THE FOOT OF PATHFINDER HILL

Through my optics, I saw Billy bending down over the bodies, examining their heads carefully. George had pulled one of the Afghans aside with Khybar, and the three of them were involved in an intense talk out of earshot of the rest of the truck's occupants, who were squatted against the hill under the watch of Jack's and Jamie's rifles.

"Andy," Billy said again over the radio, "these Afghans are saying the girl and the woman were killed by one of our bombs. But it is clear they weren't killed by us."

"What do you mean?" Andy asked.

"They were shot. Recently. Maybe a few hours ago. It looks like close range. Single gunshot to the side of the head. Both of them. Probably by a 7.62 round."

Aside from Mark's M40 and SR-25, the only other 7.62mm weapons we had on the hill were our M240 machine guns, Zohan's PKM, and a few AKs the ANA guys had yet to actually use. Nobody on Pathfinder had fired a shot all day.

"That couldn't have been us," Mark said.

"No," Pat agreed.

I heard all this and saw my life restored in a blink of an eye. I was not responsible for this. A queer sense of relief and elation rushed through me, like adrenaline. Then it was gone, driven away by the realization that there was still a dead child and her mother down there. A moment later, I felt guilty for being relieved.

Combat magnifies and intensifies every human emotional response.

Your system gets used to the radically new highs and extreme depths you bounce between from minute to minute as a battle unfolds. There is unpredictability in those extremes. One minute, we are cheering and exultant. The next, we face the death of a brother or the horrors of civilian casualties and are tormented by what we witness. Back home, those emotional highs and lows no longer exist. The middle ground—the normal realm of life back in the States—becomes impossibly dull to some of us who grew hooked on the highs. That will always be a consequence of sending warriors into battle, then bringing them home to a quiet and unspectacular life. For some of us, that is nothing short of soul death.

Post-traumatic stress (PTS) is magnified when a warrior realizes that for as long as they may live, they will never be as fucking awesome as they are in this moment. They will have to live with just being mediocre.

The radio sparked to life again. Billy explained that the driver said he'd been given permission to go into Kapeh Baba to recover the bodies of two civilian women killed by the air strikes. That permission was granted so that the women could be laid to rest within the Muslim custom of burying their dead within the period prescribed by the Koran.

The other man in the cab with the driver claimed to be a local doctor. They'd been evasive over who the other men were, and what they were doing in the car.

"Who gave them permission, Billy?"

"He says the district governor did."

The district governor was sitting with PRO 6 at the ANP Castle. Did that mean a battalion commander from the 82nd Airborne had promised these guys safe passage, then failed to tell any of us?

As Billy finished relaying all that to Andy, George waved him over. The two of them conferred for a bit, then Khybar joined them, well away from the one Afghan he'd been talking to. The three huddled together and spoke for a long time. Finally, Billy stepped away and called Andy again.

"That son of a bitch right there"—Billy said, pointing to the lone Afghan—"that's the husband and father. He just admitted to Khybar that the other three told him his wife and daughter had to be killed, and if he protested, he would be buried in the grave next to them."

"What are you saying here, Billy?"

"These two fuckers got permission to drive into the village, not to bring out a couple of bodies, but to extract these four guys. The bodies were just the ploy to make the rescue possible."

The four men had been the last survivors of the enemy element inside Kapeh Baba. They knew they had no safe escape route out of the village after we'd flattened the ratline and killed their buddies. If they'd tried to break cover and run for it, the 240s or Mark and Elvis would have cut them down without another thought.

But they had an ace in the hole: a cell phone and a direct line to the Entourage at the ANP Castle. As soon as they'd arranged safe passage for the truck, they needed bodies to pull off their ruse.

One unlucky family that had remained behind when the village was abandoned became part of the Taliban's twisted gambit. In their radical version of Islam, women have almost no value; they are things to be traded or used. They could be stoned to death if raped. They could be murdered by their husbands if they dared to leave their homes unattended by a male in their family. The Taliban had gone to great lengths to ensure girls would receive no education. In several cases, they had killed dozens of female students with poisonous gas as they sat in their classrooms.

So here, in this miserable, crumbling village, a father fighting along-side the Taliban acquiesced in the murder of his little girl. Did he pull the trigger? Did he murder his wife as well? Khybar had not been able to find that out. But they were killed as part of a last-ditch escape plan. That much was clear.

My emotions had ping-ponged to extremes ever since the bodies were removed from the truck. Now, all I felt was cold, merciless rage. I wanted those six bastards dead. I wanted their bodies dumped in some anonymous hole. I suspected the rest of the team had similar emotions. Billy and George looked particularly affected. Jack, too. He was a father, standing guard over child murderers and wrestling with the reality of life's value to these people.

But what would be the consequences? If we were to kill them, sooner or later the truth would come out, and we would be prosecuted for murder. We'd seen it happen, both within the Marine Corps and the Army. There were no extenuating circumstances. Perhaps, there should not ever be, anyway. Murder is murder, whether the victim is a six-year-old girl or that girl's unarmed killer.

Still, we could not just let the enemy go. Free pass from the district governor or not, they were still Taliban. The four bedraggled ones had been shooting at us for three days. Hell, they could have been the PKM team I'd missed with my last bomb at the end of day one.

Yes. There had to be a reckoning. But how? They ditched their weapons and had the equivalent of a Get Out of Jail Free card, even though we'd seen through their ruse.

The district governor had assured them they would have safe passage. Now, even as one of them admitted their guilt, the others still demanded they be released and sent on their way.

As we tried to figure out what to do, news of the civilian casualties had traveled like lightning throughout Western Afghanistan. Whenever non-combatants were killed, a CIVCAS (civilian casualties) report had to be sent up the chain of command. Such incidents usually attracted the attention of divisional headquarters, and an automatic investigation would be undertaken.

The 82nd Airborne's divisional HQ in Herat was going berserk. Back at the operations center at FOB Todd, Danny was simultaneously trying to coordinate all his forward observers, work with PRANKSTER 42 and relay information to the command node at the Castle—all the while dealing with increasingly strident demands from higher as to why we were dropping bombs all over the place in this supposedly peaceful valley. The second-guessing, ass-covering, and accusations apparently had already begun to fly. All by people who had not been out here getting attacked by the "peaceful" Taliban, of course.

Andy reported the situation to FOB Todd, looking for guidance. We wanted all those who came out of the village detained as prisoners of war. We wanted to make sure justice was served for those who committed the double homicide. But we had no place to hold them. Pathfinder Hill was a war zone, not a detention facility. Our mission was the hill, and we could not spare the men to stand security over detainees. How we would handle prisoners was never detailed in Operation Good Morning's original plan. I don't think anyone thought we'd capture any enemy fighters.

No, holding them here would not be an option.

We needed to get their biometrics—DNA samples, eye scans, fingerprints. If we could run those things through our database, we could see if they were already in the system. Chances were, at least one of them would probably have a file detailing a long history of fighting the Coalition.

Even more important, the bodies would need a full forensic analysis. If the gunshots were made from close range, there would be powder residue on their skulls. An autopsy would reveal that conclusively.

The fact was, we were dealing with a crime scene. We aren't cops, we are gunfighters and unequipped to handle this type of situation.

Without guidance from the FOB, Andy had to make a hard decision. He couldn't order them killed. He couldn't just let them walk, and he couldn't detain them. It was a terrible choice, and in that moment I didn't envy him or his position as our team leader one bit.

"Let's hand them off to the 82nd at Prius and they can transport them to the FOB. They can stop them. I'm sure they've got the gear to gather their biometrics," he finally said.

The truck wasn't going anywhere at the moment. Mark's bullet had destroyed the tire, and the vehicle lacked a spare. After some discussion, the doctor was allowed to use his cell phone to call for another truck. We waited in silent anger until the second truck finally drove down the Bowling Alley, past Prius, and linked up with the scene below us.

The Afghans swapped out the wrecked tire as George and Billy, Jamie, Jack, and Khybar stood nearby watching, their faces frozen with a look of cold, professional distance. I observed from the hilltop, no longer numb by the thought of my culpability in the deaths of those that lay by the truck's back gate. Instead, I was wrenched between frustration and fury, trapped in a sense of helplessness that our enemy was about to escape with our help.

What would the guys who fought in Normandy think of this? Our grandfathers who created the 82nd Airborne's legend with their blood? The Marine Raiders of Guadalcanal's Bloody Ridge—we wear their patch. What would they say if they could see the kind of war their grandsons found themselves fighting?

In that moment, as we watched men who had tried to kill us change a flat directly under our guns, the war ceased to make any sense at all to me. Lofty ideals meant nothing in the face of such reality as this. Cold politics and planning, tactics and counterinsurgency manuals were so much rubbish. Those were things that had led us to this travesty.

In Afghanistan, justice was as elusive as hope.

Joe was right. He loved us like his own family, we all knew that. But he'd seen this reality, knew how it could sear the warrior's heart, and he could not bear to see us lose ourselves to this cause.

No right and wrong. Only each other. That was the only thing worth dying for in this valley and country.

The Taliban finished changing the tire. They slid the bodies back under the tarp. Then they climbed into their tracks and drove off toward Prius.

The COP was expecting them. Andy had called over to Captain Perry and detailed the situation. Instead of stopping the trucks and detaining our foe, the soldiers at Prius were told to stand down. PRO 6, not wanting to offend the village elder or tarnish the district governor's authority, told his men to let the enemy go. The trucks were not stopped. The Taliban ruse had worked. The last three surviving enemy fighters in Kapeh Baba bailed out of the truck when it reached the Bazaar and vanished into the back alleys.

I have often wondered if any of those four later went on to kill a Coalition soldier in another fight. Or did they torture or murder more innocents? We'd validated that approach, so surely their close brush with us didn't dissuade them from such tactics.

We'd been played. By the enemy, by the elders, by the Entourage. As the truck rolled from sight, they seemed one and the same to us.

With the Taliban dropped off in the Bazaar, the doctor, the husband-father, and the driver drove the bodies to FOB Todd. Still clinging to the story that one of our bombs had killed the girl and her mom, they demanded compensation from the American government for their loss. Their *Get Out of Battle Free* victims were now seen as cash cows to these *men*.

The medical support staff examined the bodies and concluded that they had been executed at close range by a single 7.62mm gunshot to the side of the head.

The husband, doctor, and driver were questioned and released, disappearing across the Old Bridge and into the Bazaar.

26

★ SOME GOOD ★

After the trucks departed, George asked Andy if they were *cleared* to go into Kapeh Baba on foot to make sure there were no Taliban stragglers or terrified civilians hiding out within its warren of compounds and courtyards. We'd still need to occupy Pathfinder, so Billy, Jack, Jamie, Pat, Zohan, and a few ANA and 82nd paratroopers were tasked with going down the hill while the rest of us stayed topside.

Quietly, they searched through the empty village, weapons at the ready. There were blood trails here and there around Taliban fighting positions, but no bodies. The patrol cleared each dwelling and discovered mouse holes, spent cartridges, bandages, and other medical debris, but little else. No weapons or live ammunition were discovered. The enemy had either shot every round they had, or they'd buried their weapons and ammo in caches we wouldn't be able to find without a more thorough search. Right now, with the battlefield still so fluid, we didn't have time to do that.

In the southern part of Kapeh Baba, the men heard movement inside a compound's courtyard. The ANA went through the outer gate to investigate the noises. Instead of a human, they encountered a single, starving puppy. Traumatized and filthy, the animal had been abandoned to his fate when the Taliban had pulled out earlier in the day. Billy and George approached him and gave him a little bit of food. The pup wolfed it down even though he shivered with fear at the sudden onset of strangers gathered around him. He was the only living creature left in Kapeh Baba.

There were plenty of rules against keeping pets on the FOB, but by this time we were so sick of bullshit regulations and restrictions that they

meant little to us. Here, in this moment, the guys could do something—
the right thing—without any moral ambiguity or without any second-
guessing from distant eyes peering over our shoulders. There was no
option here. American Marines meet a lost dog on a bullet-riddled battlefield? Come on.

They scooped him up and carried him back to Pathfinder.

When they reached the hill, the rest of us greeted the pup with an out-
pouring of affection. We cuddled him. We stroked his cublike ears and
stuffed him full of MREs until he couldn't eat another bite. We shared
our water with him, which he lapped gently from our cupped hands.

He sat in my lap, his face nuzzled against my chest, as we discussed
what to do with him. Dark eyes, with a cream-colored nose and light
brown fur, the pup had a peculiar gray marking on either side of his snout,
like vertical stripes that bent around the edges of his eyes. It gave him a
simultaneous look of badass and complete adorability.

"I've never seen a dog like this before," I said while scratching his ears.
"What breed is he?"

Khybar cleared that up. "He's a Koochie dog."

His actual breed is Central Asian Shepherd.

They were used as guard dogs throughout Afghanistan. While most
Afghans have little regard for animals, especially dogs, they did see them
as useful tools. Koochie dogs were legendary for their hearing and ability
to sense strangers, so they made excellent organic early warning systems
for their owners. Families used them to watch over their compounds. The
ANA liked them, too, as they could be used on remote outposts to detect
any approaching humans.

"He looks like a bear cub," I said, marveling at his short cropped ears.

"Yeah he does," Mark agreed as he offered a piece of beef jerky to the
pup. The dog studied the morsel, balancing his already bloated stomach
with the chance of seeing more food later. Like most abandoned animals,
he settled on the here and now. He stuffed the jerky down and closed his
eyes happily. I doubt he'd ever been so full in his short life.

"Bear," I said. The pup looked up at me, as if in response. He licked my
thick red beard and I feigned disgust. Truth was, I hadn't felt this good
since setting foot in this country.

"Bear," George said.

"Guess he has a name," I said.

"Wonder who owned him," Jack muttered as he came over to sit in the trench line beside Bear and me.

"Doesn't matter. He's ours now," I said.

A couple of the ANA came over to visit the pup. It became clear that they wanted him. We were not having any of it. They grew angry, but we were not going to budge. Bear was ours, even if the ANA did find him first.

The Afghans grumbled and protested. But they weren't walking away with him. At length, they backed down and returned to their positions.

Bear curled up next to Mark in his sniper nest as our interlude came to an end and we picked up our weapons again. Kapeh Baba may have been cleared, but much of the battlefield had not, and Prius was reporting movement to the south of them again.

With binoculars and scopes, we searched the valley floor for targets. Bear fell asleep, his cub ears twitching whenever the wind picked up. Periodically, Mark would reach over and stroke his head. The pup's eyes would open, wary and distrustful at first. Then they would soften as he relaxed into the pleasure of Mark's fingers scratching his neck.

"Bear's been through a lot," George said. "Gonna take some time for him to get used to us."

"Well, George, he'll figure out he's on the right side now soon enough."

George crawled over and gave Bear another piece of beef jerky. "He's probably got fleas."

"So do you."

"You thirsty, boy?" he asked him in a goofy, little-kid-sounding voice. I'd never seen George like this. Brash, obnoxious, badass George lay in a trench, baby-talking to a Taliban puppy.

Unfuckingbelievable.

"We'll keep you safe, little guy," he cooed as he gave him some water.

Andy watched the scene and started to laugh.

"What?" George asked.

"Dude, gimme your man card," Billy teased.

"Fuck you."

"I wouldn't fuck you with Ski's dick," Billy shot back. Andy lost all composure at that one. Next to him, Mark stifled a chortle, his eye still in Elvis's scope.

"Hey, leave my dick out of this," I protested.

Bear finished his snack and drink and curled back up beside Mark. George returned to his fighting position, and the hill grew silent but for the sound of the wind whistling overhead. We lay in the earth, searching for the enemy and waiting for something to happen.

"Hey, Mark?"

"What is it now, George?"

"What kind of name is Elvis anyway?"

"I'm a fan."

"Of Elvis Presley? Really?"

"Yeah, really," Mark said a bit defensively.

"Why?"

"Guy was badass. Larger than life, you know? Ever hear 'American Trilogy'?"

"No," George said. He sensed the conversation was turning serious. In the past, George tended to push buttons well beyond the acceptable limits. Recently, he'd been more nuanced, and was learning when to back off. This was one of those times. That song, and Elvis, obviously meant something to Mark.

"You should listen to it sometime," Mark said quietly. Then he added, "Play it at my funeral."

"Well, that got morose fast," George said.

" 'Just Pretend' is a good song, too," Mark offered, a little less intensely.

"How do you feel about 'Do the Clam'?"

"George, you are such an asshole."

But Mark was laughing in his scope again.

In the valley, an AK-47 barked. Another one joined in. Prius was getting hit again. In a heartbeat, the relaxed atmosphere on Pathfinder vanished, and we were all business again.

"Where are they?" I asked Mark.

"Don't see anyone yet."

One of the AK's went cyclic. The Taliban fighter emptied his thirty-round magazine in a couple of seconds and his weapon fell silent while he reloaded.

The gunfire had a profound effect on Bear. With every burst from those AKs, he trembled with fear and whined.

"Seems like only a couple of guys at most," Billy said. He sounded disappointed.

"I'm on one," Mark said. A second later, he pulled his trigger and Elvis boomed.

Bear went absolutely berserk. The sound of the M107 followed by its concussion wave sent him fleeing to the far side of the hill.

We would have to find him later. Work needed to be done.

"Ski, help me reload," Mark yelled.

With the SASR still damaged and only firing one manually loaded round at a time, I fell against the berm and grabbed a handful of .50 caliber cartridges. Mark kept his eye in the scope and jerked the charging handle back.

I reached up and slid the round in. "Loaded," I said to him.

"Shot."

"Load."

"Shot."

Like a well-oiled machine sending nine rounds downrange. Two men working in sync with one purpose, to kill.

The men with Captain Perry started returning fire. Mark took several more shots. The two Taliban did not last long. Soon, silence filled the valley again.

The afternoon shadows grew long. Bear had taken shelter in a deep hole near the ANA. He returned to his search for more food as time had passed since the last gunshot was fired.

First Sergeant Z showed up with the daily resupply convoy. As his men unloaded boxes of ammo and food, he walked up the hill to check on his boys. Moving from foxhole to foxhole, he broke the news from FOB Todd. The Taliban had threatened to torture and kill the ANA soldier's family if he didn't attack and kill Americans on post. Perhaps out of guilt, perhaps to steel himself to his almost certain death, he smoked opium before walking to the helicopter pad. When he got there, he seemed to struggle with what he had to do. At first, he waved frantically to the men and women unloading the Mi-8, as if warning them away. Then he lowered his AK and shot the nearest man, a medic named Staff Sergeant Spino. Spino had volunteered to come up to FOB Todd from Herat to help out during Operation Good Morning. He shouldn't have even been there.

Fate can be unbearably cruel. What were the odds that he would be on that pad at that exact moment, and find himself directly in front of a reluctant killer?

The ANA soldier killed him instantly, though that did not stop the medical support staff from trying to resuscitate him in the base medical tent. Long after there was no hope, they kept working on their fallen comrade. The scene must have been indescribably tragic.

For a medical staff to be working on one of their very own, it must have been heartbreaking that they couldn't save him.

The ANA soldier was gang-tackled by a group of Italian, American, and Afghan soldiers. In the scrum to subdue him, somebody shot him in the leg and bashed him in the head with a rock. He was removed from the FOB that afternoon, and was awaiting the hangman's noose in Herat.

Staff Sergeant Spino's wife was also a noncommissioned officer in the 82nd. She worked in the office responsible for handling all communication with the families of wounded and fallen soldiers.

Quietly, we kept watch over the valley as the sun dropped beneath the clouds and turned the sky gold and crimson. I watched it as it briefly perched above one of the jagged hilltops to the west beyond FOB Todd, absorbed in memories of Sabrina and Devlyn and my life back in Colorado. Why had I left them again?

If I get back, I will burrow deep in my little mountain town and never leave. Easy civilian job. PTA meetings. Coffee downtown. I'll take Devlyn to play video games in the arcade and start playing music again. In the spring, we'll go to music festivals and lie together on blankets, letting the tunes fill our ears. And in winter, we'll hit the slopes. I'll teach my girl to snowboard. We'll play and live and keep it simple. Love each other. That's all that will matter.

"And beer. I want to drink good beer whenever the fuck I want one," I whispered to myself.

Something made me look down the trench. In the pre-dusk shadows, Bear sat staring at me, his face drawn and sad. He looked almost guilty. His cub ears rotated toward me as he caught my eye.

"C'mere boy," I said. He padded down the trench, noticed now by Andy, George, and Mark.

The mood on the hill changed instantly. The banter returned, more subdued than before, but at least it was back. George cracked wise. Billy bitched about lack of targets. Mark took notes on his range card.

Bear climbed into our area, and I laid my poncho liner down for him. He intuited what that meant, and he circled atop it before curling up in a tan ball, his snout buried in the comfort of his own fur.

That night Bear slept beside me on his blanket. Standing watch that night was brutal. The temperature plummeted again, and we shivered through subzero weather as a splinter moon occasionally shone through the clouds drifting overhead.

I had more time than I wanted to think, and my mind wallowed in the events of the past three days. I thought of Bear being carried up the hill and how his arrival had been like an adrenaline shot to our morale. I thought of Mikey and his unique brand of courage.

But most of all, I thought of Jack's words earlier that day.

I wonder whom he belonged to?

Bear had somebody. Once. The fighting had made him an orphan. Had we killed his Taliban owners?

George stirred in his hole. It would be his turn to stand watch in thirty minutes, but he was already awake, fumbling with an MRE.

"Hey George?" I whispered.

"Yeah, Ski?"

"Where exactly did you guys find Bear?"

George thought about that, then said, "You remember the compounds you took out with a two-thousand-pounder?"

"Yeah." It was the one we dropped in the middle of the road, between a few compounds.

"He was in the next compound over. Why?"

"Curious is all."

"You know, Ski, for a place like this, you think too much."

"Maybe."

"I got watch. Go to sleep," he said, his voice barely a whisper. Mark had actually drifted off, the first time I'd seen him get any shut-eye since we'd gotten here, and George was being careful not to wake him.

"Thanks, have fun, brother."

I crawled back into my frozen bag and threw some of the excess to cover Bear.

The sight of the little girl and her mother lying in the dirt returned to me. Had Bear been the family's newest protector? Had the little girl played with him within the safety of the family's compound? My imagination drifted, picturing her in the courtyard, her green dress clean and tended, Bear at her side.

Was he her dog?

I couldn't stop thinking of her and her mom. I begged my imagination to stop, tried to shut my brain off, but nothing worked. I came back each time to the same question: Where had they been murdered?

I pictured a grim and spartan room, sleeping mats on the dirt floor. Mud walls, a window overlooking the courtyard. Bear sitting out there alone as the scene played out. The girl, beside her mom, crying and confused. Her mother, stoic, knowing the score in this hellish culture, knowing that her life meant little to even the man bound to her by marriage.

Donkeys have more value than women to these people.

I prayed in the darkness that the little girl had not seen her mother killed.

What was the last thing she'd seen?

Stop it.

Had she glanced out the doorway? Had she seen her would-be protector, as helpless to stop this horror as we were unknowing and unable to intervene atop Pathfinder?

There would never be an answer to that. But of this I had no doubt: Bear was mine now. We were bound together by this place and the horrors we had both experienced.

27

★ EXFIL ★

In the afternoon of day four, PRO 6 decided to take the Entourage on a grand tour of the battlefield. They convoyed down the Bowling Alley and stopped first at Prius. The enemy had made no appearance that morning, so the engineers and 82nd were busily hard pointing Prius and turning it into a true fortified position. After a whirlwind visit, they saddled back up and drove to the base of Pathfinder Hill. When we realized they were coming to see us, Mark made a point of hiding his sniper rifles. He stashed them beneath a sleeping bag and a couple of poncho liners just as PRO 6's convoy pulled up alongside the base of the hill.

"What a fucking circus," Pat muttered from behind his 240. He was looking down as PRO 6 stormed about, shaking hands and making bombastic comments he clearly thought would bolster morale.

"The king has paid us a visit," George sniped.

"With his fucking minions," Billy added.

They stayed at the base of the hill only for a few minutes before starting up toward us.

"Here they come," Pat warned.

"Play it cool, guys," Andy said.

PRO 6's head appeared over the crest. He strutted over the berm and stepped over the trench. The leather-jacket-wearing NDS spook joined him and peered around at us without comment or expression. Colonel Ali appeared beside him, followed by Chief Lewal. Both men were red-faced and winded, their huge guts heaving as they struggled to catch their breath.

Even the ANA, normally stoic and accepting of whatever fate threw at them, looked on with disgust.

The district governor was the last to make it up the hill, huddled in his clothes against the cold, his weasel eyes scanning around.

"Can you believe this shit?" Billy said bitterly.

"What a fucking clown show," said George.

PRO 6 went over to Lieutenant Robinson, the 82nd Airborne's platoon leader on the hill, and pumped his hand. Vacant, meaningless words were exchanged. PRO 6 looked pompous and puffed up. He was clearly in charge now, and this was his hill. It made our stomachs turn.

He and the Entourage made their way to Andy, shaking hands and slapping shoulders with ANA, paratroopers, and Marines.

"Good job, men! Well done!" he repeated over and over.

He reached Andy and held court. Andy played the game, shaking hands with the Entourage and giving a very brief description of the past four days.

More back slapping and hand pumping ensued.

The Entourage began to wander around, looking at us in our fighting positions. Chief Lewal drifted over to our side of the line, stopping to examine Mark's sniper position. He bent down and peered through the loophole Mark had made with sandbags, and seemed to study the field of view he had from it. Then he looked down at the sleeping bag and poncho liners that concealed Elvis and Mark's M40 and SR-25.

Mark put an end to his curiosity. "Sshhhhhhh," he said, his index finger to his lips. "Sleeping, he has been working very hard." He feigned sleep to get his point across.

"Ahhhh!" the Afghan said. He looked down again at the stash of weapons.

"That fucker looked like he was casing the place," George said.

I stood next to Andy as he spoke with PRO 6 about the situation.

"And here's the man who drops the bombs!" PRO 6 suddenly announced. I looked at him in shock.

PRO 6 turned to his terp and said again, "This is the man who drops the bombs!"

The terp translated. Heads bobbed. They all made eye contact with me. *I cannot believe he just said that.*

I was the only one with a red beard on the hill. So far, the shooter had not made an appearance on our battlefield. Or if he had, he'd been shooting at Prius, not at us. But what Taliban commander wouldn't want to know that the only red-bearded American on Pathfinder was the one who rained bombs down on his brethren?

They shook my hand, one at a time. It felt like I was consorting with the enemy. As they turned to leave, I wanted to punch PRO 6 in the face. How dare he identify me as a JTAC to these people, these so-called allies? The man had just put a gigantic X on my forehead.

After he led the Entourage back down to the vehicles, said. "Andy, do you fucking believe he just pointed me out like that. What the fuck? He's put my life at risk. If any of those assholes with him decide to talk to their Taliban buddies, they're going to be looking for me."

"I know, Ski. This is seriously fucked up."

We watched Colonel Ali and the chief waddle back to PRO 6's convoy and stuff themselves inside the rigs. The district governor climbed into another one. Soon, the whole circus took off in a cloud of dust, bound for the FOB. It was the sum total of PRO 6's presence on the battlefield.

Thank God.

We stayed on the hill one more freezing-cold night. Bear made the rounds between all of us, but ultimately settled beside me again on the blanket I'd laid out for him. In the morning, we stood full security, everyone on their weapons as dawn broke over the valley one more time.

Day five was quiet. The enemy had been defeated. At noon, the 82nd sent out another platoon to replace us and begin work on a combat outpost atop the hill. They brought some Italians out with them, and as we picked up our gear they began to settle in around us as we turned over our position to them.

Mark hauled all his rifles down to the RG and stuffed them inside. He came back up the hill, grabbed the rest of his gear, and picked up Bear.

"You got him?" I asked.

"Yeah. I'll put him in one of the GMVs."

I stood up from my gear I was packing, and Mark came over to me. We shared a look and knew. This place, these days—we may be leaving, but part of us will always remain here, lost forever like the Russian soldier whose grave we had unearthed.

"Why is it that the worst moments of your life always seem to last forever?" Mark said.

"And the best ones never seem long enough."

George joined us. So did Pat. Billy slung his SAW and walked past us. "Let's get some of that hot Italian chow, all of this smoke checking has got me hungry."

"I would like a nap first," Pat said. Dirt had coated his face paint like another layer of skin. He looked like he'd just stepped out of a Norman Rockwell painting. *Portrait of the American Warrior.*

"Get down to the trucks," Andy told us from across the main trench line. He was holding his M4, his assault pack bulging with stuff and dangling from one shoulder.

"Hey, Mark."

"Fuck you, George."

"You think you can get me a job with the Dallas PD?"

"No. They don't take assholes."

Pat started to laugh. "Home Depot does."

"Excellent."

"Come on, George," Mark said. Together, the two brothers walked off the hilltop, Bear still in Mark's arms.

Pat walked back over to his fighting position and picked up the last of his stuff. "Ski?"

"Yeah, I'll be there in a minute."

"You did a good job."

"Thanks."

He vanished over the crest.

I wanted to be the last of us to leave. I don't know why that was important to me, but it was. This place was seared into us. The memories of it will be carried through whatever length of life remained to each of us. I was too weary to be philosophical. I just wanted a moment's peace. Standing there, exposed to the world, the breeze in my face felt good. The lack of gunfire and exploding RPGs felt even better, like against all odds we had accomplished something important.

I looked down at Kapeh Baba. Is this what victory looks like? Even if we rid BMG of the Taliban, there was another valley on the other side of the mountains. And another beyond it. And another. There would always be another valley.

"Hey Ski. Let's go." I heard Rob's voice call on my radio.

I keyed my handset. "Roger."

"You know, I'm pissed you guys got to have all the fun while Paddy and I sat on our hands."

"That's what you get for being late to the party."

"Yeah, sorry about that." Rob sounded genuinely bummed. He had the warrior soul, just like George and Billy and Pat. I'd never be like them, I knew that now. I could be here with them. I could fight alongside them. But in my heart I was just a regular guy wanting to return home. Until then, I would give this team everything I had. They were my family now.

"Well, there's always tomorrow, brother," I said into my mic, thinking of the shooter and the midget, and the shadow governor. They were all still out there, and if we were going to win this, they would have to die.

"Yeah. Another Level Zero CONOPS."

"Level Zero my ass."

I put my back to the wind and headed down to join my brothers.

Operation Good Morning was the biggest Coalition offensive in BMG up to that time. It succeeded in bisecting the valley, and with the establishment of COP Prius and Pathfinder, the Taliban could no longer control the north–south communication lines that the drug trade relied upon. In those five days of fighting, we killed about fifty to sixty Taliban fighters and left many more wounded.

In the weeks that followed, the Task Force Professional intel guys busily scratched dozens of names off their white board that listed all known enemy operatives. Some of those deaths we confirmed through video footage of their funerals. The NDS agent received them electronically from members of the network he'd established. We watched them with deep satisfaction, thinking only of our own pain from the losses they'd inflicted on us. Besides Staff Sergeant Spino, one ANA soldier had been killed in action. Two more, plus Mikey, had been wounded. He recovered quickly, though, and rejoined us.

Once we returned to FOB Todd, it took me a few days to try to understand what had been going on around us while we fought for our lives on Pathfinder. I truly hoped that what I was thinking was not the truth.

The Entourage was at the Castle, and PRO 6 kept them in close company. I couldn't help but think that the lines had blurred between friend, foe, and the unknowns. On more than one occasion in PRO 6's COC, I had personally witnessed classified imagery on a 60-inch flat screen displaying friendly locations and routes and objectives being discussed with the Entourage present. This type of incorporation had become commonplace since Hero Recovery. Why would Operation Good Morning be any different? As I requested bomb drop approval, Danny was relaying it to PRO 6's radio operator. Dropping aircraft ordnance in a village is a huge deal; you have to incorporate Afghan National Security Forces (ANSF) and Government of the Islamic Republic of Afghanistan (GIRoA) elements, which the Entourage fell under. But to what extent? How much information is too much information? Every time I saw the district governor and the ANP chief, they were glued to their cell phones. The district governor many times would walk off by himself and speak in a very low voice, almost a whisper. On the FOB, while touring COPs, during operations . . . all the time. Who were they talking to? A paid insider, a cell leader, or a village elder who was also a Taliban sympathizer? Were the district governor and the ANP chief being asked to confirm the presence of civilians in those compounds I had targeted? Would you have trusted these people while U.S. service members were under fire?

There was no way to know where that information was going. Were the Taliban fighters within Kapeh Baba being tipped off about an incoming bomb drop, causing them to vacate the compounds as quickly as possible? I had sensed that something not right was going on toward the end of the first day. Was the decision to drop a bomb being based in part on information that the Entourage had provided in the past? The Entourage was a part of PRO 6's battle staff. Was real-time battlefield information getting out to unknown people in the valley, which could easily be relayed to the Taliban? It felt like the only logical conclusion to me based on everything I had witnessed or experienced up to that point. The sad part is that I was no longer shocked or surprised at the possibility.

PRO 6 would have to have had a say in allowing the truck into Kapeh Baba to pick up the girl and her mother. As the senior U.S. commander on scene, all decisions of that nature would have had to go through him. It was inconceivable to think they didn't. Paratroopers at Prius must have been instructed not to interfere with the truck or its occupants. If PRO 6 did allow the truck in, maybe he was trying to show the Afghans he trusted them, and thought maybe with this act of good faith he could help end the fighting. The cold reality on the ground that we were facing was another matter. The truck could have had anything in it: more ammo, supplies, or weapons. And because the truck was never searched, you could even assume that the bodies could have been loaded elsewhere and driven into Kapeh Baba as part of the cover for the rescue operation. We'll never know for sure. Who allows a civilian vehicle onto the battlefield without being searched? This whole act defied basic security and could have endangered many lives. As it was, the truck had come and gone with no impede. We all knew in our guts that those guys coming out of Kapeh Baba were straight Taliban and were being allowed to walk out of the fight scot-free. I could not grasp the concept of what was going on here. All of my military training was telling me, "This is wrong."

King documented all of the concerns that had been raised and sent a lengthy report up to our MSOC explaining what was going on under PRO 6's command, which eventually made it to the SOTF. It would only have been a matter of time until PRO 6's brigade commander caught wind of the report. Days later, PRO 6 flew out of BMG and back to Camp Stone in Herat. We saw him only one more time during the rest of our deployment at FOB Todd.

Captain Perry finally regained tactical control over his unit. The 508th elements at FOB Todd were good soldiers, and they never questioned the orders of their battalion commander, but they followed Perry because he was a leader we all trusted. Dynamic, creative, intelligent, and deeply concerned about his men, Captain Perry was an exemplary officer who engendered loyalty no matter service or nationality. He quickly saw the Entourage for what it was. In the months that followed, he played a key role in ensuring there would be a reckoning for that.

Nine months after I left Pathfinder Hill, I returned home to Sabrina and Devlyn. I shed the uniform forever and sought the quiet life I'd dreamt of on those subzero nights in my fighting position. We bought a house in a small mountain town in Colorado. I found a job as a writer for a local publisher after a failed attempt at government contract work. I work nine to five and come home to my little girl and wife. I live in a town where I know the people by name, and can step into any business and hear mine called in greeting. It is comfortable, and healing, and I would not have it any other way.

★ ★ ★

As I type these final words in the early spring of 2014, I know that I was lucky enough to never get addicted to the highs of battle. That said, there are plenty of nights I miss the simplicity of combat. Life gets boiled down to the barest elements. There are no bills to pay, no complexities in relationships. There are no nights spent with a sense of utter helplessness as you hold your sick daughter while she shivers with a fever. There are no road rage incidents or piles of junk mail to sort through. No family dynamics with your mom and dad or siblings. There are no worries of taxes and house loans, car repairs, or keeping up with the latest smartphone.

No. Life in combat is much simpler. It boils down to survival and loyalty. In the former, we find elation after every brush with death. In the latter, we find family among our brothers in arms. There is a brutal elegance to our experiences in combat. And when life here at home gets too complicated, it is easy to flee to the memories of BMG for solace.

But there is pain there as well. Pain of loss, pain of separation from my Marine family. Pain from those things we witnessed but could not control. On bad nights, I sleep on the couch and try not to think of the little girl and her mother. But their faces always revisit me.

Though I have a civilian life and job again, my mind never wanders far from my brothers. That is something time will never change; we are bound forever by the crucible of BMG.

I started writing of our experience in the valley on a sleepless night almost three years ago. I'd been collecting photos, video, and memories from everyone I could find who had been there with us, so I could paint this picture the right way. It started as a sort of catharsis for me, but quickly grew into a mission. I wanted people, my fellow Americans, to meet their warriors, those few who voluntarily carry the fight to the enemies of our nation. I wanted to show the measure of men like George and Mark and Andy and Billy, Pat, Jack, Paddy, Ryan, Floyd, Jamie, Jay, and Rob. They did not join the Corps for college money, or because they couldn't find a job back home. They joined to defeat the enemy. They are the best men I've ever known. And when the best of a generation leaves chunks of their souls on soon forgotten battlefields half a world away, the least we can do as Americans is listen, know their stories, and respect what they have given up for us.

The nights are cool here in Colorado. From my deck, the sky is crystal clear. Pollution doesn't exist here—a traffic jam for us is five cars at a stop sign. So the stars always seem to shine brightest in the Rockies, just as they did that night atop Sabzek Pass.

I cast my eye to the window. Upstairs, Sabrina and Devlyn are sleeping soundly. We're happy here. And that is more than I could ever ask for after Afghanistan.

In the remaining five months of the deployment I saw a lot of things, a lot of deep dark things. But I also saw hope. I saw men from all branches of service; all ranks and nationalities. I witnessed a brotherhood battle through the winter to become triumphant during the Spring Offensive. I watched more than a hundred Afghan Commandos rise up and claim their country and their place in our warrior culture. They are the last great hope for Afghanistan, the weight of the country rests on their shoulders and they are ready for the challenge. The rules of engagement that had almost stifled us to the point of failure, finally gave away to sane reasoning when General David Petraeus took command of Afghanistan a few months after I left the country.

I miss my brothers of Dagger 22 every day. The loss of their constant presence in my life makes me feel lonely at times. It is a loss that no amount of e-mails or phone calls or Facebook messages can ever overcome. Those days are gone, and my fellow veterans of BMG have been scattered to the wind by life. Some we have lost forever. We will never stop mourning them.

Something big and furry leans into my leg. I reach down and scratch those giant cublike ears.

"Okay, Bear. Let's go for a walk."

Turns out, Bear loves the stars and mountains and cool nights of Colorado as much as I do.

★ LIST OF CHARACTERS ★

DAGGER 22

Andy – team leader
Joe – team chief
Ski – JTAC/fire support
Licon – EOD technician
James – signals intelligence
West – all-source intelligence
King – human-intelligence chief
John – Joint Fires Observer
Paddy – human intelligence/scout sniper
Rob – human intelligence/operator
George – operator/breacher
Mark – scout sniper
Billy – operator
Ryan – SARC/medic
Heath – SARC/medic
Pat – element leader/operator
Jack – element leader/operator
Mikey – operator
Russo – operator
Cox – data communications
Jay – communications/operator
Jamie – communications/operator
Floyd – mechanic
Hatch – combat photographer

MARSOC INTERPRETERS

Naqib (Mike)
Khybar (K-bar)
Ahmed (Ez)
Shiraz (Ross)
Abdul (TJ)
Mohammad (John)

82ND AIRBORNE

Danny – fire support chief
PRO 6 – battalion commander
Captain Perry – battery commander
First Sergeant Zappala – battery first sergeant
Matt – Air Force JTAC

AFGANS

Chief Lewal – ANP chief
Colonel Ali – ANA commander
Shawa Ali – BMG district governor
Haji Wakil Jailan – Daneh Pasab cell leader
Wakil – Daneh Pasab village elder
Mullah Muslim – IED maker
Colonel Nordeen – NDS chief
Mullah Ishmil – provincial shadow governor

★ FALLEN HEROES ★
BALA MURGHAB, AFGHANISTAN

HM2 Anthony M. Carbullido (U.S. Navy)

SFC David J. Todd (U.S. Army)

SGT Benjamin W. Sherman (U.S. Army)

SGT Brandon T. Islip (U.S. Army)

SSG Ronald J. Spino (U.S. Army)

SGT Dillon B. Foxx (U.S. Army)

SPC Matthew D. Huston (U.S. Army)

SPC Josiah D. Crumpler (U.S. Army)

GySgt. Robert L. Gilbert (MARSOC)

PFC Billy G. Anderson (U.S. Army)

SSgt. David P. Day (MARSOC)

Sgt. William J. Woitowicz (MARSOC)

SFC Wyatt A. Goldsmith (Special Forces)

SSgt. Patrick R. Dolphin (MARSOC)

First Corporal David Tobini (Italian Army)

Sgt. Justin M. Hansen (MARSOC)

GySgt. Daniel J. Price (MARSOC)

GySgt. Jonathan W. Gifford (MARSOC)

★ Acknowledgments ★

MICHAEL GOLEMBESKY

Many people have helped me along the way; this book would not have been possible without them. Sabrina Golembesky, John Bruning, Mark Terrell, George Callum, Dan Hatfield, Matt Scott, Andy Jarosz, Will Perry, David Tamburin, Mindy Kane, Marc Resnick, the entire team at St. Martin's Press, and everyone else who put up with my shit, frustration, and sometimes unstable personality. Thank you for sticking with me and believing in the purpose of telling this story.

—Ski

Level Zero Heroes LLC proudly supports the MARSOC Foundation and their efforts.

The foundation aims to meet needs unmet by the government with an emphasis on building personal and family resiliency and supporting the full reintegration of MARSOC Marines and sailors following wounds, injuries, and extended deployments.

The MARSOC Foundation is a 501(c)(3), tax-exempt, national nonprofit charitable foundation.

To learn more, visit www.marsocfoundation.org.

JOHN BRUNING

Working with Michael to tell the story of Dagger 22 has been a tremendous professional and personal joy. From the outset, Michael and I shared a sense of mission and purpose to bring the experience of BMG to the American people. After meeting in Colorado (and nearly being stomped on by a moose), I found Michael's modesty and desire to give others credit solidified my respect for him. Thank you, Ski, for giving me the chance to help see your book to print.

Marc Resnick, your staunch support and encouragement were vital, and flattering. Thank you for believing in us and our vision of what *Level Zero Heroes* should become. A big thanks to the staff at St. Martin's Press—you are all so pro and so talented it makes working together tons of fun.

Renee and Ed—I know there were many days and nights we didn't get to spend time together as I was squirreled away in the woods, at Capitola or the Bunker writing *Level Zero Heroes*. Your understanding, love, and support made it possible for me to focus and get the words on the page. Bringing each chapter to you and reading them aloud has become a vital part of the process for me. Renee, being a national-caliber, small-bore shooter in her own right, particularly loved hearing more about Mark. I'm hoping we'll all be able to get together someday.

Jenn—family, always. Thank you for all the support and encouragement.

Jim Hornfischer, you've transformed my life too many times to count with your dedication and hard work on my behalf. Thank you for all you've done for my family. One of these days, we need to meet. After all, it has only been eight years!

Allison Serventi Morgan, once again you've played a significant role in my work. Incisive, literate, and profoundly intelligent, you're not only a gift as my most trusted sounding board, but as one of the closest friends I've ever known. Thank you for all your support, suggestions, and faith. This could not have been possible without you.

Lastly, Taylor Marks. I live to honor you. I carry your spirit with me and never lose sight of your sense of adventure. My successes are yours. That's the way it will always work. The enemy may have taken you from us, but you will never be forgotten.

—John

★ Bonus Material ★

Want more Level Zero Heroes? Visit the book-extras portion of the official Web site for exclusive maps, photos, and videos provided by the veterans of Bala Murghab, Afghanistan.

VISIT ONLINE AT

http://levelzeroheroes.com/protected/book_extras.html
Username: levelzeroheroes
Password: dagger22
Video passwords are located inside the hardback copy of *Level Zero Heroes*. Password locations are described above each video.

LEVEL ZERO HEROES ON SOCIAL MEDIA

Facebook: https://www.facebook.com/LevelZeroHeroes
Twitter: https://twitter.com/LevelZeroHeroes
Vimeo: https://vimeo.com/channels/levelzeroheroes

★ GLOSSARY ★

A&S	Assessment and Selection
ABP	Afghan Border Police
ACU	Army Combat Uniform
AFSOC	Air Force Special Operations Command
AIRO	air officer
ANA	Afghan National Army
ANP	Afghan National Police
AO	area of operations
AP	armor-piercing
BDU	battle dress uniform
BMG	Bala Murghab
CAG	Combat Applications Group
CAS	Close Air Support
CDS	Container Delivery System
CMDO	Afghan Commandos
COC	Command Operations Center
COMISAF	Commander ISAF
Commandos	Afghan Commandos (Special Forces)
Conex box	large metal storage container
CONOPS	Concept of Operations
COP	Combat Outpost
CRP	Combat and Reconnaissance Patrol
DMPI	Desired Mean Points of Impact
DUSTWUN	Duty Status Whereabouts Unknown
DZ	Drop Zone
EOD	Explosive Ordnance Disposal
FalconView	PC-based mapping application for plotting and navigation

FLIR	Forward Looking Infrared (camera)
FMV	Full Motion Video
FOB	Forward Operating Base
GBU-31	2,000-pound, GPS-guided bomb
GBU-38	500-pound, GPS-guided bomb
GFC	Ground Force Commander
GMV	Ground Mobility Vehicle
GPS	Global Positioning System
GRG	Grid Reference Graphic
HE	High-explosive
Hellfire	High-explosive air-to-ground missile
Hesco	a wire basket full of dirt used for force protection
HET	Humint Exploitation Team
HLZ	hasty landing zone
HME	homemade explosives
HUMINT	human intelligence
HVT	high-value target
IDF	indirect fire (mortars and rockets)
IED	Improvised Explosive Device
infantillery	an artillery unit operating as an infantry unit
IR	Infrared
ISAF	International Security Assistance Force (the Coalition)
JAG	Judge Advocate General (military lawyer)
JDAM	Joint Direct Attack Munition
JFO	Joint Fires Observer
JTAC	Joint Terminal Attack Controller
JTAR	Joint Tactical Airstrike Request
KA-BAR	knife attachment, Browning Automatic Rifle (BAR)
Kit	tactical vest and interceptor plate carrier
LGB	laser-guided bomb
LZ	Landing Zone
Ma Deuce	Military slang for the M2 .50 caliber machine gun

MARFLIR	Maritime Forward Looking Infrared system
MARSOC	Marine Corps Special Operations Command
MARSOF	Marine Special Operations Force
MBITR	AN/PRC-148 Multiband Inter/Intra Team Radio
MEDCAP	Medical Civil Action Program
medevac	medical evacuation
mIRC chat	Internet Relay Chat (IRC) client
MOS	Military Occupational Specialty
MRAP	Mine Resistant Ambush Protected (vehicle)
MRE	Meal, Ready to Eat
MSOB	Marine Special Operations Battalion
MSOC	Marine Special Operations Company
MSOT	Marine Special Operations Team
NCIS	Naval Criminal Investigative Service
NCO	noncommissioned officer
NDS	National Directorate of Security
NVG	Night Vision Goggles
ODA	Operational Detachment Alpha
OP	Observation Post
OPSEC	operational security
PAX	personnel, people
POI	Point of Impact
POO	Point of Origin
PPIED	Pressure Plate Improvised Explosive Device
PR	Personnel Recovery
PRT	Provincial Reconstruction Team
qalat	Arabic for "fortified place"
QRF	Quick Reaction Force
ROE	Rules of Engagement
RON	remain overnight
ROZ	Restricted Operating Zone
RPG	rocket-propelled grenade

SARC	Special Amphibious Reconnaissance Corpsman
SASR	Special Application Scoped Rifle
SATCOM	satellite communications
SIGINT	signals intelligence
SIPRNet	Secret Internet Protocol Router Network
SNAFU	Situation Normal, All Fucked Up
SNCO	staff noncommissioned officer
SOCOM	United States Special Operations Command
SOF	Special Operations Force
SOP	standard operating procedure
SOTF-W	Special Operations Task Force–West
SVoIP	Secure Voice-over Internet Protocol
TACP	Tactical Air Control Party (USAF)
Tango(s)	military slang for Taliban
TIC	Troops in Contact
TOC	Tactical Operations Center
TOF	Time of Flight
TOT	Time on Target
T-SCIF	Temporary Sensitive Compartmented Information Facility
VideoScout	rugged laptop used to view Full Motion Video from aircraft
VSO	Village Stability Operations
Yo-Yo Ops	routing aircraft to a fueling point

MICHAEL GOLEMBESKY

Born in 1976, Michael moved from his hometown of Levittown, Pennsylvania, to Colorado in 1997 to begin a new life. There he worked as a truck driver for a local dairy before enlisting in the Marine Corps shortly after the events of 9/11 to help support the United States in the global war on terrorism.

Upon graduating MCRD San Diego in 2002, he was assigned to 3rd Battalion, 10th Marines, as a field artillery cannoneer, deploying to Okinawa (2003) and Iraq (2005) with Regimental Combat Team 2, where he served as a provisional rifle company squad leader.

Upon returning from Iraq, Sergeant Golembesky made a lateral move in primary MOS (Military Occupational Specialty) to become a Fire Support Man (0861). He served his following two deployments attached to 2nd Battalion, 2nd Marines, as a forward observer and Fire Support Chief as part of the 26th Marine Expeditionary Unit (2006) and Task Force 2/2 in Iraq (2008).

While on his second deployment in Iraq, Staff Sergeant Golembesky was selected to become an aircraft controller with the newly formed Marine Corps Special Operations Command (MARSOC). He reported to 2nd Marine Special Operations Battalion in January 2009 and immediately attended the Joint Terminal Attack Controller course in Norfolk, Virginia. After graduating and obtaining 8002 MOS, he was assigned as a team JTAC with Marine Special Operations Company G, Team 2. His fifth and final deployment was served in Afghanistan (RC-W) with Marine Special Operations Team 8222 from 2009 through 2010 in the Bala Murghab River valley.

Honorably discharged in October 2010 after eight years of military service, Michael, along with his wife, Sabrina, and daughter, Devlyn, returned to Colorado, where he works as a defense contractor and writer.

Michael's personal military awards include the Navy and Marine
Corps Commendation Medal (Valor), two Navy and Marine Corps Combat Action Ribbons, and the Afghanistan and Iraq Campaign Medals.

JOHN R. BRUNING

John R. Bruning is the author or collaborating writer of nineteen non-
fiction books, including the *New York Times* bestseller *Outlaw Platoon*
with Sean Parnell, and such critically acclaimed works as *Shadow of the
Sword* with Jeremiah Workman (Ballantine), *How to Break a Terrorist*
with Matthew Alexander (Free Press), *House to House* with David Bella-
via (Free Press), *The Devil's Sandbox* (Zenith), and *Ghost: Confessions of a
Counterterrorism Agent* with Fred Burton (Random House, a *New York
Times* expanded-list bestseller). He has been called "one of a handful of
great military historians" and his writing has been described as "excep-
tional historical reporting."

Bruning embedded with an Oregon National Guard unit, the 2-162
Infantry, during Operation Southern Comfort, the stability and support
operation in New Orleans following Hurricane Katrina.

From 2007 to 2011, John founded, funded out-of-pocket, and ran the
973rd Civilians on the Battlefield, an all-volunteer, nonprofit organization that provided training support for the Oregon National Guard's infantry units, FBI SWAT, Oregon State SWAT, WMD response teams, and
other law enforcement agencies. The 973rd accurately modeled Afghan
and Iraqi insurgent tactics and served as the "bad guys" during counterterrorism training exercises. The perspective this gave John significantly
enhanced his understanding of military operations, and the 973rd's effectiveness was praised repeatedly by the Oregon National Guard's commanding officer, Major General Raymond Rees. He founded a new veteran-based
OPFOR nonprofit in 2012 called the 503rd Rogue Cell, which has supported National Guard field exercises and MOS transition courses throughout Oregon.

In 2010, John embedded with Task Force Brawler, a combat aviation helicopter unit based in eastern Afghanistan. While with TF Brawler, he flew

over a hundred hours in combat. Additionally, Bruning went out on numerous foot and vehicular patrols with Brawler's Ground Combat Platoon and later with a counter-IED unit, the 162 Combat Engineer Company, which was supporting elements of the 1st Marine Division.

For his reporting in Afghanistan, the Department of Defense presented John with a prestigious 2010 Thomas Jefferson Award for journalism. For his work with the Oregon National Guard, he was inducted into the 162nd Infantry Regiment in September 2011 as an honorary member.

John lives in Independence, Oregon, with his two children, Ed and Renee.